Study Guide

for Plotnik's

Introduction to Psychology
3rd Edition

Matthew Enos
Harold Washington College

Brooks/Cole Publishing Company
Pacific Grove, California

Brooks/Cole Publishing Company
A Division of Wadsworth, Inc.

Printed in the United States of America

10 9 8 7 6 5 4 3 2

ISBN 0-534-16448-X

Sponsoring Editor: *Vicki Knight*
Editorial Associate: *Heather L. Graeve*
Production Coordinator: *Dorothy Bell*
Cover Design: *Katherine Minerva*
Printing and Binding: *Malloy Lithographing, Inc.*

Contents

Introduction

Welcome to Psychology

You are taking a challenging course, but I think you will enjoy it, because psychology is one of the most exciting and relevant fields of college study today. An explosion of new ideas and research in psychology is creating a vast accumulation of knowledge that is radically changing the way we understand ourselves and other people. To participate fully and effectively in today's world, we need a kind of psychological literacy, just as we need computer literacy and other new technological abilities. This course can help you acquire the skills and information you need to be psychologically literate.

Let's work together

Forgive me for using the personal pronoun "I" in this Study Guide. As a teacher, I can't help imagining you working your way through psychology and Rod Plotnik's exciting new textbook, and I'd like to help. I want to speak to you as directly as I can. Even though I don't know you personally, I've probably had students like you in my own classes.

Rod Plotnik's new *Psychology (3rd Edition)*

You're going to love your new psychology textbook. Dr. Rod Plotnik, a psychologist and professor on the faculty of San Diego State University, is a teacher and writer who sees examples of psychology's importance everywhere he looks and loves sharing his observations with us. You'll find Dr. Plotnik's book as fresh as your morning newspaper or your favorite talk show. At the same time, you'll see that his book meets the requirements of solid scholarship. He covers the relevant research and carefully explains the major theories. It's how Rod tells it that I think you will find especially rewarding.

Rod's book is different. An expert in learning psychology, Rod knows we *understand* what we can visualize in a picture and *remember* what we can organize into a story. Consequently, he filled his book with pictures and stories (and not many words like "consequently").

Excellent as his book is, I wouldn't want you to passively agree with everything Rod says. Instead, try to become actively involved in a dialogue with the book. You'll notice how often Rod *asks you a question.* Argue with him. Write notes in the margins. Highlight the important stuff. Make reading and studying this new textbook an adventure.

Kick the tires and slam the doors

By now you've probably paged through your new psychology textbook to see what it's like. If you haven't, I suggest that you do so as soon as you finish reading this introduction. It's a good idea to get the feel of a new book before you begin working in it. That way, you have some sense of where you are going and how to pace yourself for effective study.

What is a module?

You may have noticed that there are about as many chapters as there are weeks in the semester, permitting instructors to organize their courses logically, but what are the two "modules" in each chapter?

Perhaps you have seen modular furniture. You can arrange the pieces in different ways to best suit your tastes and the space available. If there is a part of the modular couch or computer desk you don't need, you can leave it out without destroying the integrity of the set.

Each module in a chapter complements the other, yet explains a separate element of psychology and can stand on its own. If you studied all the modules with great care, you would have a near-perfect understanding of modern psychology. (You might also be flunking your other courses.) If you read only a single module, you would learn something important about one aspect of psychology.

Pay attention to the modules your instructor has assigned (our first job is to pass the tests, after all), but remember that there's no law against reading an unassigned module that interests you. [Hint: if you do, tell your instructor about it and you'll make a good impression.]

How this Study Guide works

The bottom line is that this Study Guide must help you earn the grade you want in your psychology course. I tried to include materials that have helped my own students attain their goals. Some information is highly specific, aimed straight at getting more questions right on the next test. There are observations about the field of psychology, because, as I explain in Chapter 1, if you can't tell the forest for the trees, you're lost. Still other parts have a general goal — helping you become a more effective student (and where better than in a psychology course?).

The organization of the Study Guide parallels the chapters and modules in your textbook. Here is what you will find in the Study Guide.

Chapter introductions

Each chapter in the Study Guide begins with an observation I think may help you tackle the chapter in the textbook more successfully. These observations are not summaries, but thoughts about how to orient yourself toward understanding what is in the chapter.

In some chapters, I included a box titled "**For psych majors only...,**" in which I try to suggest ideas of interest to students who intend to take more psychology courses. I guess I wouldn't really mind if an English major or chemistry major reads these boxes.

Outline

Each module begins with a topic outline. Sometimes I added a phrase or definition to help you grasp a difficult idea. I placed the most important names, terms, and phrases in **boldface**, to suggest that they are the key ones to learn.

There is one thing wrong with the outlines — I wrote them instead of you. Much of the benefit of using an outline comes from the process of building it. Therefore, your job is to turn each outline into your own by writing all over it and revising it as you study. Make each outline a personal set of notes that will help you prepare for your tests.

Self-Tests

Three kinds of Self-Tests follow the outline. First, you will find 10 True-False questions intended to indicate how well you understand the main ideas in the module. Next, there are 10 Matching questions that attempt to pick up the more important new vocabulary terms and names in the module. Finally, 15 Multiple-Choice questions explore important facts, concepts, and theories presented in the module. You will find the answers for all the questions at the end of each chapter.

By the way, if you laugh while reading my questions... I'll be delighted. I've never believed learning has to be deadly serious all the time. So when I was writing questions and couldn't take it any longer, I sometimes indulged myself in what I hoped would be a bit of humor. The results may be too corny, but you be the judge.

Becoming a more effective student

Finally, in each chapter of the Study Guide, you will find a tip on how to become a more effective student. These tips are based on my belief that all humans have a deep-seated urge to be effective and on my experience of working with students who were trying to become more effective in college. Some tips tell you how to study better, but most are general ideas about the psychology of effectiveness. I'll begin with a tip I hope you read right away and really take to heart.

Chapter 1: Discovering Psychology

An explosion of knowledge

The other day I found a box of my old college textbooks. I was delighted to discover the textbook I used when I took *my* first psychology course, years ago. Would you believe I still remembered some of the pictures and lessons?

I was shocked, though, to see how slender a book it was. It had a chapter on the eye, another on the ear, and others on the rest of the senses. There was some material on Freud, but not much on anyone else. I was struck by how much less knowledge there was in the field of psychology back then.

The explosion of research and thinking in psychology has created a problem for teachers and students. Textbooks are four times as thick, and they apologize for leaving material out. In the newer textbooks, such as the one by Rod Plotnik that you are using, the writing is lively and the graphics are superb, but there still is much more material to cover. The problem is that colleges and universities, which change very slowly, still expect you to master it all in one semester!

How to tell the forest from the trees

My experience as a teacher says the single greatest problem of introductory psychology is that the sheer mass of information thrown at students overwhelms them, no matter how diligently they study. What is really important? Where are the connections between all these facts and ideas and names? What must I remember for the tests? The study of introductory psychology presents a classic example of the old problem of not being able to see the forest for the trees.

The solution is to develop a conceptual framework for understanding psychology. If you have an overview of what questions psychology attempts to answer, how it goes about seeking answers, and what the dominant themes in the answers have been, you will be able to fit any new fact, idea, or name into a coherent picture.

That's where Chapter 1 comes in. Besides describing the kinds of work psychologists do, Rod Plotnik gives you two important tools: (1) the six major theoretical approaches to psychology, and (2) the scientific method of objective observation. These tools are vital because the six theoretical approaches and the objective methods of science guide all research and thinking in psychology.

As a student and consumer of psychology, you need to know what questions it can answer and how the major pioneers in the field have tried to answer them. Chapter 1 is the road map for an exciting journey.

Effective Student Tip 1

Attend Every Class

I shudder when I hear college teachers advise, "Come to class if it helps, but attendance isn't required." That's such poor psychology and such destructive advice. Students should attend *every* class, even the dull ones, because regular attendance leads directly to involvement and commitment, the basic ingredients of effective college work.

We aren't talking morals here, we're talking the psychology of effectiveness: (1) Good attendance makes you feel more confident, purposeful and in control. (2) Attendance is the one feature of college that is completely under your control. (3) The reason for an absence usually reveals some area in which you feel ineffective. (4) Whether they make a big deal of it or not, your professors want and need your good attendance. What if no one came? (5) There is more to a class than the lecture. Other good things happen when you attend class regularly. Your professor gets to know you. You become better acquainted with your classmates. You learn from them and you learn by helping them. (6) Most students can achieve perfect attendance if they try, and their professors will admire them for it. You can help make a good class a great one.

P.S.

I had planned to begin with a more philosophical tip, about the psychology of effectiveness, but I realized that, for obvious reasons, I should put attendance *first*. Besides, if you agreed to follow just one tip, I would choose this one. When you attend every class, good things happen automatically. Trust me.

Module 1: What Psychology Is

In this Study Guide, we will begin every Module with an **Outline**. Use it to organize your study. Write notes on it. Turn it into your personal aid for effective learning.

I. Defining **psychology** — behaviors and mental processes

   A. Goals

      1. **Explain** or understand

      2. **Predict**

      3. **Control**

   B. Approaches to psychology

      1. **Psychobiological**

         a. Genes, hormones, nervous system, brain

         b. How mind, brain, and body interact

      2. **Cognitive**

         a. How we process, store, and use information

         b. How information influences what we notice, perceive, and remember

      3. **Behavioral**

         a. How organisms learn new behaviors or modify existing ones through reward and punishment

         b. **B. F. Skinner** and strict behaviorism

         c. **Albert Bandura** and social learning

      4. **Psychoanalytic**

         a. Influence of unconscious fears, desires, and motivations

         b. **Sigmund Freud**

         c. Psychoanalytic techniques (free association, dream interpretation)

5. **Humanistic**

   a. Choice, freedom, personal growth, intrinsic worth, potential for self-fulfillment

   b. **Abraham Maslow**

   c. "Third Force" (vs. psychoanalysis and behaviorism)

6. **Cross-cultural**

   a. Influence of cultural and ethnic similarities and differences

   b. Newest approach to psychology

II. History of psychology

A. Discrimination in psychology

1. Women

2. Minorities

3. Current efforts to combat discrimination in psychology

B. Issues in the history of psychology

1. Structuralism

   a. **Wilhelm Wundt** ("father of psychology")

   b. Conscious elements of the mind

2. Functionalism

   a. **William James** (*Principles of Psychology*)

   b. Continuous flow of mental activity

3. Gestalt psychology

   a. Max Wertheimer, Wolfgang Köhler, Kurt Koffka

   b. Perception more than sum of its parts

   c. Apparent motion (phi phenomenon)

4. Behaviorism

   a. **John B. Watson**

   b. Objective, scientific analysis of observable behaviors

III. Psychology today

A. Careers in psychology

1. Psychologist

2. Clinical psychologist

3. Psychiatrist

B. Research areas in psychology

1. Personality and social psychology

2. Developmental psychology

3. Experimental psychology

4. Physiological psychology

5. Cognitive psychology

6. Psychometrics

IV. *Applying/Exploring:* Study skills

A. Exam preparation

1. Goal setting

   a. Time goal

   b. General goal

   c. Specific performance goal

2. Self-reinforcement

B. Effective study

1. Taking good notes
   a. In your own words
   b. Outline format [like this one]
   c. Associate new material with old [Concept/Glossary section]
2. Overcoming procrastination
   a. Stop thinking or worrying about final goal
   b. Break overall task down into smaller goals
   c. Write down a realistic schedule

Self-Tests

Next you will find the Self-tests described in the Introduction: true-false, matching, and multiple-choice. The answers are at the end of each chapter in the Study Guide (no peeking!).

Using the Self-tests

After studying the module carefully, which should include working on the outline, take the Self-Tests. Jot notes to yourself about questions where you are not sure of the answer, then score your answers. You should aim to get most of the questions right, because they are all written at about the same level of difficulty.

For every question you missed, go back to the textbook and find the section where the topic is discussed. Why did you miss the question? Had you noticed this material as you studied? Did you highlight the relevant words in the text? Did you read the test item carefully? Do you understand why the right answer is the right answer?

Most importantly, how can you do better on the next test? More reading? Better notes? Better test-taking skills? Don't worry about those wrong answers, though. We all make mistakes. The trick is to learn from them.

Getting the general idea... Is the statement true or false?

T 1. The goals of psychology are to explain, predict, and control behavior.

F 2. There are as many different approaches to psychology as there are psychologists writing about psychology.

T 3. Techniques like free association and dream interpretation are products of the psychoanalytic approach to psychology.

T 4. Abraham Maslow wanted humanistic psychology to be a "third force" against the dominance of psychoanalysis and behaviorism.

F 5. It is best to pick one of the general approaches to psychology and organize your thinking and work around it exclusively.

F 6. There has been ethnic discrimination in psychology, but at least women have always been equally represented.

T 7. Modern psychology began with Wilhelm Wundt's attempt to accurately measure the conscious elements of the mind.

F 8. The key idea of behaviorism is that perception is more than just the sum of its parts.

F 9. Not only do you have several career choices in psychology — whichever one you choose, you are almost certain to make big bucks!

F 10. There is no special program for overcoming procrastination: just get off your duff and get to work.

Knowing the essential vocabulary... Which phrase matches the term?

Answer	Term		Phrase
G	1. psychobiological	a.	unconscious motivation
D	2. cognitive	b.	personal growth and self-fulfillment
H	3. behavioral	c.	effect of group you were raised in
A	4. psychoanalytic	d.	information processing
B	5. humanistic	e.	polite fathers of psychology
C	6. cross-cultural	f.	mental activity as a continuous flow
I	7. structuralism	g.	brain, nervous system, heredity
F	8. functionalism	h.	reward and punishment
J	9. Gestalt psychology	i.	method of introspection
E	10. Gesundheit psychology	j.	perception of apparent motion

Mastering the material... Which answer makes the statement true?

D 1. Rod Plotnik opens his textbook with the story of the parents who discover their child is autistic to make the point that psychology
  a. is the science that has the answers to problems like this one
  b. is a rather grim science — lots of pain and suffering
  c. can answer some questions but not others
  d. comes out of our human need for answers about our behavior

C 2. Which one of the following is *not* a goal of psychology?
  a. to explain or understand behavior
  b. to predict behavior
  c. to criticize behavior
  d. to control behavior

A 3. The psychobiological approach to psychology focuses on
  a. the workings of the brain, nervous system, genes, hormones, etc.
  b. conscious processes like perception and memory
  c. the effects of reward and punishment on behavior
  d. unconscious processes

C 4. The cognitive approach to psychology studies how we
  a. are motivated by unconscious processes
  b. are motivated by the need for self-fulfillment
  c. process, store, and use information
  d. program our behavior by seeking rewards and avoiding punishments

B 5. The major contributor to the behavioral approach to psychology was
  a. Sigmund Freud
  b. B. F. Skinner
  c. William James
  d. Abraham Maslow

A 6. Among the techniques used in the psychoanalytic approach are
  a. free association and dream interpretation
  b. brain scans
  c. lever pressing for a reward
  d. asking clients about future plans and goals

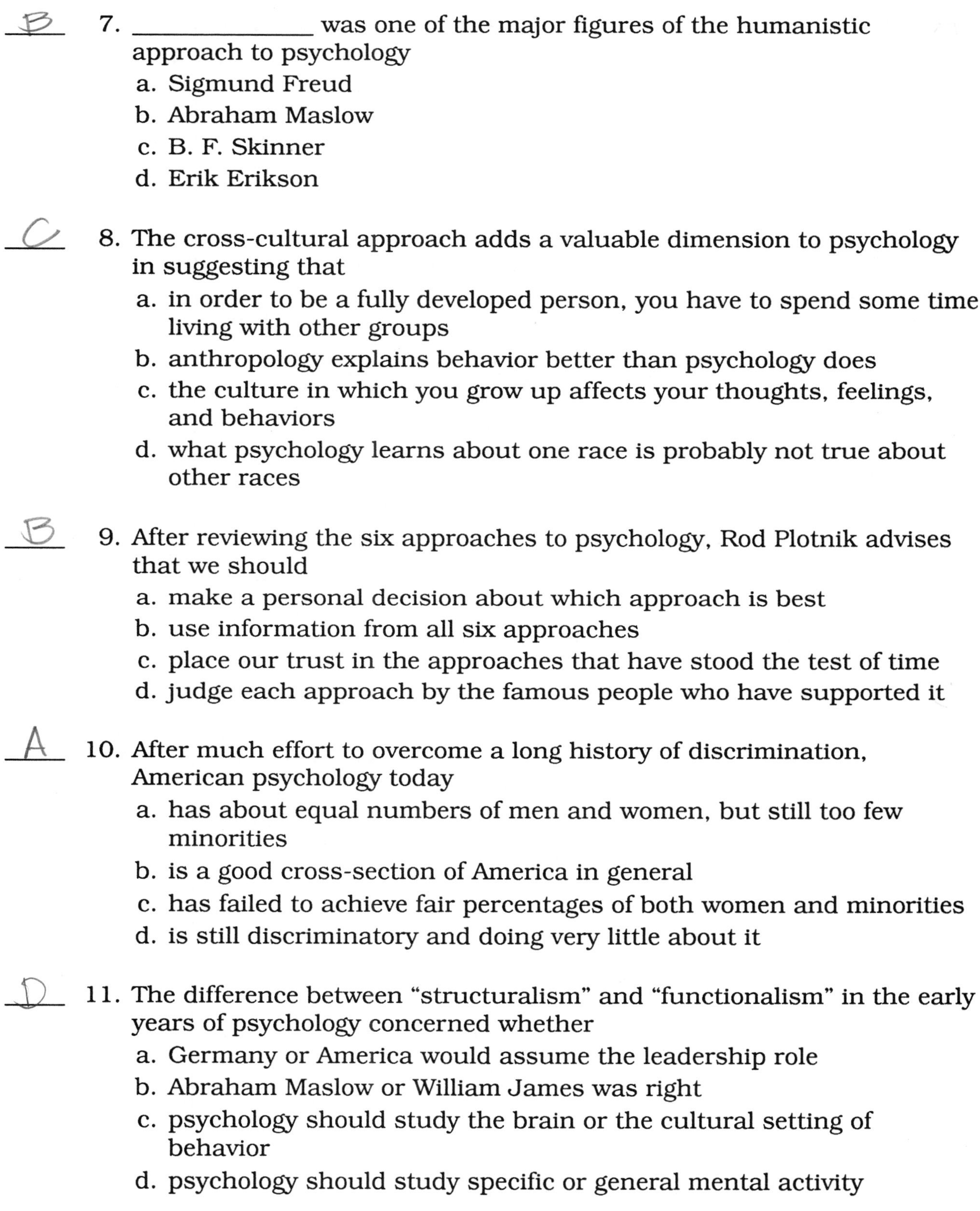

<u>B</u> 7. ______________ was one of the major figures of the humanistic approach to psychology

a. Sigmund Freud
b. Abraham Maslow
c. B. F. Skinner
d. Erik Erikson

<u>C</u> 8. The cross-cultural approach adds a valuable dimension to psychology in suggesting that

a. in order to be a fully developed person, you have to spend some time living with other groups
b. anthropology explains behavior better than psychology does
c. the culture in which you grow up affects your thoughts, feelings, and behaviors
d. what psychology learns about one race is probably not true about other races

<u>B</u> 9. After reviewing the six approaches to psychology, Rod Plotnik advises that we should

a. make a personal decision about which approach is best
b. use information from all six approaches
c. place our trust in the approaches that have stood the test of time
d. judge each approach by the famous people who have supported it

<u>A</u> 10. After much effort to overcome a long history of discrimination, American psychology today

a. has about equal numbers of men and women, but still too few minorities
b. is a good cross-section of America in general
c. has failed to achieve fair percentages of both women and minorities
d. is still discriminatory and doing very little about it

<u>D</u> 11. The difference between "structuralism" and "functionalism" in the early years of psychology concerned whether

a. Germany or America would assume the leadership role
b. Abraham Maslow or William James was right
c. psychology should study the brain or the cultural setting of behavior
d. psychology should study specific or general mental activity

A 12. By explaining perceptual phenomena like the phi phenomenon [apparent motion], Gestalt researchers gave psychology the idea that
a. the whole is more than the sum of its parts
b. research results could be profitable when applied to advertising
c. Wundt and the structuralists had been right about the importance of the individual parts
d. individual parts are more significant than resulting wholes

B 13. The early behaviorist John B. Watson wanted psychology to be
a. an introspective investigation of how people understood the workings of their minds
b. an objective, scientific study of observable behavior
c. a philosophical study of the continuous flow of mental activity
d. a program for "building" whatever kinds of people society needed

C 14. After reading the material on careers and research areas, it would be reasonable to conclude that psychology
a. requires so much education that few students should consider it
b. will have fewer job opportunities in coming years
c. offers a great variety of intellectual challenges and kinds of work
d. is one of the best paid professions today

D 15. Which one of the following is *not* a good strategy for overcoming procrastination?
a. stop thinking or worrying about the final goal
b. break the task down into smaller goals
c. write down a realistic schedule for reaching the goals
d. don't begin working until you are confident that you won't fail

Module 2: What Science Is

Remember! The more notes you write on this **Outline** the more useful your study guide will be.

I. **Scientific method**

   A. Rules and procedures for gathering information

   B. Goal: objective (unbiased) data

   C. Three research strategies for scientific investigation

      1. Case study

      2. Survey

      3. Experiment

II. **Case study**

   A. Naturalistic observation (see IV.B.1. below)

   B. **Testimonials**

      1. Sources of error and bias in testimonials

         a. Personal beliefs

         b. **Self-fulfilling prophecy**

         c. Confounded causes

      2. "Subliminal message" research

III. **Survey**

   A. Advantages and disadvantages

      1. Quick, efficient collection of large amounts of information

      2. Danger of bias through unrepresentative sample

B. **Correlation**

1. **Correlation coefficient**

2. Correlation does not prove causation

3. Correlation and prediction

4. Correlations as clues

IV. Decisions about doing research

A. Choosing a research technique

1. Interviews and questionnaires

2. Standardized tests

3. Behaviors observed in the laboratory

4. Physiological and neurological responses

5. Animal model

B. Choosing the setting for studying behavior

1. **Naturalistic** setting (case study)

a. Advantage of real-life situation

b. Disadvantage of bias in uncontrolled situation

2. Laboratory setting

a. Advantage of control of variables

b. Disadvantage of artificiality

V. **Experiment**

A. Controlled experiment in the laboratory (see IV.B.2. above)

B. Steps in conducting an experiment

1. Ask specific questions (**hypothesis**)

2. Identify variables

a. **Independent variable** (treatment)

b. **Dependent variable** (resulting behavior)

3. Choose subjects

a. Sample

b. **Random** selection

4. Assign subjects randomly

a. **Experimental group**

b. **Control group**

5. Manipulate independent variable (administer treatment)

6. Measure resulting behavior (dependent variable)

7. Analyze data

a. Experimental group vs. control group

b. Statistical procedures

C. Possible bias in effect of laboratory setting

VI. *Applying/Exploring:* Human subjects and animal research

A. **Ethical** considerations in psychological research

1. Deception and debriefing

2. **Double-blind technique**

B. Pros and cons of using animal subjects

Now take the

Self-Tests

to check your understanding and mastery of this module.

Getting the general idea... Is the statement true or false?

_____ 1. Linus Pauling knows that megadoses of vitamin C promote health because he used the scientific method to prove it.

_____ 2. The scientific technique with the lowest potential for error and bias is the survey method.

_____ 3. Testimonials have a high potential for error and bias.

_____ 4. Surveys like the famous Kinsey report are interesting but quite unscientific.

_____ 5. If there isn't a positive correlation between studying the textbook and getting good grades, you just wasted a big chunk of money.

_____ 6. If you can establish a significant correlation between two variables, you have also determined the causal relationship between them.

_____ 7. Research in naturalistic settings has greater reality, but research in the laboratory has greater control.

_____ 8. What you do to subjects in an experiment is called the dependent variable because the resulting behavior "depends" on the treatment.

_____ 9. Random selection is crucial in choosing subjects because you want them to accurately represent the larger population you are studying.

_____ 10. There is no way to justify doing research using animals.

Knowing the essential vocabulary... Which phrase matches the term?

_____	1. scientific method	a. naturalistic setting
_____	2. case study	b. statistical relationship
_____	3. testimonial	c. rules for objective study
_____	4. self-fulfilling prophecy	d. treatment
_____	5. survey	e. your posse
_____	6. correlation	f. shows effect of experimental setting
_____	7. independent variable	g. Kinsey report
_____	8. dependent variable	h. individual report
_____	9. control group	i. behavior of subjects
_____	10. good group	j. believing makes it so

Mastering the material... Which answer makes the statement true?

_____ 1. Rod Plotnik begins this module with the example of Linus Pauling because the renowned scientist
   a. finally proved that megadoses of vitamin C promote health
   b. knows you should stick to what you believe even if you can't prove it
   c. applied his training and knowledge to helping all of us enjoy better health
   d. illustrates the difference between scientific research and sincere testimonial

_____ 2. The scientific method is
   a. a set of rules and procedures for objective research
   b. a faith that precise equipment will produce accurate information
   c. all of the findings of science in the modern era
   d. a set of guidelines published by the American Academy of Science

_____ 3. Which one of the following has the *lowest* potential for error or bias?
   a. case study
   b. survey
   c. experiment
   d. testimonial

_____ 4. When you encounter a testimonial, you know that it is
   a. true, if enough other people also report it
   b. false, because it is only a personal belief
   c. true, if the person conveying it has a good reputation for honesty
   d. possibly true, but not proven by science

_____ 5. A good example of a self-fulfilling prophecy is the belief that
   a. there's no use studying for multiple-choice exams because the questions are tricky
   b. psychology requires more study than literature
   c. if you do all your studying the night before the exam you'll do better
   d. you don't have to take notes in class if you listen carefully

_____ 6. One of the main disadvantages of the survey method is that
   a. many people won't go to the trouble of filling out the survey
   b. the results will be biased if the sample is not representative
   c. it is difficult to survey enough subjects to make the results valid
   d. it takes so long to conduct survey research that the method is impractical for most purposes

_____ 7. If she wears her lucky socks, Gail wins three golf matches out of four, a _______________ correlation between wearing the socks and winning
   a. perfect negative
   b. negative
   c. positive
   d. perfect positive

_____ 8. Does this prove that the socks are the cause of Gail's winning?
   a. yes
   b. no
   c. it would if she won *every* time she wore the socks
   d. which socks Gail wears cannot possibly have anything to do with the outcome of the matches she plays

_____ 9. Whether to conduct research in a naturalistic or a laboratory setting involves the issue of
   a. comprehensiveness vs. cost
   b. testimonial vs. science
   c. realism vs. control
   d. objectivity vs. subjectivity

_____ 10. The special treatment given to the subjects in the experimental group is called the
   a. hypothesis
   b. independent variable
   c. dependent variable
   d. control variable

_____ 11. Which one of the following is an example of random sampling?
   a. winning numbers in the lottery
   b. annual National Football League player draft
   c. numbers people play in the lottery
   d. annual Miss America contest

_____ 12. The purpose of having a control group in an experiment is to
   a. show what results the opposite treatment would produce
   b. show how a different group would react to the treatment
   c. identify and rule out the behavior that results from simply participating in the experiment
   d. provide backup subjects in case any members of the experimental group are unable to continue

_____ 13. Did the famous Rowland research prove that hypnotized people will perform dangerous acts?
   a. yes, because some of them reached for the rattlesnakes
   b. no, because the control group refused to reach into the box
   c. yes, because several hypnotized subjects actually held the snakes until told to put them down
   d. no, because there is evidence that laboratory settings cause people to want to cooperate and make the experiment work

_____ 14. Should you volunteer to be a subject in a psychological experiment?
   a. no, because you are completely at the mercy of the researcher
   b. yes, because ethical guidelines protect subjects from danger or undue deception
   c. no, because they'll never tell you what the experiment was really about
   d. yes... when rattlesnakes stop biting

_____ 15. The attitude of most psychologists toward the use of animals in research is that
   a. scientists must have complete freedom to conduct their research however they see fit
   b. ethical concerns are involved in research on humans but not on animals
   c. animals have no rights
   d. the issue is complicated and calls for a balance between animal rights and research needs

Answers for Chapter 1

Module 1

True-False	Matching	Multiple-Choice
1. T	1. g	1. d
2. F	2. d	2. c
3. T	3. h	3. a
4. T	4. a	4. c
5. F	5. b	5. b
6. F	6. c	6. a
7. T	7. i	7. b
8. F	8. f	8. c
9. F	9. j	9. b
10. F	10. e	10. a
		11. d
		12. a
		13. b
		14. c
		15. d

Module 2

True-False	Matching	Multiple-Choice
1. F	1. c	1. d
2. F	2. a	2. a
3. T	3. h	3. c
4. F	4. j	4. d
5. T	5. g	5. a
6. F	6. b	6. b
7. T	7. d	7. c
8. F	8. i	8. b
9. T	9. f	9. c
10. F	10. e	10. b
		11. a
		12. c
		13. d
		14. b
		15. d

Chapter 2: Biological Bases of Behavior

Psychology as a spectrum of approaches

In Chapter 1, we got acquainted with what psychology is, learned some of its history, and saw how psychologists work. It is all interesting and important material, yet you could say that psychology itself really begins in Chapter 2.

Remember the six approaches to psychology discussed in the first chapter? I find it useful to think of them as forming a spectrum, a rainbow of ideas. At one end there is the psychobiological approach — the brain and nervous system Rod Plotnik describes in this chapter. At the other end is the cross-cultural approach — the social interactions he covers in the last chapter (Social Psychology).

I put the brain and nervous system at the beginning of the spectrum, because the brain seems like the most obvious, most elemental starting point in psychology. You could just as well put social interaction first, however, because we become experts about other people long before we know anything about the brain. It doesn't really matter; the point is that the psychobiological and cross-cultural approaches are polar opposites in how we think about psychology.

The other four approaches (cognitive, behavioral, psychodynamic, and humanistic) fall somewhere within the spectrum. How you arrange them only reveals your biases about their relative importance. (For example, which do you consider more dominant, thinking or feeling?)

Our starting point, deep in the fields of biology and chemistry

At the furthest extreme, psychology is almost pure biology and chemistry. [The longer you are in college, the more you will appreciate the great overlap in all fields of study. The way we have them neatly arranged in the college catalog is artificial. Therefore, if you are a business major, congratulate yourself on having the wisdom to enroll in psychology. You'll find many connections and tie-ins between business and psychology.] Whenever the text brings in the cross-cultural approach, you will see how deeply psychology also reaches into the fields of anthropology and sociology.

Now you can appreciate why this chapter is not an easy one to master (and probably wasn't an easy one to write, either). It involves a minicourse in biology. You could easily get lost just trying to remember the key terms. My advice is to concentrate on the *processes* involved. Try to appreciate how the brain and nervous system stand between us and the rest of the world, helping us understand it and make the best use of it. I suppose loyal Trekkies could compare the brain to the Starship Enterprise, going bravely where no man has gone before, in the name of peace and the orderly regulation of our affairs.

Effective Student Tip 2

Why You Must Be Effective in College

Effectiveness comes into play in all our endeavors, the most trivial as well as the most crucial. Consider a systems analyst, triumphant in the solution of a tricky problem (effectiveness confirmed), who then wheels around and fires a paper ball in a perfect jump shot into the wastebasket across the room (effective again). The urge behind each effort was effectiveness, but realistically it's more important that our systems analyst solve the problem than make the imaginary buzzer-beating shot.

If we were only dealing with office wastebasketball, we could afford to ignore the psychological factor of effectiveness. The stakes aren't very high. College is a different matter — probably the highest stakes in your life so far.

College is an essential rite of passage in our society, a critical bridge over which you cross into adulthood. College is more important today than ever, with at least two outcomes of great consequence: (1) College may determine whether you gain admittance to a technologically sophisticated world of commerce, industry, and the professions. (2) College helps shape your self-esteem and psychological health.

That's why you must handle your college experience effectively. Your future depends on it.

Module 3: Building Blocks of the Brain

I. The big picture

   A. Are **mind** and **brain** two things or one?

      1. Mental functions

      2. Physical functions

   B. Substance of the brain

      1. Neurons (play key role in psychological functioning)

      2. Glial cells

II. Neurons

   A. Development

      1. Billions of cells

      2. Not replaced or regrown

   B. Structure and function

      1. Three basic structures

         a. Cell body

         b. **Dendrites**

         c. **Axon** with **myelin sheath**

      2. Communicate through **synapse**

         a. Terminal buttons

         b. **Neurotransmitters**

Use this

Outline

to organize your studying. Write notes on it. Turn it into a personalized aid for effective learning.

C. **Reflex** response

1. Sensory (afferent) neurons

2. Motor (efferent) neurons

III. Axon structure and function

A. Membrane (tubelike structure)

1. Fluid with chemical particles

2. Semipermeable

B. **Ions** and electrical activity in the brain

1. Sodium ions (positive charge) outside

2. Protein ions (negative charge) inside

C. Resting state

D. **Threshold**

E. Conducting state

1. Action potential

2. Nerve impulse

3. All-or-none law

F. Neurotransmitters (keys) and receptors (locks)

1. Either excitatory or inhibitory

2. Neurotransmitters and brain disorders

a. Single function (e.g., endorphin)

b. Keys to brain disorders (e.g., Alzheimer's)

IV. Nervous system

A. **Central nervous system** (neurons)

1. Brain and spinal cord

2. Inability to regrow or regenerate

B. **Peripheral nervous system** (nerves)

1. Body

2. Ability to regrow, regenerate, or reattach

V. *Applying/Exploring:* Brain transplant — new treatment for Parkinson's

A. Parkinson's disease

1. Periods of rigidity

2. Insufficient supply of neurotransmitter dopamine

3. Treatment with drug L-dopa

B. Brain transplant

1. Human fetal brain tissue

2. Stereotaxic procedure

Now take the
Self-Tests
to check your understanding and mastery of this module.

Getting the general idea... Is the statement true or false?

_____ 1. Science has determined that the mind is a separate entity from the brain.

_____ 2. If that ad "this is your brain on drugs" scares you, add the fact that damaged neurons are not regrown or replaced.

_____ 3. Most neurons have a cell body, dendrites, and an axon.

_____ 4. Reflexes are actions you have learned to execute so fast you don't think about them.

_____ 5. The "all-or-none law" refers to the fact that ions are either positively or negatively charged.

_____ 6. Neurotransmitters are the keys that unlock the receptors of dendrites, cell bodies, muscles, and organs.

_____ 7. The steady reduction in an important neurotransmitter in the brain is part of the cause of Alzheimer's disease.

_____ 8. Nerves are located in the central nervous system; neurons are in the peripheral nervous system.

_____ 9. Of all the people you don't want to get upset, the chef preparing your puffer fish may be at the top of the list.

_____ 10. The stereotaxic procedure is the treatment of Parkinson's disease with a drug called L-dopa.

Knowing the essential vocabulary... Which phrase matches the term?

_____	1. mind	a. transmits electrical signals
_____	2. brain	b. either excitatory or inhibitory
_____	3. neuron	c. either positively or negatively charged
_____	4. axon	d. mental functions
_____	5. synapse	e. a class where snap quizzes are given
_____	6. ions	f. unlearned, involuntary reaction
_____	7. reflex	g. set point for activating axon
_____	8. threshold	h. physical functions
_____	9. neurotransmitter	i. very small space between neurons
_____	10. nervous system	j. brain cell

Mastering the material... Which answer makes the statement true?

_____ 1. Rod Plotnik begins with the example of the *readiness potential* to illustrate the fact that
a. whether awake or asleep, humans are always ready to take action
b. people can be measured by the level of their readiness potential
c. the key question is whether thinking or acting comes first
d. the key element in the functioning of the brain is electrical activity

_____ 2. Is the mind the same as the brain? Rod Plotnik says that
a. the mind must be separate — otherwise there would be no soul
b. physical and mental functions interact with and influence each other
c. the physical brain is the only thing — there is no actual "mind"
d. the question is best left to philosophers

_____ 3. The human brain contains about ________ neurons and glial cells
a. one thousand
b. 100 thousand
c. 100 billion
d. a zillion

_____ 4. Unlike nerves, neurons
a. are not replaced or regrown
b. have the ability to regrow or reattach
c. are located outside the brain and spinal cord
d. have no dendrites or axons

_____ 5. The purpose of a synapse is to
a. wrap around and insulate an axon
b. hold chemicals that act like switches to turn on or off adjacent cells
c. protect the nucleus of the cell body
d. drain dangerous electricity away from the brain

_____ 6. An unlearned, involuntary reaction to a stimulus is called
a. an explosion
b. an electrical burst
c. a conditioned reflex
d. a reflex

_____ 7. The purpose of the ions in the axon's membrane is to
- a. generate a miniature electrical current
- b. plug up the tiny holes in the membrane's semipermeable skin
- c. pump excess sodium out of the neuron
- d. dry up the watery fluid that collects in the membrane

_____ 8. Because it has a _____________, an axon does not continually generate electrical signals
- a. myelin sheath
- b. terminal button
- c. threshold
- d. sodium pump

_____ 9. The "all-or-none law" explains what happens when
- a. positively and negatively charged ions meet
- b. an impulse starts at the beginning of an axon
- c. electrical impulses spread throughout the body
- d. your brain gets the idea of a six-pack

_____ 10. If receptors in muscle fibers are thought of as locks, the keys are
- a. the action potential of the axon
- b. synapses
- c. the resting state of the axon
- d. neurotransmitters

_____ 11. The effect of a neurotransmitter on an adjacent neuron, muscle, or organ is
- a. excitatory
- b. inhibitory
- c. either excitatory or inhibitory
- d. determined by the all-or-none law

_____ 12. Endorphin, a natural pain killer in the brain, offers an example of
- a. the key role that neurotransmitters play in regulating our lives
- b. the way neurotransmitters out of control can cause diseases like Alzheimer's
- c. hope for finding a cure for Parkinson's disease
- d. left-over entities in the brain (like the appendix in the body)

_____ 13. A severed thumb could be replaced with a big toe because
a. neurons have the ability to regrow, regenerate, or reattach
b. neurons are part of the central nervous system
c. nerves have the ability to regrow, regenerate, or reattach
d. nerves are part of the peripheral nervous system

_____ 14. Rod Plotnik cited the example of the puffer fish to show that
a. the electrical activity in this fish is the exact opposite of that in the human body
b. the electrical activity of the nervous system keeps us alive
c. over generations, the Japanese have developed an immunity to certain poisons
d. sometimes $450 isn't really too much to pay for a properly prepared meal

_____ 15. The newest hope for sufferers of Parkinson's disease is treating damaged cells with
a. a new drug called L-dopa
b. massive injections of dopamine
c. genetically engineered cells grown in the laboratory
d. transplanted human fetal brain tissue

Module 4: The Incredible Nervous System

Use this **Outline** to organize your studying. Write notes on it. Turn it into a personalized aid for effective learning.

I. Overview of **nervous system** [see V below for *endocrine system*, the other major system regulating body and brain]

A. **Central** nervous system

1. Brain

2. Spinal cord

B. **Peripheral** nervous system

1. **Somatic** nervous system (voluntary)
-network of ropelike nerves connected to sensory receptors/or to muscles

a. Afferent fibers (from skin and muscles to brain and spinal cord)

b. Efferent fibers (away from brain and spinal cord to muscles)

2. **Autonomic** nervous system (involuntary)
-regulates heart rate, breathing, blood pressure

a. **Sympathetic** nervous system (**fight or flight** response)

b. **Parasympathetic** nervous system (calming down)

c. **Homeostasis**
-tendency of the autonomic nervous syst to maintain the body's internal environment in balanced state of optimum functioning

II. Major divisions of human brain

A. Hemispheres (right and left) [see VI and VII below]

B. **Forebrain** and **midbrain**
└being a person

1. **Reticular formation**

2. Unconsciousness (anesthesia)

C. **Hindbrain**

1. Pons (bridge)
2. Medulla (vital reflexes)
3. **Cerebellum** (coordination)

D. Racial myths about brain size

1. Attempts to relate brain size to race and intelligence
2. Science and bias

III. **Cortex**

A. Shape and functions

1. Folded, creased skin covering surface of forebrain
2. Four areas or lobes and their functions

B. **Frontal lobe** — regulates social-emotional behavior

1. Normal, healthy personality
    a. Adaptive social and emotional behaviors
    b. Making and carrying out plans
2. Physical damage
    a. Case of Phineas Gage
    b. Frontal lobotomies
3. **Motor cortex**
    a. Initiation of voluntary movement
    b. Opposite side wiring

C. **Parietal lobe** — receives sensory information

1. **Somatosensory cortex**

2. Receives sensations

D. **Temporal lobe** — controls hearing and speech

1. **Primary auditory cortex**

2. Wernicke's aphasia (difficulty understanding and using words)

3. Broca's aphasia (inability to speak in fluent sentences)

E. **Occipital lobe** — controls vision

1. **Primary visual cortex**

2. Transforms sensory information into visual sensations

F. Association areas (remaining 80% of cortex)

1. Add meaning or associations to sensory stimuli

2. Occur in each of the four lobes

IV. Techniques for studying a living brain

A. Scanning *structure* of brain

1. CAT (computerized axial tomography) scans

2. MRI (magnetic resonance imaging) scans

B. Scanning *function* of brain

1. **PET** (positron emission tomography) scans

2. New research on how brain processes information

V. Inside the forebrain

A. **Limbic system**, your "animal brain"

1. Central core of forebrain

2. Structures and functions of limbic system

a. Hippocampus — putting memories into permanent storage

b. Amygdala — emotional behavior

c. Thalamus — receiving and initial processing of information

d. **Hypothalamus** — motivational and emotional behavior

B. **Endocrine system**

1. Secretion of hormones controlled by hypothalamus

2. Glands

a. Pituitary

b. Thyroid

c. Adrenal

d. Pancreas

e. Gonads

VI. Organization of brain

A. **Localization of function,** or total use of brain?

B. Three common questions

1. Am I "left-brained" or "right-brained?" [see VII below]

2. Which hemisphere is more dominant? (specialization)

3. Does the left hemisphere always know what the right is thinking?

VII. *Applying/Exploring:* Split-brain research

A. Independent functioning (after operation) illustrates specialization of hemispheres

B. Basic functions

1. Left hemisphere

a. Verbal

b. Mathematical

c. Analytical

2. Right hemisphere

a. Nonverbal

b. Spatial

c. Holistic

Now take the

Self-Tests

to check your understanding and mastery of this module.

Getting the general idea... Is the statement true or false?

_____ 1. The brain and the spinal cord make up the central nervous system.

_____ 2. The right and left hemispheres of the brain make up the peripheral nervous system.

_____ 3. The general tendency of the autonomic nervous system is homeostasis.

_____ 4. It is the operation of the hindbrain that makes you a person.

_____ 5. It is silly to believe that skull size affects human intelligence, but brain size obviously does.

_____ 6. When Igor hands Dr. Frankenstein a fresh brain, what we see quivering in his hands is the cortex.

_____ 7. As human society evolves, the limbic system incorporates cooperative and positive tendencies and feelings into the brain.

_____ 8. In the endocrine system, glands secrete hormones that affect many important bodily processes.

_____ 9. Science has finally explained why people are so different: each human being is either left-brained or right-brained.

_____ 10. The need to perform split-brain operations for medical purposes gives science a rare look at the degree of specialization in the brain's two hemispheres.

Knowing the essential vocabulary... Which phrase matches the term?

	Term		Phrase
_____	1. forebrain	a.	ancient, "animal" brain
_____	2. cerebellum	b.	coordinates voluntary movements
_____	3. cortex	c.	control center of the endocrine system
_____	4. frontal lobe	d.	thin folded layer covering forebrain
_____	5. temporal lobe	e.	Chapter 2 (Ha ha... just kidding)
_____	6. limbic system	f.	verbal, mathematical, analytical
_____	7. hypothalamus	g.	critical to hearing and speech
_____	8. left-brained	h.	visual, creative, intuitive
_____	9. right-brained	i.	involved in social-emotional behaviors
_____	10. no-brainer	j.	behaviors that make us human

Mastering the material... Which answer makes the statement true?

____ 1. Rod Plotnik tells the story of the man checking into a hotel who suddenly found himself unable to read a clock or tie his shoes to show that

a. one side of the brain controls both of those activities
b. brain damage can strike almost anyone at any time
c. the human nervous system is incredibly complex
d. the brain will never be fully understood

____ 2. Which one of the following is *not* a part of the peripheral nervous system?

a. somatic nervous system
b. autonomic nervous system
c. sympathetic nervous system
d. limbic nervous system

____ 3. When we see Michael Jordan flying toward the hoop, we are witnessing a modern version of the

a. fight-or-flight response
b. homeostatic reaction
c. parasympathetic push
d. arouse-or-die response

____ 4. The autonomic nervous system kept Karen Ann Quinlan alive because it maintained her body in a state of

a. autonomy
b. homeostasis
c. arousal
d. coma

____ 5. The human brain contains all of the following divisions *except*

a. the forebrain
b. the midbrain
c. the hindbrain
d. the topbrain

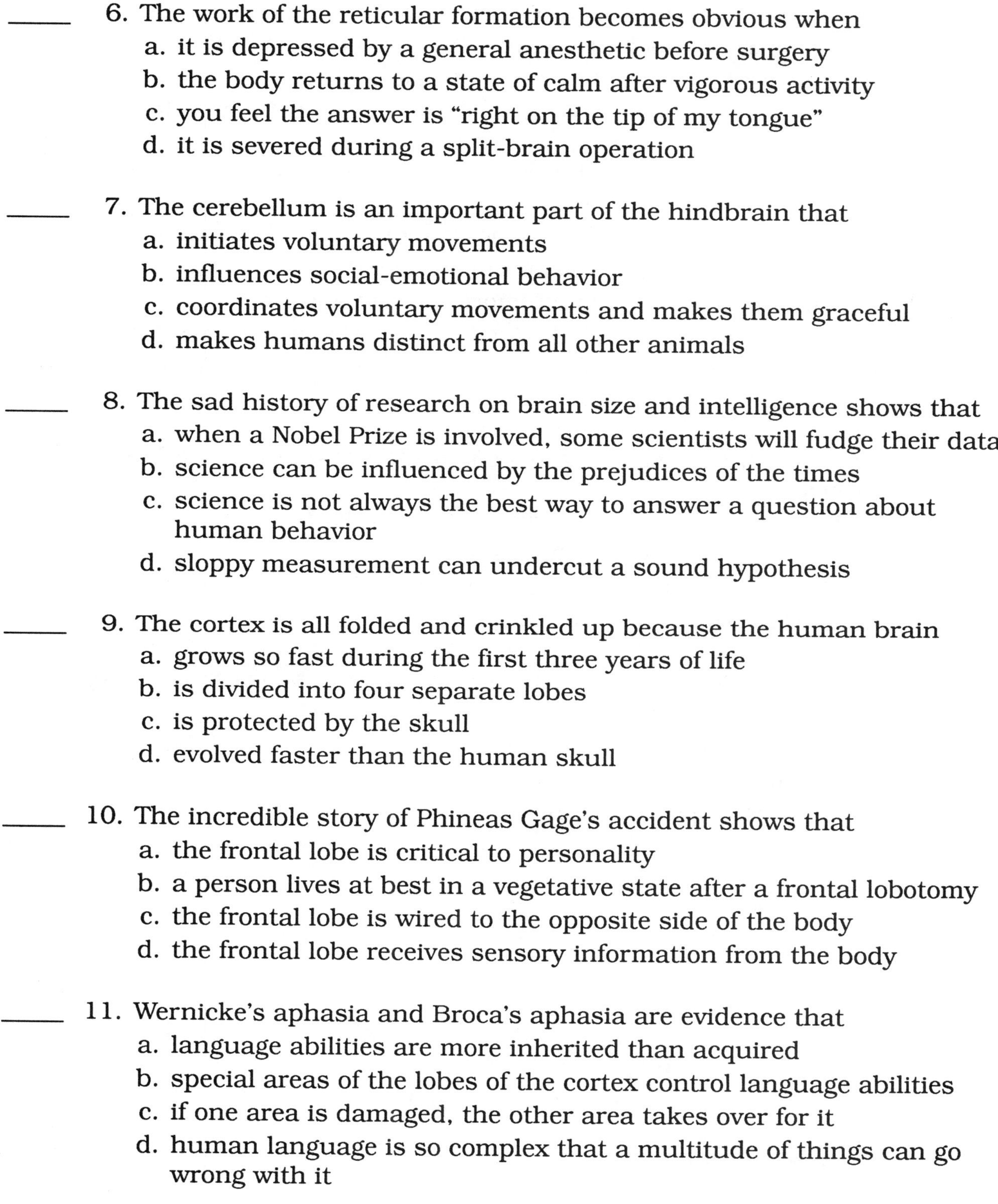

_____ 6. The work of the reticular formation becomes obvious when
   a. it is depressed by a general anesthetic before surgery
   b. the body returns to a state of calm after vigorous activity
   c. you feel the answer is "right on the tip of my tongue"
   d. it is severed during a split-brain operation

_____ 7. The cerebellum is an important part of the hindbrain that
   a. initiates voluntary movements
   b. influences social-emotional behavior
   c. coordinates voluntary movements and makes them graceful
   d. makes humans distinct from all other animals

_____ 8. The sad history of research on brain size and intelligence shows that
   a. when a Nobel Prize is involved, some scientists will fudge their data
   b. science can be influenced by the prejudices of the times
   c. science is not always the best way to answer a question about human behavior
   d. sloppy measurement can undercut a sound hypothesis

_____ 9. The cortex is all folded and crinkled up because the human brain
   a. grows so fast during the first three years of life
   b. is divided into four separate lobes
   c. is protected by the skull
   d. evolved faster than the human skull

_____ 10. The incredible story of Phineas Gage's accident shows that
   a. the frontal lobe is critical to personality
   b. a person lives at best in a vegetative state after a frontal lobotomy
   c. the frontal lobe is wired to the opposite side of the body
   d. the frontal lobe receives sensory information from the body

_____ 11. Wernicke's aphasia and Broca's aphasia are evidence that
   a. language abilities are more inherited than acquired
   b. special areas of the lobes of the cortex control language abilities
   c. if one area is damaged, the other area takes over for it
   d. human language is so complex that a multitude of things can go wrong with it

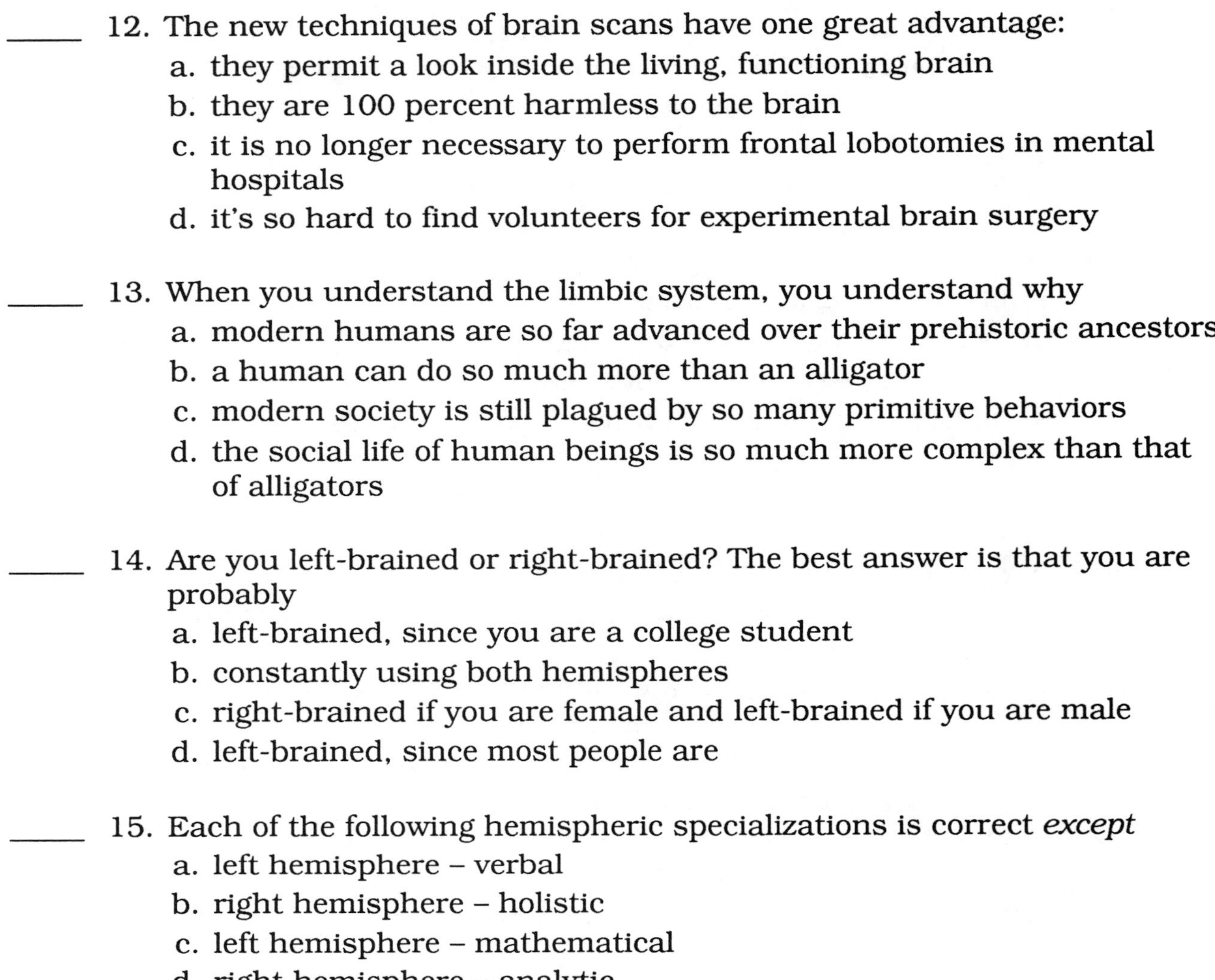

_____ 12. The new techniques of brain scans have one great advantage:
- a. they permit a look inside the living, functioning brain
- b. they are 100 percent harmless to the brain
- c. it is no longer necessary to perform frontal lobotomies in mental hospitals
- d. it's so hard to find volunteers for experimental brain surgery

_____ 13. When you understand the limbic system, you understand why
- a. modern humans are so far advanced over their prehistoric ancestors
- b. a human can do so much more than an alligator
- c. modern society is still plagued by so many primitive behaviors
- d. the social life of human beings is so much more complex than that of alligators

_____ 14. Are you left-brained or right-brained? The best answer is that you are probably
- a. left-brained, since you are a college student
- b. constantly using both hemispheres
- c. right-brained if you are female and left-brained if you are male
- d. left-brained, since most people are

_____ 15. Each of the following hemispheric specializations is correct *except*
- a. left hemisphere – verbal
- b. right hemisphere – holistic
- c. left hemisphere – mathematical
- d. right hemisphere – analytic

Answers for Chapter 2

Module 3

True-False	Matching	Multiple-Choice
1. F	1. d	1. d
2. T	2. h	2. b
3. T	3. j	3. c
4. F	4. a	4. a
5. F	5. i	5. b
6. T	6. c	6. d
7. T	7. f	7. a
8. F	8. g	8. c
9. T	9. b	9. b
10. F	10. e	10. d
		11. c
		12. a
		13. c
		14. b
		15. d

Module 4

True-False	Matching	Multiple-Choice
1. T	1. j	1. c
2. F	2. b	2. d
3. T	3. d	3. a
4. F	4. i	4. b
5. F	5. g	5. d
6. T	6. a	6. a
7. F	7. c	7. c
8. T	8. f	8. b
9. F	9. h	9. d
10. T	10. e	10. a
		11. b
		12. a
		13. c
		14. b
		15. d

Chapter 3: The Senses

If a tree falls in the forest...

Does it make any sound if there is no one there to hear it? Rod Plotnik discusses this old puzzler in the module on hearing. As you might imagine, the answer depends on how you define the word "sound." Is it the sound waves generated when the tree crashes to earth? Is it the vibrations of the inner ear stimulated by the sound waves? Is it the activity of the auditory cortex in the brain receiving electrical impulses from the ear? Or is it the accumulated auditory experience that causes us to say, "Darn! It sounds like a tree just fell in the forest!"

What is reality?

Studying this chapter on sensation, and the next one on perception, might cause you to ask what reality is, or even whether there is any reality at all. Some philosophers have taken the extreme position that there is no reality — just ideas in our minds (or in God's).

If you can answer these questions, congratulations (and sign up for philosophy next semester), but for a student of psychology it is more important to appreciate the processes that run from something physical "out there," to electrical activity in our sense organs and brain, and finally to mental interpretations of what that reality is (this is perception).

Try to think about all the stimuli that are bombarding your senses right now — everything your eyes, ears, nose, skin, and taste buds are picking up. It is impossible to think about all of them at once. Imagine the problem your sense organs have, gathering it all and sending it to the brain. That enormous problem of data collection and transmission is what you should attempt to grasp and appreciate in this chapter.

Effective Student Tip 3

Stay Focused

You may be away from home for the first time, trying to get along with your roommates, cheering on your college team, and worrying about how to get a date. You may be returning to college and finding out how difficult it is to squeeze extra hours into the day. In either case, you are discovering how easy it is to become distracted from your basic purpose for being in college.

No matter how important a party, your friend's need to talk all night, or extra work at the office may seem at the time, learning and succeeding are what college is really all about. The most important attributes of college are what happens in your classrooms and at your desk, when it's time to study.

Keep your emotional radar attuned to incoming distractions. When all you hear is the beep, beep, beep of threats to learning and succeeding, it's time to defend yourself. Remind yourself why you are in college. Then make the necessary adjustments to get back to the work you came to college to do.

Module 5: Vision

Use this

Outline

to organize your studying. Write notes on it. Turn it into a personalized aid for effective learning.

I. Overview: do eyes see and ears hear?

A. Characteristics of all senses

1. **Transduction** — changing physical stimuli into impulses

2. **Adaptation** — gradual decrease in responding

3. **Sensory experience** — physical stimuli plus processing by the brain produces a psychological experience

B. How sense organs and brain create sensations

1. Sense organs react to stimuli and send impulses to brain

2. Brain creates psychological experience of seeing, hearing, smelling, touching, tasting, positioning

II. Components of vision

A. Light waves

1. **Visible spectrum**

2. Colors

B. Eye

1. Structure

a. **Cornea**

b. Pupil

c. Iris

d. **Lens**

2. Function
    a. **Nearsightedness**
    b. **Farsightedness**
    c. Cataracts

C. **Retina**
1. Photoreceptors
2. **Rods**
3. **Cones**
4. Transduction
    a. Convergence
    b. Night blindness
    c. Dark adaptation
    d. Light adaptation

D. From eye to brain
1. **Primary visual cortex**
2. **Association area**

E. Color vision
1. Wave lengths
2. Theories of color vision
    a. **Trichromatic** theory
    b. **Opponent-process** theory
3. Color blindness

III. *Applying/Exploring:* Visual experiences

A. Preferred eye

B. Blind spot

C. Afterimage

D. Color blindness test

Now take the

Self-Tests

to check your understanding and mastery of this module.

Getting the general idea... Is the statement true or false?

_____ 1. All of the senses share three characteristics: transduction, adaptation, and the experience of "sensing" something.

_____ 2. The visible spectrum consists of the very short light waves — those that humans are able to see.

_____ 3. The reason you can "see" a giraffe is that the animal emits light waves that humans can detect.

_____ 4. As they age, all humans are doomed to become either nearsighted or farsighted.

_____ 5. The retina performs the work called transduction.

_____ 6. Both rods and cones help us see detail by producing a great deal of convergence of visual stimuli.

_____ 7. The images you "see" are created by the primary visual cortex and related association area of the brain.

_____ 8. We see in color because the eye can detect the texture of most objects.

_____ 9. Color blindness is found mostly in males.

_____ 10. *All you baseball players, listen up!* If your preferred eye is the left eye, you should bat left-handed.

Knowing the essential vocabulary... Which phrase matches the term?

_____ 1. transduction — a. gradual decrease in responding

_____ 2. adaptation — b. bends and focuses light waves

_____ 3. visible spectrum — c. allow us to see color

_____ 4. cornea — d. used for precise sighting

_____ 5. lens — e. hot student in your psych class

_____ 6. retina — f. large amount of convergence

_____ 7. rods — g. perceptible wave lengths

_____ 8. cones — h. where transduction occurs in the eye

_____ 9. preferred eye — i. covering of the eye

_____ 10. eyes for — j. from physical stimuli to sensation

Mastering the material... Which answer makes the statement true?

_____ 1. Rod Plotnik tells the story of the man blinded by a gunshot wound to illustrate the fact that
   a. once the eyes are destroyed, sight is lost forever
   b. once the skull is shattered, blindness usually occurs
   c. we "see" because of our visual cortex
   d. we "see" because of our cornea and lens

_____ 2. The process by which a sense organ changes physical stimuli into impulses is termed
   a. transduction
   b. adaptation
   c. sensing
   d. experiencing

_____ 3. A decline in responding with prolonged or continuous stimulation is called
   a. transduction
   b. adaptation
   c. sensing
   d. experiencing

_____ 4. The sensations of which we are constantly aware are produced by the
   a. sense organs
   b. eyes, ears, nose, skin, and tongue
   c. spinal cord
   d. brain

_____ 5. The reason why we can't see X-rays is that
   a. they are a form of electromagnetic energy
   b. their wave length is too short
   c. X-rays have no color
   d. X-rays overstimulate the receptors in our eyes

_____ 6. When you get that new road rocket for graduation, you may want a radar detector, too, because those things
   a. see the pulses of light that radar guns use
   b. hear the faint vibrations of radar guns
   c. see long wave lengths you can't
   d. make your car look cool

_____ 7. The function of the cornea is to
a. bend and focus light waves into a narrower beam of light
b. screen out irrelevant light waves
c. prevent convergence from occurring too soon
d. add color to light waves entering the eye

_____ 8. The purpose of the lens is to
a. protect the eye from damage by irritants in the air
b. magnify the image you perceive
c. control the amount of light that enters the eye
d. bend and focus light waves into an even narrower beam

_____ 9. If you see close objects clearly but distant objects appear blurry, you are
a. nearsighted
b. farsighted
c. normal
d. abnormal

_____ 10. The work of the retina is to
a. add sharp focus to what you are seeing
b. transform light waves into impulses
c. turn the inverted image we see right side up
d. change impulses into light waves we can see

_____ 11. One difference between rods and cones is that
a. rods help us see details
b. rods help us see color
c. cones help us see details
d. cones help us see in dim light

_____ 12. The best explanation of how color vision works is the
a. trichromatic theory
b. opponent-process theory
c. existence of different wave lengths
d. all three explanations are needed

_____ 13. A person who has difficulty distinguishing red from green is referred to as a

a. monochromat
b. dichromat
c. trichromat
d. quadromat

_____ 14. Researchers have discovered that good hitters in baseball usually have

a. their preferred eye on one side and their preferred hand on the other
b. both their preferred eye and preferred hand on the same side
c. eyeballs that are slightly elongated
d. optic nerves that are more sensitive

_____ 15. The blind spot everyone has is caused by

a. extremely slow ocular deterioration that occurs from birth on
b. areas where rods and cones overlap
c. the small circular area where the optic nerve exits from the back of the eye
d. stop worrying — there is no actual blind spot, it's just a figure of speech

Module 6: Hearing and Other Senses

Use this

Outline

to organize your studying. Write notes on it. Turn it into a personalized aid for effective learning.

I. Hearing

A. **Sound waves**

1. Amplitude (loudness)

2. Frequency (pitch)

3. Hearing range

B. Structure and function of the ear

1. Outer ear

a. External ear

b. Auditory canal

c. **Eardrum** (tympanic membrane)

2. Middle ear

a. **Ossicles** (hammer, anvil, stirrup)

b. Oval window

3. Inner ear

a. **Cochlea**

b. **Basilar membrane**

C. Neural pathways to the brain

1. Primary auditory cortex

2. Association areas

D. Interpreting sound waves

1. **Direction** (ears set apart)

2. **Loudness** (rate of impulses)

3. **Pitch** (sound waves)
    a. Frequency theory
    b. Place theory

E. Deafness

1. Conduction deafness
2. Neural deafness

II. Perceiving movement and **position (vestibular system)**

A. Vestibular organs

B. Motion sickness

III. Chemical sense: Taste

A. Tongue

1. Surface
2. **Taste buds**
3. Four basic sensations
    a. **Sweet**
    b. **Salty**
    c. **Sour**
    d. **Bitter**

B. Taste and smell

C. Cultural differences in taste

IV. Chemical sense: Smell

A. Smell and taste

B. Process of smelling

1. **Volatile** stimuli

2. Receptors for olfaction (mucus)

3. Olfactory sensations

C. Functions of smell

1. Intensify taste of food

2. Warn of dangerous foods

3. Elicit strong memories

V. Sense of touch

A. Sensations: pressure, temperature, and pain

B. Receptors for sense of touch

1. Skin

2. Free nerve endings

3. Hair receptors

4. Pacinian corpuscle

VI. *Applying/Exploring:* Experience of pain

A. Receptors and sensations

1. Many different stimuli

2. Intensity involves psychological factors

B. **Gate control** theory

C. Attention and emotion

D. **Endorphins**

E. Acupuncture explained

Getting the general idea... Is the statement true or false?

_____ 1. Sound waves vary in amplitude and frequency.

_____ 2. Infants have the widest range of human hearing.

_____ 3. The outer ear contains the ossicles and oval window.

_____ 4. The cochlea transforms vibrations into nerve impulses.

_____ 5. The vestibular system provides feedback on your body's position in space by interpreting sound waves from your environment.

_____ 6. The tongue has receptors for only four basic tastes.

_____ 7. Humans won't eat just anything — we have biologically determined preferences for some foods and feelings of disgust at the thought of others.

_____ 8. The sense of smell is 10,000 times more sensitive than that of taste.

_____ 9. The sensations of touch, temperature, or pain are created by three specific sensors on the surface of the skin.

_____ 10. Acupuncture often produces pain relief — probably by causing secretion of endorphins in the brain.

Knowing the essential vocabulary... Which phrase matches the term?

	Term		Phrase
_____	1. amplitude	a.	three small bones
_____	2. frequency	b.	wear out in ten days
_____	3. ossicles	c.	pitch
_____	4. cochlea	d.	coiled, fluid-filled apparatus
_____	5. vestibular system	e.	how Flipper's friends ride
_____	6. taste buds	f.	motion sickness
_____	7. volatile	g.	turns impulse into feeling
_____	8. somatosensory cortex	h.	natural pain killers
_____	9. endorphins	i.	loudness
_____	10. on dolphins	j.	give off molecules

Mastering the material... Which answer makes the statement true?

_____ 1. To the traditional "five senses," science now adds others, such as
   a. divining
   b. intuition
   c. positioning
   d. extra-sensory perception

_____ 2. How loud a sound seems is determined by the ______________ of the sound waves
   a. amplitude
   b. frequency
   c. pitch
   d. cycle

_____ 3. If a tree falls in an uninhabited forest, does it make any sound?
   a. obviously, it does
   b. not if there is no human there to "hear" it
   c. it depends on whether we define "sound" as the waves of air or the subjective experience of hearing
   d. I thought this was psychology, not philosophy

_____ 4. At about 120 decibels, a live rock band is
   a. safe as long as you don't attend every day
   b. in the danger zone for permanent damage
   c. just barely within the safety zone
   d. safe for some persons but not for others

_____ 5. Infants have the widest range of human hearing because
   a. babies need to keep track of where their mothers are at all times
   b. hearing is an important part of language acquisition
   c. they're brand new
   d. science has not determined the reason

_____ 6. Which one of the following is *not* a part of the outer ear?
   a. external ear
   b. auditory canal
   c. tympanic membrane (eardrum)
   d. cochlea

_____ 7. The function of the middle ear is to
   a. funnel sound waves into the eardrum
   b. reduce the pressure on the three small bones called ossicles
   c. transform vibrations of the tympanic membrane into vibrations of the ossicles
   d. help determine position and balance

_____ 8. The function of the cochlea is to
   a. turn vibrations into nerve impulses
   b. move fluid forward toward the oval window
   c. house the hammer, anvil, and stirrup
   d. house the band of fibers called the auditory nerve

_____ 9. The actual experience we know as "hearing" occurs in the
   a. eardrum (hammer, anvil, and stirrup)
   b. primary auditory cortex and neighboring association areas
   c. cochlea of the inner ear
   d. outer, middle, and inner ear working together

_____ 10. We are able to tell where a sound is coming from because
   a. we are able to move our ears slightly toward the sound
   b. we can rotate our heads toward the sound
   c. human ears stick out from the skull
   d. our ears are about six inches apart

_____ 11. Our sense of movement and position in space is determined by
   a. movement of fluid in the arches of the vestibular system
   b. the primary visual cortex and related association areas
   c. faint echoes from surrounding objects that the brain can decode
   d. the movement of fluid in the eardrum

_____ 12. Which one of the following is *not* one of the four basic tastes?
   a. sweet
   b. sharp
   c. salty
   d. sour

_____ 13. Is the relationship between taste and smell important in marketing?
   a. no
   b. only when it brings in the culturally determined "disgust" reaction
   c. it cancels out, since smell only contributes a small amount to taste
   d. uh huh!

_____ 14. Our sense of touch comes from
   a. a half dozen miniature sensors located in the skin
   b. millions of tiny nerves on the surface of the skin
   c. special glands for pressure, temperature, and pain
   d. stimulation of the tiny hairs that cover the body

_____ 15. Can the ancient Oriental procedure called acupuncture actually relieve pain? Modern science says
   a. yes, because there are some mysteries Western science is not equipped to explain
   b. yes, because stimulation of certain points causes secretion of endorphins
   c. no, because there cannot be a relationship between twirling needles in the skin and pain caused by the nervous system
   d. no, because there is no research to date that supports acupuncture

Answers for Chapter 3

Module 5

True-False	Matching	Multiple-Choice
1. T	1. j	1. c
2. F	2. a	2. a
3. F	3. g	3. b
4. F	4. i	4. d
5. T	5. b	5. b
6. F	6. h	6. c
7. T	7. f	7. a
8. F	8. c	8. d
9. T	9. d	9. a
10. F	10. e	10. b
		11. c
		12. d
		13. b
		14. a
		15. c

Module 6

True-False	Matching	Multiple-Choice
1. T	1. i	1. c
2. T	2. c	2. a
3. F	3. a	3. c
4. T	4. d	4. b
5. F	5. f	5. c
6. T	6. b	6. d
7. F	7. j	7. c
8. T	8. g	8. a
9. F	9. h	9. b
10. T	10. e	10. d
		11. a
		12. b
		13. d
		14. a
		15. b

Chapter 4: Perception

How to ruin a professor's day

When I took experimental psychology, years ago, our professor enjoyed bedeviling us with the same classic perceptual illusions that Rod Plotnik discusses in this chapter. The one that really got us was the famous Müller-Lyer illusion. It is so powerful that it fooled us every time, even after we already knew the lines were the same length. Then a trouble-maker in the back row asked, "But *why* does it work?" Our professor hung his head and had to admit, "I don't know."

Today, cognitive psychology has an intriguing answer (see your textbook). Besides the fascination of discovering how sensation and perception function, understanding these processes can be personally liberating. Here's why.

The task of self-management

Step on a rattlesnake and it whirls and strikes. Step on a human and... a hundred different things could happen. Instinct governs much of the snake's behavior, but almost none of the human's. That's why we humans constantly face the task of self-management, or self-regulation. We also face parallel tasks of managing physical objects and other people, but self-management is the most difficult because it's so subjective. As you will see in the chapter on mental disorders, it's easy for things to get out of whack. Normally, the activity of self-management goes on so automatically it seems unconscious, but we are constantly working at it.

That's what I like about the twin chapters on sensation and perception. They help us appreciate the incredibly complex processes of apprehending and interpreting reality, and in so doing can help us be more realistic about ourselves. There are many things in life to worry about and to fear. An important part of self-management is deciding which stimuli represent real threats and which do not. The disadvantage of our limitless freedom to create wonderful new things is our equally great ability to create fears where they are not appropriate. When we get a better handle on our processes of self-management, however, we begin to appreciate that some apparent perceptions are really glitches in the self-managing process, and we realize that we are scaring ourselves needlessly.

The chapters on sensation and perception remind us that, in a sense, we constantly create reality. Just as illusions can fool us, we can torment ourselves with worries and fears about dangers that are illusory, not real.

Effective Student Tip 4

Adopt a Strategy of Effectiveness

You're probably getting more specific advice about how to be successful in college than you know what to do with. Implicit in all that advice is something more important — the need for a *strategy* of success. An overall strategy is important because it gives you a way of evaluating any particular suggestion and of adjusting to whatever condition arises. It is more than a single game plan, because it is both more comprehensive and more flexible. If your game plan for the next test is to work like the devil, what do you do if hard work doesn't seem to be enough?

The strategy of effectiveness is simply this: (1) You recognize that you have a basic need to be effective in everything you do — especially your college work, since that's your most important task right now. (2) You measure everything you do in college by asking, "Is this procedure getting the job done?" (In other words, is it effective?) (3) Whenever a method isn't working, instead of continuing to do the same old ineffective thing, you make a specific procedural change — to a technique that works better.

Module 7: Basic Perceptual Processes

Use this

Outline

to organize your studying. Write notes on it. Turn it into a personalized aid for effective learning.

I. Overview of perception

A. Three basic questions

1. At what point are we aware of a stimulus?
2. At what point do we know stimulus intensity has increased (or decreased)?
3. At what point does sensation change into meaningful perception?

B. Perceptual thresholds

1. Absolute threshold (Gustav Fechner)
2. Just noticeable difference (E. H. Weber)

C. Sensations and perceptions

1. Sensation — meaningless bits of raw information from sensory receptors
2. Perception — meaningful pattern or image assembled by the brain

D. Process of **perception**

1. Any change in energy in environment creates **stimuli...**
2. which activate **sense organs** to trigger electrical signals or impulses...
3. which are transformed by the **brain** into...
4. **sensations** or meaningless bits of sensory information...
5. to which **experience** automatically adds meanings, feelings, and memories...
6. which result in meaningful patterns or images known as **perceptions**

II. Principles of perceptual organization

A. Is the whole more than the sum of its parts?

1. Structuralist argument

2. **Gestalt** psychology argument

3. Principles of organization

B. Perceptual rules for **grouping** stimuli

1. **Figure-ground**

2. **Closure**

3. **Simplicity**

4. **Similarity**

5. **Proximity**

6. **Continuity**

C. Depth perception

1. **Binocular** cues (both eyes)

a. **Convergence**

b. **Retinal disparity**

2. **Monocular** cues (single eye)

a. Interposition

b. Linear perspective

c. Relative size

d. Atmospheric perspective

e. Texture gradient

f. Light and shadow

g. Motion parallax

D. Perceptual **constancies**

1. **Size**

2. **Shape**

3. **Color**

4. **Brightness**

E. **Illusions**

1. **Ames room**

2. **Müller-Lyer** illusion

3. Thatcher illusion

4. **Impossible figures**

5. Moon illusion

III. *Applying/Exploring:* Creating perceptual experiences

A. Real motion

B. **Apparent motion**

1. Movies

2. **Virtual reality**

3. Moving lights (phi movement)

4. Changing reality

Now take the
Self-Tests
to check your understanding and mastery of this module.

Getting the general idea... Is the statement true or false?

_____ 1. A threshold is a point above which we are aware of a stimulus.

_____ 2. When you replace a 100 watt bulb with a 200 watt bulb, the lamp becomes twice as bright.

_____ 3. A physiologist calls it "sensation" and a psychologist calls it "perception," but they are both talking about the same thing.

_____ 4. The brain follows a number of perceptual rules to make sense out of the mass of visual stimuli it receives.

_____ 5. You see in three dimensions because your eyes can differentiate the varying lengths of waves coming in.

_____ 6. A person using only one eye can still tell depth, thanks to a phenomenon known as telescopic vision.

_____ 7. If it were not for perceptual constancies, the world would seem ever-changing and chaotic.

_____ 8. In the Müller-Lyer illusion, one boy looks like a giant and the other like a midget.

_____ 9. Illusions are interesting because they remind us that perception is an active process.

_____ 10. Horses at the track, real motion; movie replay of race, apparent motion.

Knowing the essential vocabulary... Which phrase matches the term?

	Term		Phrase
_____	1. threshold	a.	each eye has a slightly different view
_____	2. perception	b.	a depth cue
_____	3. Gestalt	c.	making sense out of sensations
_____	4. closure	d.	whole is more than sum of its parts
_____	5. retinal disparity	e.	that there is nothing to worry about
_____	6. linear perspective	f.	is one arrow longer?
_____	7. Ames room	g.	at first you can't, and then you can
_____	8. Müller-Lyer illusion	h.	movie theater marquee
_____	9. apparent movement	i.	filling in the missing parts
_____	10. Alfred E. Newman illusion	j.	mad scientist takes up carpentry

Mastering the material... Which answer makes the statement true?

_____ 1. An absolute threshold is the intensity level that you
  a. can detect every time it is presented
  b. know is there, even if you can't quite detect it
  c. can just barely detect
  d. can detect 50 percent of the time

_____ 2. Weber's law of the just noticeable difference explains why
  a. your parents don't believe you really turned your stereo down
  b. kids like heavy metal and their parents like Montovani
  c. you study better if you have the radio on
  d. many teenagers knew Milli-Vanilli weren't really singing

_____ 3. Perception is to sensation as _______________ is to _______________
  a. a child ... a grownup
  b. unfinished ... complete
  c. a story ... words
  d. reality ... a movie

_____ 4. To complete the work of perception, the brain also draws on
  a. neurotransmitters
  b. experience
  c. hormones
  d. reality

_____ 5. The perceptual rule that makes important things stand out is called
  a. closure
  b. proximity
  c. figure dominance
  d. figure-ground

_____ 6. The perceptual principle that creates a group out of objects that are close together is called
  a. proximity
  b. similarity
  c. continuity
  d. closure

_____ 7. The advantage to the human species of having two eyes is
a. figure-ground discrimination
b. monocular cues
c. retinal disparity
d. glasses balance on the nose better

_____ 8. Which one of the following is *not* a monocular cue for depth?
a. interposition
b. similarity
c. relative size
d. texture gradient

_____ 9. Motion parallax explains why we are able to
a. move faster than usual in dangerous situations
b. pick out the most important elements in what we are seeing
c. tell how fast something is moving even though it is far away
d. use the speed of moving objects to tell distance

_____ 10. Thank goodness for size constancy! Without it, you would
a. never know for sure which is the figure and which is the background
b. immediately get bigger after a single large meal
c. be overcome by grief when your sweetheart walks farther and farther away from you
d. see things change in size whenever the light changes in brightness

_____ 11. The reason why people seem to change size as they move around in the Ames room is that
a. the room isn't rectangular
b. hidden mirrors distort the images you see as you look in
c. a lens in the peephole forces you to view them upside down
d. the subtle coloring of the walls creates a hypnotic trance in the viewer

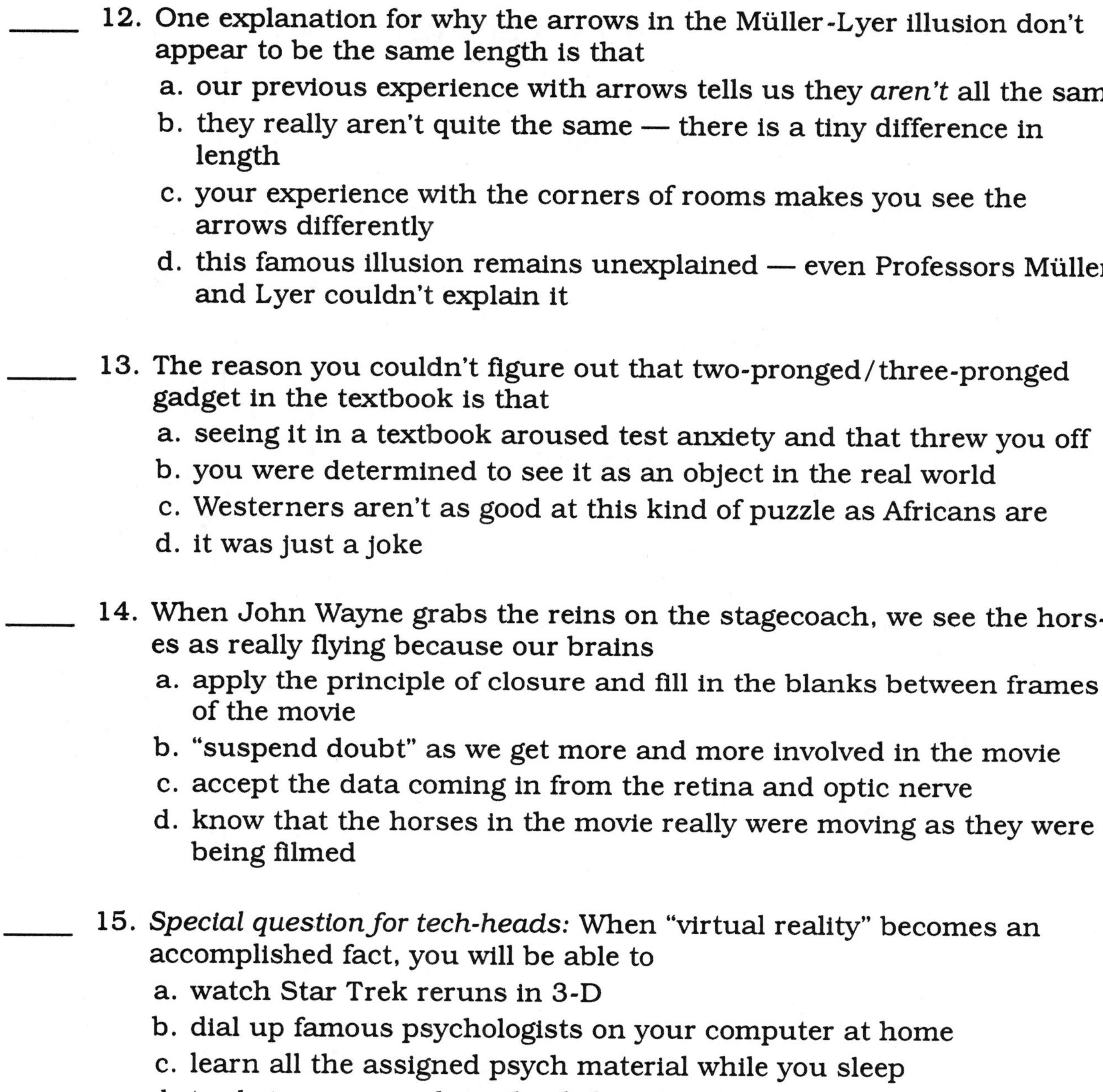

_____ 12. One explanation for why the arrows in the Müller-Lyer illusion don't appear to be the same length is that

a. our previous experience with arrows tells us they *aren't* all the same
b. they really aren't quite the same — there is a tiny difference in length
c. your experience with the corners of rooms makes you see the arrows differently
d. this famous illusion remains unexplained — even Professors Müller and Lyer couldn't explain it

_____ 13. The reason you couldn't figure out that two-pronged/three-pronged gadget in the textbook is that

a. seeing it in a textbook aroused test anxiety and that threw you off
b. you were determined to see it as an object in the real world
c. Westerners aren't as good at this kind of puzzle as Africans are
d. it was just a joke

_____ 14. When John Wayne grabs the reins on the stagecoach, we see the horses as really flying because our brains

a. apply the principle of closure and fill in the blanks between frames of the movie
b. "suspend doubt" as we get more and more involved in the movie
c. accept the data coming in from the retina and optic nerve
d. know that the horses in the movie really were moving as they were being filmed

_____ 15. *Special question for tech-heads:* When "virtual reality" becomes an accomplished fact, you will be able to

a. watch Star Trek reruns in 3-D
b. dial up famous psychologists on your computer at home
c. learn all the assigned psych material while you sleep
d. trade in your psych textbook for a headset and a computer disk

Module 8: Influences on Perception

Use this

Outline

to organize your studying. Write notes on it. Turn it into a personalized aid for effective learning.

I. Heredity and experience in perception

   A. Research methods

      1. Developmental

      2. Experimental

      3. Case study

   B. Effects of restricted experience with external environment

      1. Kittens in a striped world (**critical period**)

      2. Salamanders with rotated eyes (**heredity**)

      3. Humans in an upside down world (**perceptual adaptation**)

   C. Effects of restricted experience with internal environment (brain damage)

      1. **Agnosia**

         a. Faces

         b. Objects

      2. **Neglect syndrome**

II. Learning influences

   A. Weight and media pressures

   B. **Gender differences**

      1. Ambiguous objects

      2. Rotating figures

C. **Perceptual sets**

D. **Culture** and perception

1. Images (black and white photo)

2. Constancy and depth ("insects" that were water buffalo)

3. Motion (conventions to depict movement)

III. *Applying/Exploring:* **Extrasensory Perception** (ESP)

A. Varieties of ESP experiences

1. **Telepathy**

2. **Precognition**

3. **Clairvoyance**

4. **Psychokinesis**

5. **Out-of-body experience**

B. Debate over psychic abilities

1. Inability to repeat positive results

2. Lack of convincing research results

Now take the
Self-Tests
to check your understanding and mastery of this module.

Getting the general idea... Is the statement true or false?

_____ 1. All perceptual processes, by definition, are inherited.

_____ 2. The most useful approach to studying influences on perception is the correlational method.

_____ 3. Research on kittens living in a striped world showed the importance of critical periods for experience.

_____ 4. Human subjects learned to perform complex behaviors like riding bicycles even though they were seeing the world upside down.

_____ 5. As is demonstrated by the effects of brain damage, changes in the internal environment can affect perception.

_____ 6. Even though the media promotes ultra thinness, people know if they are overweight or not.

_____ 7. It seems logical that there would be gender differences in perception, but extensive research has failed to find any.

_____ 8. A perceptual set is a kind of stubbornness that makes subjects stick to the first answer they give even if they realize they were wrong.

_____ 9. Anthropologists have discovered that how you see things depends on the culture in which you were raised.

_____ 10. There is a large body of accepted scientific evidence that supports the existence of ESP.

Knowing the essential vocabulary... Which phrase matches the term?

	Term		Phrase
_____	1. critical period	a.	limited window for learning
_____	2. perceptual adaptation	b.	seeing what you expect to see
_____	3. agnosia	c.	why a drawing can seem to be moving
_____	4. neglect syndrome	d.	humans have it; salamanders don't
_____	5. gender differences	e.	taking all the fun out of it
_____	6. perceptual set	f.	agnosia for the left side
_____	7. cultural influences	g.	dinner plate or target?
_____	8. artistic conventions	h.	sensory input but no perception
_____	9. clairvoyance	i.	pressures to conform to shared values
_____	10. Amazing Randi	j.	perceiving something out of sight

Mastering the material... Which answer makes the statement true?

_____ 1. The case of the man in his fifties who regained his sight after a lifetime of blindness shows that
a. visual experience that was missed in childhood can't be made up
b. near-normal vision comes back very quickly after operations such as his
c. perception can be restored surgically
d. perception depends on both inherited and learned factors

_____ 2. Eleanor Gibson invented the visual cliff in order to study
a. whether Sam (in the question above) had acquired a sense of depth
b. when infants develop depth perception
c. how kittens and human infants differ in depth perception
d. at what age children begin to develop common sense

_____ 3. Raising newborn animals in total darkness shows that
a. without visual stimulation, animals go blind
b. animals can learn to "see in the dark"
c. a minimal amount of visual stimulation is necessary for normal development
d. both too little and too much stimulation is harmful to the development of vision

_____ 4. Raising kittens in a world of only vertical lines demonstrated that
a. experience missed at a critical period can't be made up later
b. cats can adapt to almost any situation if fed and cared for
c. most animals (including humans) are either vertically or horizontally oriented
d. the kittens learned to ignore the stripes

_____ 5. Those poor salamanders with the surgically rotated eyes at least taught us about the relationship between
a. vision and food
b. vision and hunting
c. heredity and adaptation
d. heredity and genetics

_____ 6. When human subjects wore goggles that turned their world upside down, they demonstrated that
a. distorted visual experience usually causes motion sickness
b. humans have great powers of perceptual adaptation
c. inverted vision produces some of the same symptoms as agnosia
d. once you learn to ride a bicycle, you never forget

_____ 7. The existence of the neglect syndrome shows the importance of
a. experience in perception
b. constant practice in maintaining visual acuity
c. agnosia in activities on the right side of the body
d. association areas in perception

_____ 8. Answers to the question, "Am I overweight?" show that perception is influenced by
a. personal feelings
b. what other people say about you
c. objective data (scales)
d. realistic appraisals of yourself and others

_____ 9. When shown ambiguous objects, males and females tend to "see"
a. the same things
b. different things
c. it varies greatly from individual to individual
d. the same things within a culture; different things across cultures

_____ 10. You probably saw the bodybuilder pictured in the textbook as huge because
a. the background showed other small people
b. he was shown in the Ames room
c. a perceptual constancy was operating
d. a perceptual set was operating

_____ 11. Seeing water buffalo as "insects" shows that size constancy and depth perception are strongly affected by
a. cultural beliefs about animals
b. seeing a black-and-white photo for the first time
c. previous visual experience
d. racial inheritance

_____ 12. The ability to foretell events is called
  a. telepathy
  b. precognition
  c. clairvoyance
  d. psychokinesis

_____ 13. The ability to move objects without touching them is called
  a. psychokinesis
  b. precognition
  c. clairvoyance
  d. telepathy

_____ 14. Despite the fact that many people believe in it, convincing evidence of ESP has been undercut by the
  a. hocus-pocus that surrounds ESP demonstrations
  b. refusal of psychologists to investigate it seriously
  c. inability to repeat positive results
  d. fact that some people have it and others don't

_____ 15. Tops on the list of people *not* to invite to an ESP demonstration:
  a. Gustave Fechner
  b. E. H. Weber
  c. Max Wertheimer
  d. Amazing Randi

Answers for Chapter 4

Module 7

True-False	Matching	Multiple-Choice
1. T	1. g	1. d
2. F	2. c	2. a
3. F	3. d	3. c
4. T	4. i	4. b
5. F	5. a	5. d
6. F	6. b	6. a
7. T	7. j	7. c
8. F	8. f	8. b
9. T	9. h	9. d
10. T	10. e	10. c
		11. a
		12. c
		13. b
		14. a
		15. d

Module 8

True-False	Matching	Multiple-Choice
1. F	1. a	1. d
2. F	2. d	2. b
3. T	3. h	3. c
4. T	4. f	4. a
5. T	5. g	5. c
6. F	6. b	6. b
7. F	7. i	7. d
8. F	8. c	8. a
9. T	9. j	9. b
10. F	10. e	10. d
		11. c
		12. b
		13. a
		14. c
		15. d

Chapter 5: States of Consciousness

1. Do dreams have meaning?

Freud is dead... Freud is dead... Freud is dead.... Keep repeating it long enough, and maybe Freud will go away. He has a way of coming back, though, no matter how often psychology pronounces him dead wrong.

One of Freud's most provocative ideas is the notion that all dreams have meaning. He thought it was his most important discovery, and wrote, "Insight such as this falls to one's lot but once in a lifetime." Dreams were important to Freud because they allowed the best look into the workings of the unconscious. When you learn more about Freud's theory of personality (in Chapter 12) and his technique of psychoanalysis (in Chapter 15), you will see that he thought of dreaming, with unconscious meanings hidden beneath innocent-sounding surface stories, as a model for all human psychic life.

The newer theories of dreaming discussed in Chapter 5 discount or reject Freud's theory, perhaps partly because — you knew this was coming — Freud says dreams represent sexual wishes. Building on research into sleep and brain biology, the new theories are filling in blanks Freud could only guess at. Still, these theories do not disprove Freud completely.

The deciding evidence may be your own dreams. Try an experiment: Tell yourself the story of a recent dream, then ask how the dream connects to your life. What feelings does it arouse? What thoughts (none sexual, of course) pop into your mind? How do the feelings and thoughts associated with the dream relate to issues in your psychological life? Is it possible that your dream does have meaning?

2. Why do we use drugs?

In textbook after textbook I've seen, the section on drugs reads like something you would get in pharmacy school. Good, solid technical information on psychoactive drugs, including the most recent illegal drugs to hit the streets, but nothing on the really important issue — why we use psychoactive drugs at all, let alone to such excess.

Rod Plotnik raises that question, and provides provocative answers about the biology and history of drug use. Personally, I'm dead set against any use of psychoactive drugs [...he typed, after setting down his can of caffeine-laced diet cola!], but I don't believe that it does any good for me to tell you that. Rod has it right. Instead of moralizing, let's investigate the psychological processes by which almost all of us "self-medicate," in our continual attempt to manage our thoughts, feelings, and behavior. This is exciting stuff.

Effective Student Tip 5

Build Effective Routines

Anyone who loves computers also values orderly procedures. To get the most out of your computer, you must learn procedures and follow them.

Why not apply the same tactic to your college studies? When it comes to advice about how to do better in college, there are tons of useful techniques, hints, tips, tricks, and shortcuts out there. Become a consumer of useful procedures. Adapt them to your needs. Invent your own. Gather advice about how to be successful in school, but do it with a difference.

First, take a *procedural* point of view. Pay less attention to advice that is mainly sloganeering (You must work harder!) and more to specific procedures (Three Secrets of Effective Writing). [Hey, that's tip #9.]

Second, gather all these useful procedures under the umbrella of *effectiveness*. Judge every procedure by whether it makes you a better student. If it works, keep it in your arsenal of useful procedures. If it doesn't, drop it. I once had a friend who decided to make himself lean and strong by eating *nothing but apples*. Excited about his new plan, for several days he was never without his bag of apples. It didn't work. He went back to burgers and fries.

Module 9: Consciousness, Sleep, and Dreams

Use this **Outline** to organize your studying. Write notes on it. Turn it into a personalized aid for effective learning.

I. **Consciousness**

A. Continuum of consciousness

1. **Controlled processes**

2. Automatic processes

3. Daydreaming

4. **Altered states** of consciousness

5. Sleep

6. **Unconscious** (psychological)

7. Unconsciousness (physical)

8. Coma

B. Rhythms of sleeping and waking

1. **Biological clock**

a. Suprachiasmatic nucleus

b. Highly responsive to changes in light

2. **Circadian rhythm** (25-hour day)

3. Resetting (**jet lag**)

a. Light

b. Melatonin

II. Sleep

A. Studying sleep in the laboratory

1. Electroencephalogram (EEG)

2. Amplitude and frequency of waves

B. Stages of sleep

1. Relaxed, drowsy state (alpha waves)

2. Stage 1 (theta waves)

3. Stage 2 (sleep spindles)

4. Stages 3 and 4 (delta waves)

C. **Rapid eye movement** (**REM**) (and non-REM) sleep

1. **Paradoxical sleep**

2. Dreaming

3. REM rebound

D. Causes of sleep and wakefulness

1. Brain

a. Reticular formation

b. Neurotransmitters

c. Body temperature

2. Changing patterns of sleep across lifetime

3. Theories of why we sleep

a. **Repair theory**

b. **Adaptive theory**

4. Sleep deprivation and performance

III. Dreams

A. General

1. Everyone dreams

2. Varieties of dreaming

a. Recurrent dreams

b. Color

c. Prediction

B. Interpretation of dreams

1. **Freud's** theory of dreams

a. **Wish fulfillment**

b. Disguise and **symbols**

2. **Activation-synthesis theory** (J. Alan Hobson and Robert McCarley)

a. Random, meaningless activity of nerve cells in brain

b. No reason to interpret dreams

3. **Extension of waking life** (Rosalind Cartwright)

a. Provide clues to dreamer's personal problems and feelings

b. Problem of very incomplete recall of dreams

4. **Lucid dreaming** (Stephen LaBerge)

a. Awareness of dreaming

b. Dreaming for a purpose

IV. *Applying/Exploring:* Sleep problems and treatments

A. **Insomnia**

1. Psychological causes

2. Physiological causes

a. Circadian rhythms

b. Sleep apnea

3. Behavioral treatment programs

a. **Stimulus control** method

b. Progressive relaxation method

c. Visual imagery method

B. **Night terrors** in children

C. **Nightmares**

D. **Sleepwalking** (somnambulism)

E. **Narcolepsy**

Now take the
Self-Tests
to check your understanding and mastery of this module.

Getting the general idea... Is the statement true or false?

_____ 1. Human beings are always in one of two distinct states: awake and conscious or asleep and unconscious.

_____ 2. One adjustment problem faced by humans is that the circadian rhythm of our biological clocks is set closer to 25 hours than to 24.

_____ 3. Exposure to bright light is a fast way to reset our biological clocks.

_____ 4. Researchers study sleep by measuring brain waves.

_____ 5. Once you sink into true sleep, your bodily activity remains constant until you awake in the morning.

_____ 6. The existence of the REM rebound effect suggests that dreaming must have some special importance to humans.

_____ 7. Research on sleep deprivation and performance proves that the "repair theory" of sleep is correct.

_____ 8. Everyone dreams.

_____ 9. As with everything else in his theories, Freud's explanation of dreams has a sexual twist.

_____ 10. The activation-synthesis theory of dreams places great importance on getting to the underlying meaning of each dream.

Knowing the essential vocabulary... Which phrase matches the term?

	Term		Phrase
_____	1. circadian rhythm	a.	dreams as meaningless
_____	2. non-REM sleep	b.	REM sleep
_____	3. paradoxical sleep	c.	awareness of dreaming
_____	4. REM rebound	d.	not enough hours in the day
_____	5. repair theory	e.	date hot number in your psych class
_____	6. adaptive theory	f.	Freud's theory of dreams
_____	7. wish fulfillment	g.	no dreams
_____	8. activation-synthesis theory	h.	need more dreams
_____	9. lucid dreaming	i.	sleep to stay out of trouble
_____	10. "in your dreams"	j.	sleep to recharge batteries

Mastering the basic facts and concepts... Do you know the answer?

_____ 1. Rod Plotnik opens the module on consciousness with the story of Stefania's three-month stay in a cave to illustrate the fact that
a. body time runs slower than celestial time
b. without sunlight, humans begin to lose their grip on reality
c. without sunlight, Stefania's night vision became very acute
d. we would all be much more cheerful if there were no clocks around

_____ 2. We naturally think in terms of the two states called "conscious" and "unconscious," but actually there
a. are three states, including the "high" from drugs
b. are four states: conscious, drowsy, dreaming, and unconscious
c. is a continuum of consciousness
d. is no measurable difference between consciousness and unconsciousness

_____ 3. Psychologists call activities that require full awareness, alertness, and concentration
a. automatic processes
b. altered states
c. comas
d. controlled processes

_____ 4. Have you noticed that you often wake up just before the alarm clock goes off? Credit it to the fact that we humans have a built-in
a. aversion to jangling noise, which we try to avoid
b. biological clock
c. sense of responsibility
d. brain mechanism that is always monitoring the external environment, even during sleep

_____ 5. If human beings were deprived of all mechanical means of telling time (like clocks), they would
a. still follow schedules and be punctual, thanks to their biological clocks
b. follow a natural clock with a day about 30 hours long
c. not stick to strict schedules the way we do now
d. lose all sense of when things should be done

_____ 6. The most promising new treatment for jet lag appears to be
   a. periods of bright light
   b. avoidance of food for 24 hours before a long flight
   c. surgical resetting of the biological clock
   d. drugs that induce sleep in the new time zone

_____ 7. Modern research on sleep suggests that most of us need
   a. about 10 hours of sleep a night
   b. about 8 hours of sleep a night
   c. short naps every 4 hours rather than a long night of sleep
   d. varying amounts of sleep — there is no general pattern

_____ 8. Dreams are most likely to occur during
   a. stage 1 (theta waves)
   b. EEG sleep
   c. non-REM sleep
   d. REM sleep

_____ 9. REM sleep is often called "paradoxical sleep" because
   a. you appear to be looking around even though obviously you can't see anything
   b. you have dreams, but they don't make any sense
   c. your body is in a state of arousal and your brain waves are like those when you are awake and alert
   d. your body is tense and ready for action even though you are asleep

_____ 10. As logical as the repair theory of sleep seems, it is not consistent with the fact that
   a. people are able to function fairly well even after long periods of sleep deprivation
   b. there is a marked secretion of growth hormones during sleep
   c. archaeological evidence suggests that early humans did not sleep much at all
   d. some people are "short sleepers" and others are "long sleepers"

_____ 11. According to Freud's famous theory, at the heart of every dream is a
   a. hate-filled thought
   b. clue to the future
   c. shameful sexual memory
   d. disguised wish

_____ 12. The activation-synthesis theory says that dreams result from
  a. a biological need to pull together and make sense of the day's activities
  b. "batch processing" of all the information gathered during the day
  c. random and meaningless activity of nerve cells in the brain
  d. the need to express hidden sexual and aggressive impulses

_____ 13. Sleep and dream researchers point out that you may not always understand what your dreams mean because
  a. you only remember small fragments of them
  b. they are expressed in a code only an expert can understand
  c. they simply don't mean anything significant in your life
  d. you may be one of those people who don't dream every night

_____ 14. The best advice for combating insomnia is to
  a. get in bed at the same time every night and stay there no matter what happens
  b. get out of bed, go to another room, and do something relaxing if you can't fall asleep
  c. review the problems of the day as you lie in bed trying to go to sleep
  d. try sleeping in another room, or on the couch, if you can't fall asleep in your bed

_____ 15. Which one of the following is *not* a sleep problem?
  a. night terrors
  b. sleepwalking
  c. narcolepsy
  d. oversleeping

Module 10: Hypnosis and Drugs

Use this

Outline

to organize your studying. Write notes on it. Turn it into a personalized aid for effective learning.

I. **Hypnosis**

A. An altered state of awareness

1. Anton Mesmer and "animal magnetism"
2. Hypnotizability

B. Four steps in inducing hypnosis

1. Establish sense of trust
2. Make subject concentrate on something
3. Suggest what subject will feel during hypnosis
4. Observe subject and suggest behaviors that seem to be occurring

C. Behaviors under hypnosis

1. Age regression
2. Imagined perception
3. Posthypnotic amnesia
4. Posthypnotic suggestion
5. Hypnotic analgesia

D. Explanations (theories) of hypnosis

1. **Special process** (special state)

a. Special state (trance) unlike consciousness

b. **Hidden observer** experiments

c. Consciousness divided into two parts by hypnosis

2. **Sociocognitive theory** (suggestibility)
    a. Pressures to conform and go along with hypnotist
    b. Not faking, but **role playing**
    c. Consciousness intact

E. Applications of hypnosis
1. Medical and dental uses
2. Police investigations
3. Behavioral change programs

II. Drug usage

A. Aspects of drug use
1. **Tolerance**
2. **Addiction**
3. **Withdrawal symptoms**
4. **Psychological dependency**

B. The most important question: **why do people use drugs?**
1. Example of Sigmund Freud's nicotine addiction (and experiments with cocaine)
2. Concept of the "**fourth drive**" (Ronald Siegel)

C. **Psychoactive drugs**
1. Chemicals that affect nervous system
    a. Alter consciousness, perception, mood, and thinking
    b. Cause changes in behavior
2. Lessons from history of usage and suppression

D. How drugs affect **nervous system** and change behavior

1. Increase release of neurotransmitters

2. Mimic action of neurotransmitters

3. Block the locks of receptors

4. Block the removal of the neurotransmitter (reuptake)

III. Kinds of psychoactive drugs

A. **Cocaine**

1. Short bursts of energy, arousal, and alertness

2. Vicious circle of cocaine use

B. **Amphetamines**

1. Once heavily prescribed

2. Reemergence as "crystal meth" or "ice"

C. **Caffeine**

D. **Nicotine**

1. Health risks

2. Difficulty of quitting

E. **Marijuana**

1. Dangers first exaggerated ("reefer madness") then underestimated

2. Respiratory risks, possible psychological dependency

F. Hallucinogens

1. **LSD**

2. **Psilocybin** (magic mushrooms)

3. **Mescaline** (peyote cactus)
4. Designer drugs
   a. **PCP** (angel dust)
   b. **MDMA** (ecstasy)

G. Opiates (opium poppy)
1. Opium
2. Morphine
3. **Heroin**

IV. **Alcohol**

A. Response to alcohol

B. Rates of alcoholism

C. Risk factors
1. Environmental
2. Genetic

V. *Applying/Exploring:* Alcohol effects and treatment for drug abuse

A. Alcohol abuse

B. Drug treatment programs
1. Admitting to a drug problem
2. Entering a treatment program
3. Preventing relapse
4. Measuring success

Now take the
Self-Tests
to check your understanding and mastery of this module.

Getting the general idea... Is the statement true or false?

____ 1. Stage hypnotism isn't so remarkable, since everyone can be hypnotized.

____ 2. The essence of the four steps used to induce hypnosis is increasing suggestibility.

____ 3. One good use for hypnosis is to reduce pain during medical or dental procedures.

____ 4. The debate in psychology about hypnosis concerns whether entertainers should be allowed to exploit hypnosis for profit.

____ 5. Hypnosis is more effective than any other technique in helping people quit smoking.

____ 6. Humans seem to have an almost natural urge to get high.

____ 7. History shows that if our government would follow a consistent policy, one by one all illegal drugs could be eradicated.

____ 8. Psychoactive drugs create effects on behavior by interfering with the normal activity of neurotransmitters.

____ 9. The most harmful drugs are the illegal ones; the legal drugs may not be good for you, but they don't do any serious harm.

____ 10. Your risk for becoming an alcoholic rises significantly if members of your family were alcoholics.

Knowing the essential vocabulary... Which phrase matches the term?

	Term		Phrase
____	1. animal magnetism	a.	unhypnotized part of mind
____	2. suggestibility	b.	physical need and intense craving
____	3. hypnotic analgesia	c.	strong psychological need
____	4. hidden observer	d.	key to hypnosis
____	5. tolerance	e.	who you don't want as a roommate
____	6. addiction	f.	painful physically, psychologically
____	7. withdrawal	g.	chemicals that affect nervous system
____	8. dependency	h.	Anton Mesmer
____	9. psychoactive drugs	i.	built-up resistance
____	10. psycho active druggie	j.	dentist's friend

Mastering the basic facts and concepts... Do you know the answer?

_____ 1. Rod Plotnik tells the story about attending a stage hypnotist's act to illustrate the point that
   a. a trained psychologist cannot be hypnotized
   b. entertainment pays better than psychology
   c. hypnotism produces remarkable effects, but we don't understand what it really is
   d. hypnotism is an art that many have attempted to learn, but only a rare few have mastered

_____ 2. Which one of the following is *not* a necessary part of inducing hypnosis?
   a. establish a sense of trust
   b. swing a watch slowly back and forth until the subject's eyes glaze over
   c. suggest what the subject will experience during hypnosis
   d. closely observe the subject and "suggest" what seems to be happening

_____ 3. All of the following are claimed effects of hypnosis *except*
   a. age regression
   b. imagined perception
   c. hypnotic analgesia
   d. superhuman acts of strength

_____ 4. The hypnotist tells Janet, "When you wake up, you will not remember what you did on stage tonight." This is an example of
   a. posthypnotic amnesia
   b. hypnotic suggestion
   c. posthypnotic ordering
   d. hypnotic analgesia

_____ 5. The main issue in the psychological debate over hypnosis is
   a. not whether it exists, but how it is induced
   b. why subjects tend to play along with the hypnotist
   c. whether hidden observers really can spot stage hypnotist's tricks
   d. whether it is a special state of consciousness

_____ 6. Courts are reluctant to admit testimony obtained under hypnosis because
a. hypnotized witnesses can remember so much that it wouldn't be fair to the other side
b. hypnotized witnesses are highly suggestible
c. hypnosis has been shown to be fakery
d. it would seem like bringing witchcraft into the courtroom

_____ 7. Research into the use of hypnosis to change problem behaviors suggests that hypnosis
a. is a miracle treatment in changing behavior
b. does not help in attempts to change behavior
c. can be useful in combination with other treatments
d. is useful in helping people quit smoking, but not in weight loss

_____ 8. Many students are shocked to learn that the great psychologist Sigmund Freud had a serious drug problem —
a. cocaine
b. nicotine
c. alcohol
d. marijuana

_____ 9. "Tolerance" for a drug means that the brain and the body
a. adjust to the drug and use it with no ill effects
b. no longer get any effect from using the drug
c. shut out the drug, which passes harmlessly through the system
d. develop a resistance to the drug and require larger doses to achieve the same effect

_____ 10. One reason it is so tough to quit smoking is that
a. tolerance of nicotine develops so quickly
b. addiction can continue for years after quitting
c. withdrawal symptoms are so painful
d. psychological dependency is deepened by the problems smoking seems to solve

_____ 11. The clear lesson of the history of attempts to suppress drugs is that
- a. when one drug becomes harder to get, people will switch to another
- b. we must abandon our on-again off-again enforcement strategies and declare an all-out war on drugs
- c. eventually people get tired of any drug
- d. legalization would reduce the problem to manageable dimensions

_____ 12. Why do we use drugs? One provocative suggestion is Ronald Siegel's theory that we humans have
- a. acquired a "fourth drive" (namely, to get high)
- b. evolved a mind so complex that it cannot tolerate boredom
- c. solved all the basic problems, and restlessly seek out others
- d. created a form of society so liberal that "anything goes"

_____ 13. All of the following are stimulants *except*
- a. cocaine
- b. caffeine
- c. alcohol
- d. nicotine

_____ 14. For all the drug abuse horror stories we hear, the truth is that _____________ are the two most costly and deadly drugs in our society
- a. heroin and cocaine
- b. marijuana and crack cocaine
- c. angel dust and mescaline
- d. alcohol and tobacco

_____ 15. Rod Plotnik quotes a great marketing slogan ("Two pills beat a month's vacation") used to sell amphetamines in Sweden in the 1940s. How many of these American advertising gems can you identify?
- a. "It's _____ time!"
- b. "Things go better with _____"
- c. "You've come a long way, baby!"
- d. "It's mountain grown"

A special quiz on psychoactive drugs... (results will be sent to campus police)

_____	1. cocaine	a.	most widely used drug in the world
_____	2. speed	b.	severe bad trips could lead to psychotic reactions
_____	3. caffeine	c.	designer drug
_____	4. nicotine	d.	responsible for most drug deaths
_____	5. marijuana	e.	profound, long lasting sensory and perceptual distortions
_____	6. LSD	f.	creates a vicious circle of highs, intense craving for more
_____	7. mescaline	g.	opium poppy
_____	8. ecstasy	h.	oldest drug made by humans; society's biggest drug problem
_____	9. heroin	i.	refer madness
_____	10. alcohol	j.	reemerging as crystal meth or ice

Scoring:

1 to 3 correct	*You've been in a monastery, right?*
4 to 6 correct	*I'm new on campus, myself!*
7 to 9 correct	*This seems very suspicious.*
all 10 correct	*Report to student health immediately — you know too much!*

Answers for Chapter 5

Module 9

True-False		Matching		Multiple-Choice	
1.	F	1.	d	1.	a
2.	T	2.	g	2.	c
3.	T	3.	b	3.	d
4.	T	4.	h	4.	b
5.	F	5.	j	5.	c
6.	T	6.	i	6.	a
7.	F	7.	f	7.	b
8.	T	8.	a	8.	d
9.	T	9.	c	9.	c
10.	F	10.	e	10.	a
				11.	d
				12.	c
				13.	a
				14.	b
				15.	d

Module 10

True-False		Matching		Multiple-Choice	
1.	F	1.	h	1.	c
2.	T	2.	d	2.	b
3.	T	3.	j	3.	d
4.	F	4.	a	4.	a
5.	F	5.	i	5.	d
6.	T	6.	b	6.	b
7.	F	7.	f	7.	c
8.	T	8.	c	8.	b
9.	F	9.	g	9.	d
10.	T	10.	e	10.	c
				11.	a
				12.	a
				13.	c
				14.	d
				15.	*

*Miller, Coke, Virginia Slims, Folger's

A special quiz on psychoactive drugs...

1. f 2. j 3. a 4. d 5. i 6. b 7. e 8. c 9. g 10. h

Chapter 6: Learning

The paradox of behaviorist psychology

Most general psychology students begin reading the chapter on learning with good intentions, but soon give up. It's just too darn complicated. They have run smack into The Paradox.

In truth, the basic principles of learning discovered by Pavlov, Skinner, and others are elegantly simple, wonderfully powerful, and among the most useful products of psychology. They are so easy to grasp that once you do understand them you'll say, "I sort of knew that already." The problem is the language they come wrapped in.

Ivan Pavlov was a pure scientist, a Nobel Prize winner. Naturally, he used the precise, mathematical language of the laboratory. The psychologists who followed Pavlov, the ones we call behaviorists, also prided themselves on being laboratory scientists. One of the strongest points in favor of the behaviorist approach is its insistence that psychology stick to observable, measurable phenomena (no murky, mentalistic concepts like Freud's unconscious).

When students discover behaviorism, however, they do not enjoy the luxury of a long period in which to learn the technical language. We expect them to swallow it all down at one gulp. Most gag instead.

These poor psychology students have a point. Reform in our terminology is long overdue. The first term we could do without is "conditioning." We're really talking about *learning*. Classical conditioning, operant conditioning, and vicarious conditioning are also learning, each by a different route, but learning all the same. Even the terms "stimulus" and "response" say more about Pavlov's fame than about how human life really works. B. F. Skinner knew that, but still didn't come up with easy ways to describe the situation in which behavior occurs, the behavior itself, and what happens next.

We're mad as Hell and we're not going to take it anymore!

Your instructor will tell you which terms to learn, but as you study you can make some mental translations. Keep in mind that we're always talking about *learning*. When you read "classical conditioning," remind yourself that you are reading about Pavlov's kind of learning, where a dog's natural reflex to drool at meat got connected to something else (a bell). When you bump into a technical term like Skinner's "positive reinforcement," make up an everyday-life story that illustrates the term: "If my little brother cleans up his room and my parents reward him with extra allowance money, he will be more likely to clean up his room again next week."

Don't let yourself be cheated out of what may be the most useful ideas in psychology, just because the language is difficult. Fight back!

Effective Student Tip 6

No One Is Lazy

All right, go ahead and call yourself "lazy," if it makes you feel better, but it's not good psychology. First, it may be what cognitive psychologists call a self-handicapping strategy (see Chapter 9), where you excuse yourself in advance for poor performance. ("I probably won't pass the test... because I'm too lazy to study!") Well, at least they can't say you're dumb, just lazy.

Second, I would argue that no one is lazy. Oh, sure, we humans lie around and goof off a lot, but that probably has more to do with defending our freedom and autonomy against the regimentation of organized work. The natural tendency of all animals is activity. Look at the time and energy we put into second jobs, sports, and social activities. Normally, we prefer to do something, because that feeds our constant hunger to be effective.

When we feel lazy we really are feeling ineffective. The task before us is too difficult, too unrewarding, or too lacking in novelty and challenge. When you feel 'too lazy' to tackle your schoolwork, the real problem is that you haven't figured out how to handle it effectively, or how to make it deliver positive feedback of effectiveness.

Module 11: Classical Conditioning

> Use this
>
> **Outline**
>
> to organize your studying. Write notes on it. Turn it into a personalized aid for effective learning.

I. Overview of **learning**

A. Definition

1. Relatively permanent change in **behavior**...
2. Resulting from **experience**

B. Three approaches to learning

1. Classical conditioning
   a. Ivan Pavlov's famous experiment
   b. Conditioned reflex
   c. Learning through pairing stimuli
2. Operant conditioning
   a. Law of effect (E. L. Thorndike)
   b. Consequences and learning (B. F. Skinner)
   c. Learning through effects or consequences of actions
3. Cognitive learning
   a. Mental processes
   b. Observation and imitation
   c. Learning through observing and thinking

II. **Classical conditioning (Pavlov)**

A. Establishing conditioning (Pavlov's famous dog experiment)

1. Natural (unconditioned) **reflex** (stimulus – response)

a. Unlearned, involuntary physiological reflex

b. **Unconditioned stimulus** (UCS) (food) produces **unconditioned response** (UCR) (salivation)

2. **Pairing** neutral (tone) and unconditioned (food) stimuli

a. Present tone, immediately followed by food

b. Dog salivates because of food

c. Continue presenting paired stimuli

3. Testing for presence of **conditioned reflex**

a. Present neutral stimulus alone

b. Dog (soon) salivates to tone alone

c. Tone now a **conditioned stimulus** (CS) eliciting a **conditioned response** (CR)

B. The career of a conditioned reflex

1. **Generalization**

2. **Discrimination**

3. **Extinction**

4. **Spontaneous recovery**

C. Explaining classical conditioning

1. Traditional explanation

a. Stimulus substitution

b. Association

2. Modern cognitive explanation (Robert Rescorla)
    a. **Information theory** of classical conditioning
    b. Neutral stimulus **predicts** occurrence of unconditioned stimulus
    c. Supported by poor results of **backward conditioning**

D. Classical conditioning in everyday life
1. **Learned food aversions** in humans
2. Learned food aversions in animals
    a. Coyote control
    b. Rats and bait poison
    c. Bluejays and monarch butterflies
3. Conditioned objects that cause pleasure
4. Advertising
    a. Law of association
    b. Pairing what they sell with what we like

E. Impact of Pavlov on psychology
1. Made learning observable
2. Made psychology more scientific

III. *Applying/Exploring:* Chemotherapy and conditioned nausea

A. Conditioned nausea
1. Chemotherapy
2. Alcoholism treatment program

B. **Systematic desensitization** (steps in program)

1. Learn relaxation techniques
2. Construct hierarchy of stressful, feared situations
3. Progress through hierarchy making new associations while relaxed
4. Return to less stressful situation if fear occurs
5. Gradually substitute new, relaxed associations for previous fear associations

Now take the
Self-Tests
to check your understanding and mastery of this module.

Getting the general idea... Is the statement true or false?

_____ 1. Learning is a relatively permanent change in behavior as a result of experience.

_____ 2. Ivan Pavlov's famous explanation of learning was so persuasive that no other theory has challenged it since.

_____ 3. The key to Pavlov's experiment was finding a reward that would make the dog salivate.

_____ 4. At first, UCS → UCR, but after the conditioning procedure, CS → CR.

_____ 5. Once conditioning has taken place, *generalization* may cause similar stimuli to elicit the response, but *discrimination* should work to establish control by the specified stimuli.

_____ 6. The information theory says classical conditioning happens when a new stimulus replaces an old one through association.

_____ 7. Bluejays avoid monarch butterflies because they hate that orange and black pattern. [This statement is true, but can you explain why?]

_____ 8. Automobile ads often include a gorgeous model in a low-cut evening gown because women typically make the decision about buying a car.

_____ 9. If you are like most people, the sound of the dentist's drill has become an unconditioned stimulus.

_____ 10. The goal of systematic desensitization is to *uncondition* conditioned stimuli and make them neutral again.

Knowing the essential vocabulary... Which phrase matches the term?

	Term		Phrase
_____	1. unconditioned stimulus	a.	see golden arches, begin drooling
_____	2. conditioned stimulus	b.	smell of a sizzling burger
_____	3. neutral stimulus	c.	if they served nothing but tofu...
_____	4. conditioned reflex	d.	still, you might drive thru again
_____	5. generalization	e.	if you hate building arks
_____	6. discrimination	f.	if a Martian sees golden arches
_____	7. extinction	g.	when *you* see golden arches
_____	8. spontaneous recovery	h.	if you got real sick from eating one
_____	9. learned food aversion	i.	also drooling at King and Bell signs...
_____	10. learned flood aversion	j.	but don't drool at bookstore signs

Mastering the material... Which answer makes the statement true?

_____ 1. Rod Plotnik begins this module with the story of Carla, who canceled her subscription to *Zoo World,* to show how
a. learning often occurs when we least expect it
b. learning is more likely to occur in some environments than in others
c. we can learn a response simply because it occurs along with some other response
d. we can like something very much, then turn against it for no clear reason

_____ 2. All of the following are approaches to understanding how learning occurs *except*
a. classical conditioning
b. operant conditioning
c. cognitive learning
d. physical learning

_____ 3. Pavlov was studying digestion, but he quickly switched to his famous salivating dog experiment when
a. he sensed that the dogs actually understood what was going on
b. the dogs began salivating too soon
c. he got nowhere with the original experiment
d. the dogs began barking whenever they saw food

_____ 4. Since S ➔ R, then obviously UCS ➔ UCR, so naturally CS ➔
a. UCS
b. UCR
c. CR
d. neutral stimulus

_____ 5. Pavlov demonstrated that a previously neutral stimulus can acquire the response properties of an unconditioned stimulus through
a. pairing
b. shaping
c. application of rewards and punishment
d. insight

_____ 6. In Pavlov's experiment, the actual learning took place when the
a. neutral stimulus was paired with the unconditioned stimulus
b. conditioned reflex was presented again and again
c. unconditioned stimulus was paired with the conditioned stimulus
d. paired neutral and unconditioned stimuli were presented together in several trials

_____ 7. When they learned about Pavlov's discovery, many psychologists were excited because Pavlov seemed to be
a. providing the first look inside the thinking mind
b. explaining the operation of reward and punishment in learning
c. explaining learning objectively in terms of behavior you could see and measure
d. showing that the canine brain and the human brain worked in much the same way

_____ 8. It seemed to these psychologists that if Pavlov was right, psychology finally could become a
a. practical, useful profession
b. measurable, objective science
c. proven theory
d. philosophy

_____ 9. Which one of the following is an example of generalization?
a. Goldilocks tries all the beds
b. Goldilocks sleeps in Papa Bear's bed
c. Goldilocks sleeps in Mama Bear's bed
d. Goldilocks sleeps in Baby Bear's bed

_____ 10. Which one of the following is an example of discrimination?
a. Goldilocks tries all the beds
b. Goldilocks sleeps in Papa Bear's bed
c. Goldilocks sleeps in Mama Bear's bed
d. Goldilocks sleeps in Baby Bear's bed

_____ 11. When a conditioned stimulus (e.g., a tone) is repeatedly presented without the unconditioned stimulus (e.g., meat), _______________ eventually will occur
a. generalization
b. discrimination
c. extinction
d. spontaneous recovery

_____ 12. According to a modern, cognitive explanation of Pavlov's experiment, the conditioned reflex gets established because
- a. the dog wants to do what Pavlov seems to want it to do
- b. the dog learns that the tone predicts the presentation of the food
- c. Pavlov unwittingly tips off the dog by looking at the food tray
- d. Pavlov simply waits until the dog makes the right response

_____ 13. After reading about learned food aversions, you might be tempted to wonder whether
- a. little Georgie Washington hated fresh cherries
- b. little Jimmy Carter was forced to eat peanuts every day
- c. little Ronnie Reagan couldn't afford jelly beans at the five-and-dime
- d. little Georgie Bush once got sick after eating broccoli

_____ 14. Conditioned nausea works on coyotes, rats, and bluejays through a form of classical conditioning called
- a. bait poison
- b. learned food aversion
- c. chemical control
- d. learned animal avoidance

_____ 15. All of the following are necessary to the systematic desensitization procedure *except*
- a. identification of unconscious conflicts
- b. practice in relaxation techniques
- c. a hierarchy of feared situations
- d. moving up and down through the hierarchy

Module 12: Operant Conditioning and Cognitive Learning

Use this

Outline

to organize your studying. Write notes on it. Turn it into a personalized aid for effective learning.

I. Operant conditioning overview

A. **Law of Effect (Edward L. Thorndike)**

1. Goal-directed behavior

2. Effects strengthen or weaken behavior

B. **Operant conditioning (B. F. Skinner)**

1. Conditioning of voluntary behavior

2. Consequences and the laws of learning

C. Classical and operant conditioning compared

1. Classical conditioning (Pavlov)

a. Response is an *involuntary* physiological reflex behavior

b. Neutral stimulus is **paired** with natural (unconditioned) stimulus

c. After sufficient trials, conditioned stimulus also *elicits* behavior

2. Operant conditioning (Skinner)

a. Response is a *voluntary* behavior [as is most behavior]

b. Subject *emits* behavior in presence of previously reinforced stimulus

c. **Consequence** of behavior shapes future behavior

II. How operant conditioning works

A. **Shaping**

1. "Skinner box"

2. Reinforcer delivered immediately after desired behavior

3. Reinforcement of behavior that leads up to (approximates) desired target behavior

4. Consequences are **contingent** on behavior (CACOB)

B. **Consequences** applied to promoting or suppressing behavior

1. **Reinforcement** *increases* likelihood of behavior occurring again

a. **Positive reinforcement** — presentation of pleasant consequence

b. **Negative reinforcement** — removal of unpleasant consequence

2. **Punishment** *decreases* likelihood of behavior occurring again

a. Punishment by direct pain — presentation of unpleasant consequence

b. Punishment by threat — removal of pleasant consequence

C. Kinds of **reinforcers**

1. **Primary** (innately satisfying)

2. **Secondary**

a. Acquired through experience

b. Tokens (in therapeutic settings)

D. Teaching machines

E. **Schedules of reinforcement**

1. Two broad categories

    a. **Continuous** (every time) reinforcement

    b. **Partial** (only some of the time) reinforcement

2. Four common *partial* schedules of reinforcement

    a. **Fixed-ratio** (set number of responses required)

    b. **Fixed-interval** (set time must pass)

    c. **Variable-ratio** (changing number of responses required)

    d. **Variable-interval** (changing time periods must pass)

F. Everyday life examples of operant conditioning

1. Child training (toilet training)

2. Animal training (movies)

G. The career of a learned behavior

1. Generalization

2. Discrimination (**discriminative stimulus**)

3. Extinction

4. Spontaneous recovery

III. Cognitive learning

A. **Cognitive map** (Edward Tolman)

1. Rats developed cognitive map (mental picture) of maze

2. Rats performed in absence of external reinforcers

B. **Observational learning (Albert Bandura)**

1. Bobo doll experiments

2. Learning versus performance

3. Four processes necessary for observational learning

   a. Attention (see it)

   b. Memory (remember it)

   c. Motor control (possess ability to do it)

   d. Motivation (have desire to do it)

C. **Insight learning** (Wolfgang Köhler) [and Sultan]

1. "Ah ha" phenomenon

2. Neither classical conditioning nor trial-and-error learning

D. Biological factors (innate tendencies) in learning

1. Biological restraint

2. **Prepared learning**

   a. Innate sensitivity to certain cues

   b. **Imprinting** (Konrad Lorenz)

E. **Suzuki method** (teaching violin) explained in Bandura's terms

1. Attention

2. Memory

3. Motor control

4. Motivation

IV. *Applying/Exploring:* Applications of operant conditioning

A. **Behavior modification** of autistic children (Ivar Lovaas)

1. Operant conditioning principles applied

a. Shaping

b. Reinforcement

2. Success rates

B. **Biofeedback**

1. Learning to relax

2. Shaping own behavior

C. **Time out**

1. A mild punishment

2. Works by extinction of undesirable behaviors

D. Other behavior problems (see following chapters)

Now take the
Self-Tests
to check your understanding and mastery of this module.

Getting the general idea... Is the statement true or false?

_____ 1. Classical conditioning concerns involuntary (reflex) behavior while operant conditioning concerns voluntary behavior.

_____ 2. The secret of successful shaping is waiting until the animal emits the desired final target behavior, then immediately applying reinforcement.

_____ 3. The key to successful operant conditioning is making consequences contingent on behavior.

_____ 4. Positive reinforcement makes behavior more likely to occur again; negative reinforcement makes it less likely to occur again.

_____ 5. If you want effective learning, you must use primary reinforcers instead of secondary reinforcers.

_____ 6. Schedules of reinforcement are payoff rules that govern different patterns of work done and payment given.

_____ 7. Observational learning theory showed that there is a difference between learning a behavior and performing that behavior.

_____ 8. The difference between observational learning and operant conditioning is that the former does not depend on external reinforcement.

_____ 9. A good example of observational learning was when Sultan piled up several boxes so he could reach the banana.

_____ 10. The great power of reinforcement extends only so far — until it bumps into a biological restraint.

Knowing the essential vocabulary... Which phrase matches the term?

_____ 1. Law of Effect — a. Edward Tolman

_____ 2. operant conditioning — b. Konrad Lorenz

_____ 3. cognitive map — c. Albert Bandura

_____ 4. observational learning — d. E. L. Thorndike

_____ 5. insight learning — e. Mike Ditka

_____ 6. imprinting — f. Wolfgang Köhler

_____ 7. a method — g. B. F. Skinner

_____ 8. a doll — h. Shinichi Suzuki

_____ 9. *The Bear* — i. Bobo

_____ 10. "Da Bears" — j. Bart

Mastering the material... Which answer makes the statement true?

_____ 1. Rod Plotnik tells us about the starring performance of 1800-pound Bart in *The Bear* to make the point that
   a. although animals cannot begin to match human intelligence, they do have some capacity for learning
   b. the key to learning (and teaching) is perseverance: keep working
   c. you shouldn't believe that what you see in the movies reflects actual behavior in the wild
   d. operant conditioning procedures are powerful (no other technique could have produced Bart's learning)

_____ 2. Skinner gets the credit for operant conditioning instead of Thorndike because
   a. Thorndike stated a general principle; Skinner's research explained precisely how it works
   b. Thorndike's Law of Effect was essentially a restatement of Pavlov's conditioned reflex
   c. Skinner realized that there were biological limits on learning
   d. Skinner studied rats, pigeons, and other animals instead of limiting himself to cats

_____ 3. You could argue that Skinner's discoveries are more important than Pavlov's in that
   a. beginning a quarter of a century later, Skinner could build on Pavlov's discoveries
   b. Pavlov never worked with humans; Skinner did
   c. all important human behavior is voluntary (not reflex) behavior
   d. the conditioned reflex isn't fully explained until you bring in the concepts of both positive and negative reinforcement

_____ 4. The shaping procedure succeeds or fails depending on
   a. how long you are willing to wait for the target behavior to occur
   b. what behaviors you reinforce
   c. how many times you reinforce the target behavior
   d. selecting the best one of several reinforcers

_____ 5. The basic principle of operant conditioning is that
   a. consequences are contingent on behavior
   b. conditioned stimuli produce conditioned responses
   c. the performance of undesired behaviors brings swift consequences
   d. consequences = CAROB (revenge is sweet)

_____ 6. The little child who gets a good hard spanking for running out into the street is experiencing an operant conditioning procedure called
   a. positive reinforcement
   b. negative reinforcement
   c. punishment
   d. extinction

_____ 7. The student on probation who finally buckles down and begins studying in earnest is under the control of an operant conditioning procedure called
   a. positive reinforcement
   b. negative reinforcement
   c. punishment
   d. extinction

_____ 8. When your date shakes your hand and says, "I had a wonderful evening," you reply, "Gee, I was kind of hoping for a _______________"
   a. primary reinforcer
   b. secondary reinforcer
   c. token of your affection
   d. partial reinforcement

_____ 9. "Poor fool," you think to yourself when your friend tells you she lost on the lottery again, "another helpless victim of the _______________ schedule of reinforcement"
   a. fixed-ratio
   b. variable-ratio
   c. fixed-interval
   d. variable-interval

_____ 10. Skinner opposed cognitive theories of learning to the end of his life because
   a. it is difficult to admit that the work of a lifetime was misguided
   b. they are based on philosophical speculation rather than on laboratory research
   c. they bring in the "mind," which Skinner said couldn't be observed or measured directly
   d. you can't teach an old dog new tricks [just a joke!]

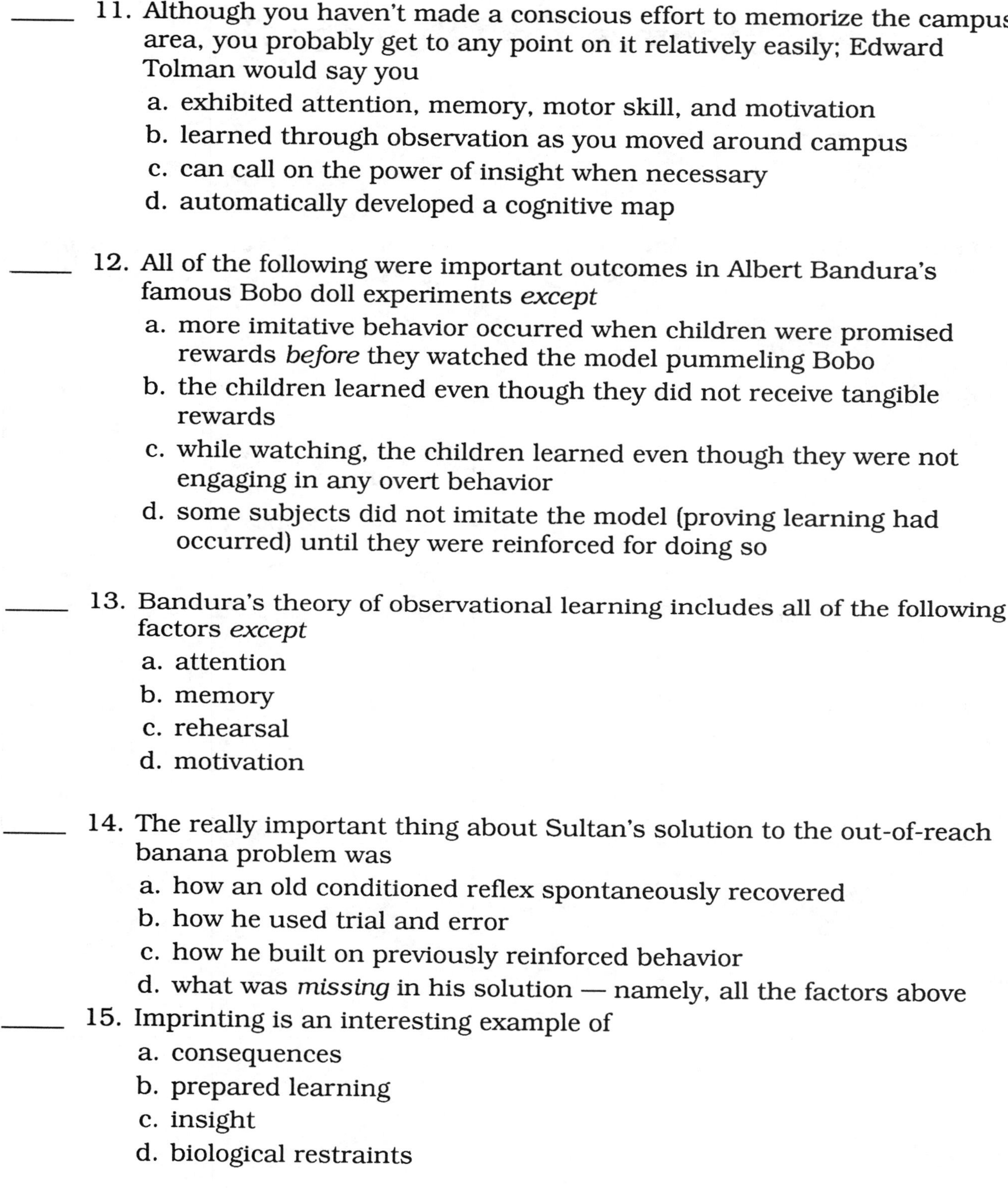

_____ 11. Although you haven't made a conscious effort to memorize the campus area, you probably get to any point on it relatively easily; Edward Tolman would say you

a. exhibited attention, memory, motor skill, and motivation
b. learned through observation as you moved around campus
c. can call on the power of insight when necessary
d. automatically developed a cognitive map

_____ 12. All of the following were important outcomes in Albert Bandura's famous Bobo doll experiments *except*

a. more imitative behavior occurred when children were promised rewards *before* they watched the model pummeling Bobo
b. the children learned even though they did not receive tangible rewards
c. while watching, the children learned even though they were not engaging in any overt behavior
d. some subjects did not imitate the model (proving learning had occurred) until they were reinforced for doing so

_____ 13. Bandura's theory of observational learning includes all of the following factors *except*

a. attention
b. memory
c. rehearsal
d. motivation

_____ 14. The really important thing about Sultan's solution to the out-of-reach banana problem was

a. how an old conditioned reflex spontaneously recovered
b. how he used trial and error
c. how he built on previously reinforced behavior
d. what was *missing* in his solution — namely, all the factors above

_____ 15. Imprinting is an interesting example of

a. consequences
b. prepared learning
c. insight
d. biological restraints

Answers for Chapter 6

Module 11

True-False	Matching	Multiple-Choice
1. T	1. b	1. c
2. F	2. g	2. d
3. F	3. f	3. b
4. T	4. a	4. c
5. T	5. i	5. a
6. F	6. j	6. d
7. T	7. c	7. c
8. F	8. d	8. b
9. F	9. h	9. a
10. T	10. e	10. d
		11. c
		12. b
		13. d
		14. b
		15. a

Module 12

True-False	Matching	Multiple-Choice
1. T	1. d	1. d
2. F	2. g	2. a
3. T	3. a	3. c
4. F	4. c	4. b
5. F	5. f	5. a
6. T	6. b	6. c
7. T	7. h	7. b
8. T	8. i	8. a
9. F	9. j	9. b
10. T	10. e	10. c
		11. d
		12. a
		13. c
		14. d
		15. b

Chapter 7: Memory

Nothing in this chapter is true

Psychobiology and cognitive psychology have made great strides in the last two decades. One of the results is a much clearer picture of how memory works. Even so, there is a sense in which none of it is true.

The answers we want are buried at least two layers down. First, how does the physical brain work? We are learning more about the brain every day, yet for all their discoveries neuroscientists have barely scratched the surface. The need to understand elusive electrical activity, not just gray matter, complicates the task. Second, how does the mind work? If the mind is an abstraction, a concept (unless you say mind and brain are the same thing), we cannot apprehend it directly, making it even more difficult to understand.

Today we are fond of comparing the mind to a computer, simply because the computer is the most powerful mechanical thinking device we know, and therefore makes a good comparison. Yet when we develop a *new* generation of thinking machines, perhaps based on liquid instead of silicone chips, we will stop comparing the mind to a computer and compare it to the new device, instead, since the new device will seem much more like the human mind. The mind is not really a computer; the computer merely makes a good model for understanding the mind, at least today.

The beauty of a good model

No wonder the dress looks so beautiful on the model sashaying down the runway in the fashion show — the model isn't an ordinary human being (how many people are that tall, that thin, that perfect?). Consequently, when draped around this ideal human body, we can see much more clearly how the clothing itself really looks.

A model helps us understand the real world because it is an ideal against which we can compare specific things. When we try to understand the mind, all we see are awkward elbows and knees. We need a model to help us visualize what it must really be like.

Many of the formulations presented in Chapter 7 are models of what the process of grasping the world and putting parts of it in our heads must be like. I think you can learn these theories better if you keep in mind the idea that they are models, not reality.

Effective Student Tip 7

Risk a New Idea

You didn't come to college to stay the same. You intend to grow in many ways. Intellectual growth requires a spirit of openness to change, of willingness to risk new ideas.

If you don't try out a new idea in college, you probably never will. As time goes on, work, family and responsibility all conspire to make most of us more cautious and more conservative. Never again will you encounter as many new and different ideas as in college. In one sense, the very mission of colleges and universities is to hit us with new ideas. If everything is dandy just the way it is now, we really don't need colleges and universities.

When a professor or student throws out a challenging idea, seriously consider whether it might be true. If true, how would it change what you believe? If false, how do your own beliefs disprove it?

Accepting intellectual challenges will strengthen your ideas and your ability to defend them. You might even solve a problem you have been puzzling over. Most of the time, however, you will augment and improve your understanding of the world and yourself only slightly. That is a great victory. We call it growth.

Module 13: Kinds of Memory

Use this

Outline

to organize your studying. Write notes on it. Turn it into a personalized aid for effective learning.

I. Overview

A. Three *processes* in memory

1. Encoding

2. Storing

3. Retrieving

B. Three *kinds* of memory

1. Sensory memory

2. Short-term (or working) memory

3. Long-term memory

II. **Sensory memory**: *recording*

A. Kinds of sensory memory

1. **Iconic memory**

a. Holds visual information for about a quarter of a second

b. Makes world appear stable and calm despite eye movements

2. **Echoic memory**

a. Holds auditory information for one or two seconds

b. Allows holding speech sounds long enough to recognize words

B. Functions of sensory memory

1. Prevents us from being overwhelmed

2. Gives us a moment or two to decide on further processing

3. Makes visual world smooth and continuous and auditory world meaningful

III. **Short-term memory**: *working*

A. Features of short-term memory

1. Limited duration

a. From two to 30 seconds

b. **Maintenance rehearsal**

2. Limited capacity

a. About seven items or bits (George Miller)

b. **Memory span test**

c. **Chunking**

3. **Interference**

4. Imagine what life would be like with *only* sensory and short-term memory

IV. **Long-term memory**: *storing*

A. *Process* of transferring information into and out of long-term memory

1. Sensory memory

a. Iconic

b. Echoic

2. Attention

3. Short-term memory

4. Encoding

5. Long-term memory

6. Retrieving

B. Difference between short-term and long-term memory demonstrated

1. **Primacy effect**

a. Better recall of items at *beginning* of list

b. Material already transferred to long-term memory

2. **Recency effect**

a. Better recall of items at *end* of list

b. Material still in short-term memory

C. Three kinds of long-term memories

1. **Episodic** information (personal information, stories)

2. **Semantic** information (general knowledge, words)

3. **Procedural** information (motor skills, conditioned reflexes)

V. **Encoding**: transferring information

A. **Automatic** encoding

1. *Episodic* information

2. *Procedural* information

B. **Effortful** encoding

1. *Semantic* information

2. Strategies of effortful encoding

a. **Maintenance rehearsal** (practice)

b. **Elaborative rehearsal** (new associations)

c. Imagery (**distinctive associations**)

VI. *Applying/Exploring:* Unusual memory abilities

A. Visualization

1. **Eidetic imagery** (some children)

2. **Photographic memory** (a rare few adults)

B. **Savants**

C. **Flashbulb memories** (concept now revised)

For psych majors only...

Here is a gloomy, possibly discouraging thought (considering how much you paid for your books): perhaps *nothing* in psychology is really true. Perhaps everything you are slaving so hard to learn is simply the best understanding we have now, soon to be replaced by better ways of understanding how psychology works.

I suggested that the computer is merely a temporary model for understanding the mind. Let's go further and suggest that *all* the wonderful theories you study in psychology are models, none ultimately "true." There is no unconscious region of the mind, no pure schedule of reinforcement, and no ethereal self. They are all fictions — fictions we need to make sense of the facts.

There is one happy possibility in these dismal thoughts. Think how eagerly psychology is waiting for the better model *you* may construct one day. Keep working on your favorite theories.

Getting the general idea... Is the statement true or false?

_____ 1. Memory involves three basic processes: encoding, storing, and retrieving.

_____ 2. There are four basic kinds of memory: flashbulb snapshots, temporary, impermanent, and permanent.

_____ 3. Without the stage called sensory memory, we would drown in a sea of visual and auditory sensations.

_____ 4. Short-term memory is capable of holding about a dozen bits of information for several minutes.

_____ 5. When you attempt to remember a list of animals, the recency effect takes precedence over the primacy effect.

_____ 6. The most difficult kind of information to store in long-term memory is semantic information.

_____ 7. Encoding is transferring information from short-term to long-term memory.

_____ 8. The best way to get information into long-term memory is to repeat it over and over again.

_____ 9. A good strategy for remembering something is to associate it with some distinctive visual image.

_____ 10. When you find someone who has unusual powers of memory, you can be fairly certain that the person possesses a photographic memory.

Knowing the essential vocabulary... Which phrase matches the term?

	Term		Phrase
_____	1. iconic memory	a.	your ability to ride a bicycle
_____	2. echoic memory	b.	story of the first bicycle you owned
_____	3. chunking	c.	I remember "Aardvark Bicycle Co"...
_____	4. primacy effect	d.	and "Ziggurat Bicycle Works" best
_____	5. recency effect	e.	Wille Nelson and his bicycle
_____	6. episodic information	f.	put bike name into long-term memory
_____	7. semantic information	g.	memorizing bike lock combination
_____	8. procedural information	h.	names of the major bicycle companies
_____	9. encode	i.	why you can read about bicycles...
_____	10. on road [again]	j.	and grasp what you hear about bikes

Mastering the material... Which answer makes the statement true?

_____ 1. Rod Plotnik discusses Rajan Mahadevan, who memorized more than 30,000 digits of pi, because Rajan's rare abilities
   a. show that extreme concentration of mental ability in one area is usually accompanied by deficiencies in other areas
   b. are possessed only by people who are otherwise retarded or autistic
   c. could be duplicated by any of us... if we put our minds to it
   d. offer an extreme example of the memory processes we all use

_____ 2. Memory is made up of three processes — all of the following *except*
   a. encoding
   b. storing
   c. deciphering
   d. retrieving

_____ 3. The function of sensory memory is to
   a. hold information in its raw form for a few seconds
   b. make quick associations between new data and things you already know
   c. weed out what is irrelevant in incoming information
   d. burn sensations into long-term memory for later retrieval and inspection

_____ 4. The process that holds visual information for about a quarter of a second is called _______________ memory
   a. chunking
   b. iconic
   c. pictorial
   d. echoic

_____ 5. Thanks to _______________ memory, incoming speech sounds linger just long enough so we can recognize the sounds as words
   a. chunking
   b. iconic
   c. verbal
   d. echoic

____ 6. The statement below that describes short-term memory is:
   a. your perceptual processes react to it
   b. you freeze it briefly in order to pay attention to it
   c. you work with it to accomplish some immediate task
   d. you retrieve it later when you need it again

____ 7. Out of change at the pay phone, you frantically repeat the number you just got from Information over and over again; that's called
   a. chunking
   b. maintenance rehearsal
   c. memory span stretching
   d. duration enhancement

____ 8. But wait a minute... You know long distance numbers are preceded by one, and you already know the area code, so you just memorize the prefix and the number, a task made easier by
   a. chunking
   b. maintenance rehearsal
   c. memory span stretching
   d. duration enhancement

____ 9. Why doesn't information in short-term memory simply become permanent? Probably because of
   a. limited storage space in the brain
   b. fascination with the new and different
   c. incompatibility with previously processed information
   d. interference caused by the constant stream of new information

____ 10. If you attempt to remember a list of animal names, you will be more likely to remember the
   a. first few names
   b. last few names
   c. both the first and last few names
   d. neither the first nor last few names, but the ones occurring in the middle of the list

____ 11. How well you did on your last psych test would be considered
a. episodic information
b. semantic information
c. consequential information
d. procedural information

____ 12. The actual knowledge required for that test would be called
a. episodic information
b. semantic information
c. consequential information
d. procedural information

____ 13. Your ability to write out the answers on the test would be called
a. episodic information
b. semantic information
c. consequential information
d. procedural information

____ 14. It takes the most effort to encode
a. episodic information
b. semantic information
c. consequential information
d. procedural information

____ 15. Rod Plotnik puts psychology to good use in his textbook by providing ______________ to help you encode the material you must learn
a. distinctive visual associations
b. elaborative rehearsal experiences
c. maintenance rehearsal drills
d. chunking strategies

Module 14: Remembering and Forgetting

Use this

Outline

to organize your studying. Write notes on it. Turn it into a personalized aid for effective learning.

I. Ways to remember

  A. **Recall**

    1. Retrieving

    2. Essay exams

  B. **Recognition**

    1. Identifying

    2. Multiple-choice tests

II. Organization of memory: two theories

  A. **Network theory**

    1. **Nodes**

      a. Memory areas containing related information organized around a specific topic or category

      b. Hierarchy of categories, from concrete to abstract

    2. Connections or associations linking nodes

    3. Gigantic interconnected network

    4. Like a map containing cities (nodes) connected by roads (associations)

  B. **Schema theory**

    1. **Schema** (mental model based on experience)

      a. Recall previous information by reconstructing schemas or scripts

      b. File and organize new information by fitting it into existing schemas or scripts

    2. **Script** (schema involving events or actions)

C. Comparison of theories

1. Network

a. Like videotapes that can be searched

b. You *recall* what happened

2. Schema

a. Like movie scripts into which new information can be fitted

b. You *reconstruct* what happened

3. A combination of both theories probably explains memory best

III. Long-lasting memory

A. Two characteristics of long-term memory

1. Holds almost unlimited amount of information

2. Retains some information for a lifetime

B. **Forgetting curves** (Hermann Ebbinghaus)

1. Nonsense syllables

2. Familiar or interesting material

IV. Forgetting

A. Reasons for forgetting

1. "Law of disuse" (old theory no longer held today)

2. **Repression** (Freud)

3. Interference

4. Inadequate retrieval cues

5. Amnesia

B. **Interference theory**

1. **Proactive** interference (interfering forward)

2. **Retroactive** interference (interfering backward)

C. **Inadequate retrieval cues**

1. **Tip-of-the-tongue phenomenon**

2. **State-dependent learning**

D. **Amnesia**

1. **Anterograde** amnesia

2. **Retrograde** amnesia

3. Both kinds of amnesia at once

a. Korsakoff's syndrome

b. Alzheimer's disease

V. Biological bases of memory

A. Memory and brain structures

1. Short-term memory — cortex

2. Long-term memory — hippocampus

3. Emotional feelings — amygdala

B. Chemical and structural changes

1. Neurotransmitters

a. Molecules

b. Chemicals

2. Structural changes

VI. Psychological bases of memory

A. **Mnemonics**: memorization methods

1. **Method of loci**

2. **Peg method**

B. Aborigines' memory cues (more visual than verbal)

VII. *Applying/Exploring:* Eyewitness testimony

A. Mistaken identities

B. Misinformation and misremembering (Elizabeth Loftus)

C. Cognitive interview technique

Now take the
Self-Tests
to check your understanding and mastery of this module.

Getting the general idea... Is the statement true or false?

_____ 1. Of the two ways to remember, recall is easier than recognition.

_____ 2. According to network theory, memory is organized like a gigantic map on which pathways connect cities of related information.

_____ 3. According to schema theory, memory is organized in a hierarchy, with less important information at the bottom and more important information at the top.

_____ 4. Forgetting curves are plots of how long pieces of information will remain in long-term memory.

_____ 5. Most psychologists explain forgetting by the law of disuse.

_____ 6. Proactive interference occurs when you are trying too hard to remember new information.

_____ 7. Anterograde amnesia is the loss of memory for events and facts that occur after brain damage.

_____ 8. Although it is the brain that does the "thinking," the spinal cord stores the actual memories.

_____ 9. The method of loci and the peg method are mnemonic strategies.

_____ 10. Psychologists have discovered that introducing misleading information during questioning can distort eyewitness testimony.

Knowing the essential vocabulary... Which phrase matches the term?

	Term		Phrase
_____	1. recall	a.	Freud's explanation of forgetting
_____	2. recognition	b.	a mnemonic strategy
_____	3. nodes	c.	interference
_____	4. scripts	d.	network theory of memory
_____	5. repression	e.	what Charlie Brown keeps forgetting
_____	6. retroactive or proactive	f.	schema theory of memory
_____	7. retrieval cues	g.	amnesia
_____	8. anterograde or retrograde	h.	associations that assist memory
_____	9. method of loci	i.	multiple-choice test
_____	10. method of Lucy	j.	essay exam

Mastering the material... Which answer makes the statement true?

_____ 1. Your brow beading with perspiration, you struggle to answer these questions, desperately summoning your best powers of
a. recall
b. reflection
c. recognition
d. recollection

_____ 2. If you just glanced through the chapter, pray that the snap quiz will be
a. essay
b. multiple-choice
c. short essay
d. oral

_____ 3. The ideas of nodes, categories, and hierarchies of information belong to the ______________ theory of how memory is organized
a. network
b. schema
c. script
d. abstraction

_____ 4. A ______________ is a mental model of a concept, event, or object that is based on previous experience
a. dialogue
b. node
c. hierarchy
d. schema

_____ 5. The bottom line on how memory is organized is that
a. schema theory is supported by most of the research
b. we have some promising theories, but no final conclusions yet
c. network theory, being the most logical, best explains memory
d. since we can't "see" the mind, we can't do objective research on it

_____ 6. Which of the following groups of items would provide the best test in research on memory over time?
   a. names and faces of childhood friends
   b. commonly studied facts, such as state capitals
   c. foreign language vocabulary
   d. nonsense syllables

_____ 7. The data yielded by such research (above) would be
   a. rates of retention
   b. memory percentages
   c. forgetting curves
   d. cognitive charts

_____ 8. You know you said something terribly embarrassing, but you can't remember what it was — this is an example of
   a. the law of disuse
   b. repression
   c. interference
   d. inadequate retrieval cues

_____ 9. You were introduced to your friend's professor recently, but there was no time to chat and now you can't recall the professor's name — this is an example of
   a. the law of disuse
   b. repression
   c. interference
   d. inadequate retrieval cues

_____ 10. Of the main explanations of forgetting, the one with the least research support is
   a. the law of disuse
   b. repression
   c. interference
   d. inadequate retrieval cues

____ 11. Proactive interference is when
- a. learning new information interferes with the retrieval of old information
- b. learning positive information interferes with the retrieval of negative information
- c. old information interferes with the learning of new information
- d. retrospective thinking interferes with potential learning

____ 12. We humans are very proud of our ability to "think," but, when we study creatures like the sea slug, "thought" begins to look more like
- a. molecular and chemical changes in the nervous system
- b. the thinking of a severely retarded person
- c. habits shaped through reward and punishment
- d. inherited tendencies somewhat modified by experience

____ 13. Both the method of loci and the peg method work by
- a. causing learning to be strengthened through repeated practice
- b. creating strong associations that will serve as effective retrieval cues
- c. connecting material to be learned to the purpose it will be used for
- d. considering material to be memorized as easy and pleasant to learn

____ 14. Aborigine children performed significantly better than white Australian children on memory tasks when
- a. only Aborigine objects were used
- b. the task involved auditory cues
- c. testing was done outdoors in a natural setting
- d. the task involved visual cues

____ 15. When evaluating eyewitness testimony, pay close attention to
- a. whether the eyewitness has anything to gain or lose by testifying
- b. how confident the eyewitness appears to be
- c. how the questions to the eyewitness are worded
- d. whether the eyewitness seems biased in favor of or against the defendant

Answers for Chapter 7

Module 13

True-False		Matching		Multiple-Choice	
1.	T	1.	i	1.	d
2.	F	2.	j	2.	c
3.	T	3.	g	3.	a
4.	F	4.	c	4.	b
5.	F	5.	d	5.	d
6.	T	6.	b	6.	c
7.	T	7.	h	7.	b
8.	F	8.	a	8.	a
9.	T	9.	f	9.	d
10.	F	10.	e	10.	c
				11.	a
				12.	b
				13.	d
				14.	b
				15.	a

Module 14

True-False		Matching		Multiple-Choice	
1.	F	1.	j	1.	c
2.	T	2.	i	2.	b
3.	F	3.	d	3.	a
4.	T	4.	f	4.	d
5.	F	5.	a	5.	b
6.	F	6.	c	6.	d
7.	T	7.	h	7.	c
8.	F	8.	g	8.	b
9.	T	9.	b	9.	d
10.	T	10.	e	10.	a
				11.	c
				12.	a
				13.	b
				14.	d
				15.	c

Chapter 8: Intelligence, Thought, and Language

Can we study ourselves scientifically?

Historians of science have pointed out that the accumulation of human knowledge seems backward. We understood the far-away phenomena of astronomy centuries ago, gradually grasped the principles of physics and biology in modern times, but only now are beginning to penetrate the mysteries of the brain and the mind. The closer we are to something, the harder it is to study it objectively. Add to this difficulty an even greater one — we *are* the very thing we want to study. Physical scientists say this problem alone dooms social science to be inherently subjective and therefore not really scientific. Social scientists disagree, naturally, but they admit that being objective about ourselves presents enormous challenges.

Three processes that make us human

As an animal lover, I welcome every discovery of an animal engaging in a behavior (like tool-using) previously thought to be the exclusive property of *Homo sapiens*. Those of us who observe animals in the wild know that they communicate very effectively. Still, is it really language? (See Rod Plotnik's fascinating discussion of whether apes can acquire language.)

In our efforts to win greater respect for the rights and inherent value of other animals, some of us argue that we humans aren't so different and shouldn't consider ourselves morally superior. Nevertheless, we have to admit that humans have strikingly unique skills and abilities in three areas that perhaps define our species. We have unmatched intellectual potential, unrivaled flexibility in exploiting that potential, and a system of communication that preserves and extends those mental powers.

In this chapter, Rod Plotnik weaves together the stories of these three quintessential human properties: intelligence, thought, and language. Discussing them in the same chapter helps us appreciate how interrelated they are. As we begin to discover the connections, we begin to understand the incredible complexity of human psychological functioning.

Science is never easy, however. We all know what intelligence, thought, and language are, yet how do we describe and explain them? Our own subjective experience seems to get in the way of objective understanding. We have to fight for every piece of knowledge.

Our own subjective experience seems to get in the way of objective understanding. We have to fight for every piece of knowledge.

Further complicating matters is the problem that science is not always neutral. Rod Plotnik describes a period in our history when racial prejudice distorted the measurement of intelligence. Science can reflect the best and worst of the times. After weighing all the evidence on whether other primates can acquire language, most psychologists have conclude that, however remarkable, the linguistic abilities of apes are not true language. So says science. Or is it our human prejudice?

Effective Student Tip 8

What Can You Do?

Some students freeze up when they get an assignment, fearing that, unless they instantly know what to do and how to do it, they're dead. The solution, if only they knew it, is right at hand. One of the best ways to tackle a new challenge is to draw on what you already do well. Step away from the course for a moment. What can you do competently right now?

Perhaps your work relates to the course (a business student at a bank, or a psychology student in a day-care center). Your experiences and observations would make great examples to use in class discussion or in written reports. Most professors delight in having students relate the subject matter of the course to the realities of the working world. If you learned how to operate a word processor at work, can you use it after hours to prepare papers so beautiful they will knock your professor's socks off? If you are an athlete, can you use your knowledge of effective training techniques to work out a schedule for gradually building up your academic skills?

Module 15: Intelligence

Use this **Outline** to organize your studying. Write notes on it. Turn it into a personalized aid for effective learning.

I. Definitions of **intelligence**

A. General opinion

1. Problem-solving skills

2. Verbal ability

3. Social competence

B. **Psychometric** approach

1. **Lumpers**

a. Intelligence as a general, unified capacity

b. Charles Spearman's **two-factor theory** ("**g**" and "**s**")

c. Gives single score, but excludes other skills and does not explain processes of intelligence

2. **Splitters**

a. Intelligence as many separate mental abilities

b. Howard Gardner's **multiple-factor theory**

c. Highlights other areas, but how many areas are there?

C. **Information-processing** approach

1. Intelligence as cognitive processes of problem solving

2. **Triarchic theory** (Robert Sternberg)

a. Analytical or logical thinking skills

b. Problem-solving skills

c. Practical thinking skills

3. Highlights practical areas missed by IQ tests, but hard to measure

II. Measurement of intelligence

A. Early attempts

1. Skull capacity (Samuel Morton) and brain size (Paul Broca)

2. Inherited factors (Francis Galton)

B. Intelligence **testing** (**Alfred Binet**)

1. **Mental age** — used to estimate a child's developmental *progress*

2. Single score

C. Intelligence quotient (**IQ**) (**Lewis Terman**)

1. Mental age divided by chronological age times 100

2. IQ — used to assign a child's innate, fixed *ability*

D. Intelligence tests

1. Stanford-Binet

2. Wechsler Adult Intelligence Scale—Revised (WAIS-R)

E. Requirements of a good test

1. **Reliability** (measures accurately and consistently)

2. **Validity** (measures what it claims to be measuring)

F. Distribution of IQ scores

1. **Normal distribution** (bell-shaped curve)

2. Mental retardation

a. Three levels of retardation

b. Organic retardation

c. Cultural-familial retardation

3. Gifted

    a. Accelerated programs, Mensa

    b. Myths about the gifted (Terman longitudinal study)

G. Problems with IQ tests

1. Labeling

    a. Racial and cultural discrimination

    b. Misapplications in educational decisions

2. Cultural bias

    a. Culture-free tests

    b. Ecological approach

3. Value of IQ testing

    a. Assessment tool

    b. Prediction of academic success

III. Intelligence testing and society

A. IQ tests and **immigration**

1. IQ scores as measures of innate intelligence and class boundaries (Terman)

2. IQ scores to classify "races" (Robert Yerkes)

3. Limiting immigration by quotas (Immigration Law of 1924)

4. Mismeasurement examined (Stephen Jay Gould)

B. The **nature-nurture question**

1. Inheritance versus experience

2. Research on contributions to intelligence

a. Twin studies: 50% is inherited

b. Adoption studies: environment does make a difference

3. Interaction of nature and nurture

a. Genes establish a broad *range* of potential intelligence

b. Environment affects development of that potential (**reaction range**)

IV. *Applying/Exploring:* Intervention programs

A. Pioneering **intervention programs**

1. **Head Start**

2. Abecedarian Project

B. Short-term benefits of intervention programs

C. Other social benefits of intervention programs

Now take the
Self-Tests
to check your understanding and mastery of this module.

Getting the general idea... Is the statement true or false?

_____ 1. The key question in defining intelligence is whether it is a single thing or a combination of skills and abilities.

_____ 2. It is generally true the larger the brain the more intelligent the person.

_____ 3. Alfred Binet gave us the concept of an intelligence quotient (IQ).

_____ 4. Lewis Terman's formula for determining IQ was mental age divided by chronological age times 100.

_____ 5. If a test is not reliable, it cannot be valid.

_____ 6. As a result of protest movements, all the major intelligence tests are now culture-free.

_____ 7. Measurements of intelligence have been used to support racial and ethnic discrimination.

_____ 8. Twin studies suggest that we inherit only a small percentage of our intelligence.

_____ 9. Adoption studies suggest that environment plays a large part in determining intelligence.

_____ 10. Research shows that programs like Head Start, while well meaning, have few long-term benefits.

Knowing the essential vocabulary... Which phrase matches the term?

	Term		Phrase
_____	1. lumpers	a.	consistency
_____	2. splitters	b.	bell-shaped curve
_____	3. reliability	c.	intelligence as one ability
_____	4. validity	d.	inherited or acquired?
_____	5. mental age	e.	"I know the answer!"
_____	6. IQ	f.	appropriateness
_____	7. normal distribution	g.	Binet's developmental idea
_____	8. culture-free	h.	intelligence as several skills
_____	9. nature-nurture	i.	Terman's innate ability idea
_____	10. teacher, teacher	j.	completely unbiased

Mastering the material... Which answer makes the statement true?

____ 1. Rod Plotnik is interested in Supreme Court Justice Clarence Thomas and his sister Emma Mae Martin because their stories
   a. show that some individuals seem destined for greatness
   b. illustrate the unpredictability of human abilities and behaviors
   c. show how unevenly intelligence is spread, even within one family
   d. illustrate the nature-nurture question in psychology

____ 2. The psychometricians known as "lumpers" believe that intelligence is a
   a. general unified capacity
   b. group of separate mental abilities
   c. set of processes for solving problems
   d. combination of biological functions of the brain and nervous system

____ 3. The strong point of the psychometricians known as "splitters" is that their approach to intelligence
   a. yields a single score that is useful for predicting academic performance
   b. measures each of the five known areas of intelligence
   c. takes into account several abilities not covered by standard IQ tests
   d. gives credit for intelligence to people with "street smarts"

____ 4. The information-processing approach to intelligence emphasizes the
   a. machine-like efficiency with which our computer minds crunch numbers and sort data
   b. cognitive processes people use to solve problems
   c. biological changes in the brain and nervous system that result from information input
   d. single core ability on which all related intellectual skills are based

____ 5. The first intelligence test was devised by
   a. Charles Spearman
   b. Lewis Terman
   c. Alfred Binet
   d. Howard Gardner

_____ 6. The formula for IQ is
  a. level of schooling divided by actual age
  b. chronological age divided by mental age
  c. test score divided by grade in school plus 100
  d. mental age divided by chronological age times 100

_____ 7. Ten times your sister jumps on the scale and ten times it reads 115 pounds. "Wow," she exclaims, "I'm taller than the average American woman!" The measurement device she used is
  a. both reliable and valid
  b. neither reliable nor valid
  c. reliable, but not valid
  d. valid, but not reliable

_____ 8. If you measured the intelligence of everyone in the United States, a distribution of all the scores would look like a
  a. curve sloping gently upward to the right
  b. bell-shaped curve
  c. flat horizon line with a skyscraper in the middle
  d. curve that rises and falls at regular intervals

_____ 9. Terman's 35-year study of gifted persons revealed their lives to be
  a. no different from the average American's life
  b. plagued by the mental instability that goes with high intelligence
  c. lonelier, sadder, and more eccentric than average
  d. healthier, happier, and more successful than average

_____ 10. The problem with IQ tests is that they are
  a. completely culture-free
  b. seldom used to get children into the right classes in school
  c. sometimes used to label people and discriminate against them
  d. unable to predict how well a child will do in school

_____ 11. The story of IQ tests and immigration shows that
  a. good research can be used for bad purposes
  b. scientific research often reflects the prejudices of the times
  c. good research can be used to right injustice
  d. scientific research is politically neutral

_____ 12. In the matter of intelligence, the nature-nurture question
a. has been essentially solved by the twin studies
b. has been essentially solved by the adoption studies
c. remains unsolved, since the concepts of "nature" and "nurture" are too vague to be resolved by scientific research
d. remains unsolved, since both nature and nurture play important roles in the formation of intelligence

_____ 13. Twin studies suggest that intelligence is
a. about 90% inherited
b. only slightly influenced by heredity
c. about 50% determined by genetics
d. a random phenomenon unaffected by heredity

_____ 14. Adoption studies suggest that intelligence
a. can be positively affected by improved environmental conditions
b. is essentially fixed at birth by heredity
c. is lessened by the loss of one's biological parents
d. does not change much, regardless of family environment

_____ 15. Studies of the effectiveness of intervention programs like Head Start suggest that
a. however well-intentioned, intervention programs don't work
b. the main benefits of these programs go to the middle-class professionals they employ
c. the short-term benefits fail to justify the high costs of these programs
d. even if differences in IQ fade over time, there are other social benefits that justify continuing these programs

Module 16: Thought and Language

Use this

Outline

to organize your studying. Write notes on it. Turn it into a personalized aid for effective learning.

I. **Concepts**

A. Functions of concepts

1. Group things into categories

2. Identify things without relearning

B. Forming concepts

1. **Definitional theory** (listing properties that define something)

a. Difficulty in listing all the defining properties

b. Exceptions, not included in list of defining properties, always occur

2. **Prototype theory** (matching to an ideal model of an object)

a. Not necessary to include all essential features of object

b. Not necessary to account for wide variations or exceptions

II. **Problem solving**

A. States in finding a plan or strategy for reaching a goal

1. **Initial state** — contemplating unsolved problem

1. **Operations state** — trying out operations, rules, plans

1. **Goal state** — reaching solution

B. Rules for solving problems

1. **Algorithms**

a. Rules that, if followed correctly, lead to solution

b. Mathematically precise

2. **Heuristics**

   a. Rules of thumb that reduce number of operations and allow taking shortcuts

   b. Human thought is supremely good at heuristics

3. Common heuristics or shortcuts (Amos Tversky and Daniel Kahneman)

   a. **Availability** heuristic — we rely on more prominent information, which seems more available, and overlook other information

   b. **Representative** heuristic — we judge the likelihood of an event by comparing it to our mental image or representation of such events

C. Developing strategies for solving problems

1. Changing one's mental set

   a. **Functional fixedness** — inability to see alternate functions

   b. **Insight** — sudden grasp of solution after many incorrect attempts

2. Using **analogies**

   a. Finding similarity between new situation and old, familiar situations

   b. Ability to use analogies increases with experience and knowledge

3. Forming **subgoals**

   a. Separate parts that, when completed in order, will result in solution

   b. *College students take note: an effective and powerful strategy for overcoming procrastination is to break a task down into smaller tasks that are easier to accomplish*

III. **Creative thinking** (five common questions)

A. What is creative thinking?

1. Combination of flexibility in thinking and reorganization in understanding to produce innovative ideas and solutions

2. **Divergent thinking**

   a. Beginning with one problem and coming up with many solutions

   b. Opposite of **convergent thinking** (beginning with one problem and coming up with the one most obviously correct solution)

B. Can creative thinking be taught?

1. Program for teaching creative thinking (Teresa Amabile)

2. **Brainstorming** (four rules)

   a. Do not criticize the suggestions of others

   b. Generate as many ideas as possible

   c. Attempt to be original

   d. Build on others' suggestions

C. What psychological traits do creative people have? [Rod Plotnik relates these traits to the famous pioneers of psychology]

1. Drive to make sense of reality, bring order out of chaos

2. Strong interest in finding and solving unusual problems

3. Believe in objectivity, or the need to *test* creative ideas

4. Not afraid to take risks

5. Have ability to change mental directions

6. Driven by internal, or intrinsic, motivation rather than money, reward, or recognition

D. Is there a relationship between creativity and IQ?

1. People recognized as creative have above-average IQs

2. Higher IQ people not automatically more creative

E. Are creative people more likely to have mood disorders?

1. Some evidence that creative people may be more likely to report mood disorders

2. In general, creativity and madness do *not* go hand in hand

IV. Rules for language

A. Characteristics of **language** [four criteria required for true language]

1. Special form of communication

2. Set of symbols

3. Complex rules

4. Ability to generate endless number of meaningful sentences

B. Four language rules

1. **Phonology** — how we make the meaningful sounds **(phonemes)** used by a particular language

2. **Morphology** — how we group phonemes into meaningful combinations of sounds and words **(morphemes)**

2. **Syntax** or **grammar** — how we combine words to form meaningful phrases and sentences

2. **Semantics** — specifies meaning of words in various contexts

V. Language acquisition

A. Structure of language (**Noam Chomsky**)

1. **Surface structure** — actual wording of a sentence, as it is spoken

2. **Deep structure** — underlying meaning, not spoken, but present in mind of listener

3. **Transformational rules** — procedures for converting ideas from surface structure into deep structure and from deep structure back into surface structure

B. Debate over how language is acquired

1. **Innate factors** (Chomsky)

a. relationship between brain and language abilities

b. **Critical language period**

2. **Learning factors**

a. **Shaping** (Skinner)

b. Social learning through observation and imitation (Bandura)

C. Stages of language acquisition

1. **Babbling**

a. One-syllable verbalizations

b. Infant quickly becomes sensitive to sound in own language

2. **Single word**

a. Objects that child can see, hear, or feel

b. "Parentese"

3. **Two-word** combinations

a. Combinations that convey meaning

b. No "three-word" stage

4. **Sentences** and rules of grammar
    a. Telegraphic speech
    b. Basic rules of grammar
    c. Overgeneralization

D. Language and thought

1. Controversial theory of **linguistic relativity** (Benjamin Whorf)
    a. Language determines how people think
    b. People with different languages think differently
2. Against: Eskimos *do not* have more words for snow (Laura Martin)
3. For: experience of thinking in two languages

VI. *Applying/Exploring:* Do animals have language?

A. Only humans meet the four criteria for true language (see IV.A.)

B. Dolphins — responders

C. Gorillas and chimpanzees — sign language

1. Koko (Francine Patterson)
2. Washoe (Beatrice and Allen Gardner)
3. Apes mainly imitating or responding to cues (Herbert Terrace)

D. Pigmy chimps — new findings

1. Kanzi (Sue Savage-Rumbaugh)
2. Language level of two-year-old human child
3. Is Kanzi actually using rules of grammar, or only using words as tools to get things?

Getting the general idea... Is the statement true or false?

_____ 1. We form a concept by constructing a complete list of all the properties that define an object, event, or characteristic.

_____ 2. A computer program like "Deep Thought" can beat all but the very best human chess players because it is so good at employing heuristics.

_____ 3. Good thinking: insight, analogy, subgoals. Bad thinking: functional fixedness.

_____ 4. Brainstorming is a form of divergent thinking.

_____ 5. Creativity is inherited — it cannot be taught.

_____ 6. Noam Chomsky bases his theory of language on the premise that humans have inborn language capabilities.

_____ 7. It is easier to learn a foreign language in grade school than in college.

_____ 8. Children complete the essential tasks of learning language during the three-word stage.

_____ 9. Eskimos probably think differently about snow because they have so many more words for it than other people do.

_____ 10. So far, only humans clearly meet the four criteria for true language.

Knowing the essential vocabulary... Which phrase matches the term?

_____ 1. prototype

_____ 2. algorithm

_____ 3. heuristic

_____ 4. analogy

_____ 5. divergent

_____ 6. syntax

_____ 7. deep structure

_____ 8. babbling

_____ 9. parentese

_____ 10. blubbering

a. a variety of solutions to a problem

b. a single syllable repeated

c. a precise rule for solving a problem

d. a set of rules for forming sentences

e. a response to seeing your test score

f. a helpful mental shortcut

g. an underlying level of meaning

h. an average of all categories

i. a similarity between new and old

j. a way of talking to infants

Mastering the material... Which answer makes the statement true?

_____ 1. Rod Plotnik is interested in the two young Hungarian sisters who are already chess champions because
a. they have disproved the notion that only adults can achieve championship-level mastery of chess
b. psychologists are always fascinated by the strange and bizarre in human behavior
c. despite their achievements in chess, they have never acquired normal language skills
d. chess involves a number of cognitive abilities and processes

_____ 2. Concepts are crucial to effective thinking because without them
a. we would not know the rules for logical thought
b. we would be overwhelmed by apparently unrelated pieces of information
c. our cognitive processes would be just like those of a dog or cat
d. our motivation to think would be greatly reduced

_____ 3. Most psychologists favor the _____________ theory of concept formation because it _____________
a. definitional ... is based on good, sound definitions
b. definitional ... accounts for the exceptions to the rule
c. prototype ... is based on complete listings of essential properties
d. prototype ... accounts for more objects using fewer features

_____ 4. Eventually, a computer program like Deep Thought will beat the best human chess player because
a. increasingly more powerful algorithms will win
b. good heuristics usually win
c. computers can "think" faster than humans can
d. there is an element of luck in any game

_____ 5. When your friend remarks pessimistically that crime is increasing ("Did you see that gruesome murder on the news last night?"), you recognize the operation of the
a. accuracy algorithm
b. availability heuristic
c. representative heuristic
d. self-fulfilling prophecy

_____ 6. If you were not able to solve the nine-dot problem, it probably was because of
   a. functional fixedness
   b. lack of insight
   c. using poor analogies
   d. failure to establish subgoals

_____ 7. One of the best ways to finish your college assignments on time is to
   a. have the problem in the back of your mind, and wait for a sudden flash of insight
   b. use the analogy of other, similar assignments you have done before
   c. fix your thoughts on the function that is involved in the assignment
   d. break the assignment down into subtasks and subgoals

_____ 8. A serious problem with too many college courses is that they place all the emphasis on ______________ thinking
   a. creative
   b. convergent
   c. divergent
   d. brainstorm

_____ 9. From most particular to most general in the rules of language, the correct order is
   a. morpheme, phoneme, syntax, semantics
   b. syntax, grammar, sentence, story
   c. phoneme, morpheme, syntax, semantics
   d. semantics, syntax, morpheme, phoneme

_____ 10. If you said "Are what you today playing?" to a child, you would see that children
   a. acquire the basic rules of grammar at an early age
   b. don't pay much attention to the exact order of words in a sentence
   c. can only handle two-word and three-word combinations
   d. pay more attention to gestures and facial expressions than to words

_____ 11. According to Noam Chomsky, we employ ______________ to go back and forth between word arrangements and meaning
   a. surface structures
   b. deep structures
   c. transformational rules
   d. learning factors

____ 12. The theoretical battle between Chomsky and Skinner concerns whether language abilities are ____________ or ____________

a. innate ... learned through shaping
b. universal ... different from one cultural group to another
c. superficial ... deep-seated
d. individual ... common to the group

____ 13. "I goed to the zoo" is an example of

a. babbling
b. parentese
c. overgeneralization
d. telegraphic speech

____ 14. Is the linguistic relativity theory correct? The fascinating observation that Eskimos have many more words for snow might prove it... except for the fact that

a. they also have fewer words for rain
b. snow is obviously such a crucial factor in their lives
c. there is no relationship between language and thought
d. it isn't true

____ 15. the bottom line in the debate over whether other animals can acquire true language seems to be that

a. dolphins may possess a system of communication far superior to human language
b. only humans meet the four criteria for true language
c. the pygmy chimp is the only animal able to learn true language
d. several of the higher primates can acquire the language skills of five-year-old children

Answers for Chapter 8

Module 15

True-False	Matching	Multiple-Choice
1. T	1. c	1. d
2. F	2. h	2. a
3. F	3. a	3. c
4. T	4. f	4. b
5. F	5. g	5. c
6. F	6. i	6. d
7. T	7. b	7. c
8. F	8. j	8. b
9. T	9. d	9. d
10. F	10. e	10. c
		11. b
		12. d
		13. c
		14. a
		15. d

Module 16

True-False	Matching	Multiple-Choice
1. F	1. h	1. d
2. F	2. c	2. b
3. T	3. f	3. d
4. T	4. i	4. a
5. F	5. a	5. b
6. T	6. d	6. a
7. T	7. g	7. d
8. F	8. b	8. b
9. F	9. j	9. c
10. T	10. e	10. a
		11. c
		12. a
		13. c
		14. d
		15. b

Chapter 9: Motivation and Emotion

Does learning interest you?

I have always thought studying psychology offers a wonderful extra payoff: learning how to become a more effective student.

You can pick up an idea about becoming a better student in every chapter of Rod Plotnik's book. Sometimes he gives you an outright suggestion, sometimes you have to make the connection yourself, but each module contains a fact or an insight you can apply to becoming more effective in your college work. One of the most important ideas concerns motivation.

Chapter 9 introduces the idea of intrinsic motivation, the kind of motivation that goes beyond working for a specific, immediate, tangible payoff. Not that there's anything wrong with motivation through reinforcement. That's what gets us to work and makes us meet specific goals. In the long run, however, sustained pursuit of complex goals requires that overt reinforcement be replaced by intrinsic motivation. That's why you get smiley faces on your papers in grade school but not in college.

It is important to understand your motivation for attending college. If the real reason you enrolled was to please your parents or because all your friends went, you may have a difficult time mustering the energy and finding the time college work demands. If you find the activity of learning itself interesting, however, your college studies should be exciting and fun.

Emotions, discussed in the second module of Chapter 9, offer a powerful tool for understanding intrinsic motivation. Emotions are like a psychological radar constantly evaluating everything in your life. Think about college for a minute. What feelings come with those thoughts? What clues do those feelings offer about your basic motivation to be in school?

Effective Student Tip 9

Three Secrets of Effective Writing

Too many students think the ability to write well is something you have to be born with. The truth is just the opposite. Any student can become a good writer. The *art* of writing requires curiosity and creativity, but we all have those qualities. The *craft* of writing is as learnable as cooking or carpentry. Three secrets of effective writing reveal how any serious student can get started on becoming a better writer.

Secret #1: Tell a **story** that is important to you. We remember stories. A well-told story is the most effective way to convey information.

Secret #2: Paint word **pictures**. We understand what we can visualize. A beautifully worded description is the most effective way to create understanding in writing.

Secret #3: Think of writing as a **craft** (artistry will come naturally). One by one, learn the skills of good writing. Start by learning how to type a beautiful paper, the easiest procedure to learn and the one that has the most immediate effect on your reader.

When you think of writing as a craft, you realize that the goal is progress, not perfection. It doesn't really matter how good your next paper is, as long as it is better than the last one.

Module 17: Motivation

I. Approaches to **motivation**

A. Four explanations of motivation

1. **Instincts** (fixed)

a. Innate or biological

b. **Fixed action patterns**

2. **Drives** and needs (internal)

a. **Homeostasis**

b. **Drive-reduction theory**

3. **Incentives** (external)

a. Reinforcers

b. Extrinsic motivation

4. Beliefs and **expectations** (cognitive)

a. Personal goals, beliefs, or expectations

b. **Intrinsic motivation**

II. Biological and social needs

A. **Maslow's** hierarchy of needs (five levels, from lowest to highest)

1. **Physiological**

2. **Safety**

3. **Love and belongingness**

4. **Esteem**

5. **Self-actualization**

Use this

Outline

to organize your studying. Write notes on it. Turn it into a personalized aid for effective learning.

B. Three important human needs illustrate motivation

1. Hunger

2. Sex

3. Achievement

III. Hunger

A. Learned cues for hunger (**body image**)

B. Biological cues for hunger

1. Peripheral cues

2. Central cues

C. Body weight

1. Inherited factors

a. Fat cells

b. Rates of metabolism

c. Set point or range

2. Learned factors

a. Psychological

b. Social-cultural

c. Physical

IV. Sexual behavior

A. Basis of sexual motivation

1. **Hormones**

2. Pheromones

3. Psychological factors

B. Human sexual response

1. **William Masters** and **Virginia Johnson**

2. Four stages of sexual response

a. **Excitement**

b. **Plateau**

c. **Orgasm**

d. **Resolution**

C. Social-cultural influences

1. Decisions about being sexual

2. **Double standard**

D. Homosexuality

1. Biological factors

2. Social-learning factors

E. AIDS

1. **HIV-positive**

2. Causes

3. Risks

4. Protection

5. Treatment

V. **Need for achievement** (David McClelland and John Atkinson)

A. Measurement (TAT)

B. Fear of failure

C. Self-handicapping strategy

D. Intrinsic motivation

VI. *Applying/Exploring:* Eating problems

A. Dieting

B. Eating disorders

1. **Bulimia** nervosa

2. **Anorexia** nervosa

Now take the **Self-Tests** to check your understanding and mastery of this module.

For psych majors only...

The most significant of all motivations may be the need to be effective. Oh sure, thirst, hunger, and sex are more immediate and can be insanely demanding, but what is it that we want all the time? We want to be effective in our dealings with the world, in our interactions with other people, and in managing our personal lives. Some call this a sense of mastery or control, but I think the word effectiveness better conveys the broad need to do things that work.

The idea comes from Robert W. White, who wrote about what he called competence motivation a half-century ago. You may study Robert White when you take a course in personality theories. Unfortunately, however, the idea of competence has become so deeply woven into the fabric of modern psychology that we tend to overlook it. I think effectiveness is such a significant need that it deserves explicit recognition.

Perhaps you see why it is so important to do well in college — success in college is the crucial measure of effectiveness at this point in your life. Examine your thoughts, feelings and behavior. Doing something well (being effective) makes you pleased and happy, but when you are ineffective, you feel lousy. Everything in your psychological makeup says you want to be effective in college. Of course this applies to your classmates, too, but it also applies to someone else in the classroom. More about that person later, in Effective Student Tip 14.

The material in general... Is the statement true or false?

_____ 1. Animals have instincts; humans have fixed action patterns.

_____ 2. The concept of homeostasis supports the drive-reduction theory.

_____ 3. The concept of intrinsic motivation rests on a recognition of the importance of external factors.

_____ 4. Maslow's hierarchy of needs nicely brings together both biological and social needs.

_____ 5. After years of research, it turns out that calories are still the most important factor in problems of weight.

_____ 6. Humans are the only animals for whom learned cues to eating are more powerful than biological cues.

_____ 7. As one might expect, the male lion gets sex whenever he wants it.

_____ 8. The percentage of people who are homosexual is rising rapidly.

_____ 9. Researchers believe they will find a cure for AIDS in the next year or two.

_____ 10. The dull truth is that the only solution to weight problems is learning better eating behaviors.

Knowing the essential vocabulary... Which phrase matches the term?

	Term		Phrase
_____	1. fixed action pattern	a.	self-starvation
_____	2. homeostasis	b.	Masters and Johnson's four phases
_____	3. self-actualization	c.	AIDS
_____	4. set point	d.	equilibrium
_____	5. human sexual response	e.	fear of fast food
_____	6. HIV-positive	f.	natural range for weight
_____	7. need for achievement	g.	animal instinct
_____	8. self-handicapping strategy	h.	fear of failure
_____	9. anorexia nervosa	i.	Thematic Apperception Test (TAT)
_____	10. golden archophobia	j.	Maslow's fifth level

Mastering the material... Which answer makes the statement true?

____ 1. Rod Plotnik tells the story of Mark Wellman's incredible climb to illustrate the fact that
   a. you can do anything you really put your mind to
   b. you should take risks in life, but also have strong ropes!
   c. the causes of human actions are complex, yet important to understand
   d. there must be a single source of motivation, as yet undiscovered

____ 2. Early in this century, most psychologists believed that motivation was explained by
   a. drives and needs
   b. instincts
   c. incentives
   d. expectations

____ 3. The newest theory of motivation places greatest emphasis on
   a. drives and needs
   b. instincts
   c. incentives
   d. expectations

____ 4. The key idea of Maslow's hierarchy of needs is that
   a. unless social needs like esteem are satisfied, one cannot deal effectively with biological needs like safety
   b. the more basic biological needs must be satisfied before the higher social needs can be dealt with
   c. unless you achieve level five, you are a defective person
   d. the higher needs are essential; the lower needs are incidental

____ 5. The term "body image" means your
   a. perception of, and satisfaction with, your body
   b. memory of when your body was at its best
   c. weight and shape compared to the national average
   d. friends' and relatives' secret thoughts about how you look

_____ 6. All of the following are biological cues for hunger *except*
a. glucose in the blood
b. the hypothalamus
c. images and odors of food
d. the walls of the stomach

_____ 7. All of the following are inherited factors that influence body weight *except*
a. fat cells
b. metabolism
c. set point
d. responsiveness to food cues

_____ 8. Perhaps the most useful recent finding about weight concerns the importance of
a. calories
b. physical exercise
c. inheritance
d. body image

_____ 9. The reason lions don't need talk shows is that their sexual behavior is kept in line by the fact that
a. females do most of the hunting
b. a lioness's bite can be fatal
c. social roles and rules predominate
d. hormones and pheromones prevail

_____ 10. Which one of the following is the correct order of human sexual response?
a. excitement – plateau – orgasm – resolution
b. plateau – excitement – orgasm – resolution
c. excitement – orgasm – plateau – resolution
d. orgasm – excitement – resolution – plateau

_____ 11. The term "double standard" means the
a. added burden modern women face of both working and caring for their families
b. biological fact that women want one man but men want more than one woman
c. social expectation that men will be more sexually active than women
d. new idea that a woman can ask a man out and still expect him to pick up the check

_____ 12. What makes a person homosexual? Much of the new evidence points to the importance of
a. social factors like having homosexual teachers
b. biological factors like brain structure and inheritance
c. family factors like overbearing mothers
d. intellectual factors like fascination with art

_____ 13. The best motivation for superior academic performance is having a
a. high need for achievement
b. high fear of failure
c. very efficient self-handicapping strategy
d. reasonable excuse for occasional failure

_____ 14. Oprah Winfrey lost her public battle with weight because, as she admitted, she
a. had secretly been bulimic for years
b. had always been terrified that she was potentially anorexic
c. did not find a way to live in the world with food
d. did not have the will power to say no to food

_____ 15. [*Warning! Trick question*] The only sure way to avoid getting AIDS is to
a. practice celibacy
b. use condoms
c. know your partner
d. just say no to drugs

Module 18: Emotion

I. Theoretical questions about **emotion**

A. Hierarchy of basic emotions

B. Theories of emotion

1. Peripheral theories (emphasize changes in body)

a. **James-Lange theory**

b. **Facial feedback theory**

2. Cognitive theories (emphasize changes in thinking)

a. **Cognitive appraisal theory**

b. Physiological arousal not necessary

3. **Primacy question**: which is true?

a. Feeling comes before thinking

b. Thinking comes before feeling

II. Basics of emotions

A. Components of an emotion

1. Physiological

2. Behavioral

3. Cognitive

B. **Adaptation level theory**

Use this

Outline

to organize your studying. Write notes on it. Turn it into a personalized aid for effective learning.

C. Functions of emotions

1. Adaptation and survival

2. Motivation and arousal

3. **Social signaling**

D. Expression and intensity of emotions

1. Universality of basic emotions

2. **Display rules** (specific cultural rules about expressing emotion)

3. Intensity of emotions

III. *Applying/Exploring:* The lie detector test

A. Administering and interpreting lie detector tests

B. Reliability of lie detector tests

Now take the **Self-Tests** to check your understanding and mastery of this module.

The material in general... Is the statement true or false?

_____ 1. People all over the world recognize the basic emotions.

_____ 2. Psychologists now agree that the James-Lange theory provides the best explanation of how emotions work.

_____ 3. Psychologists do not agree on whether feeling or thinking comes first in the process of experiencing emotions.

_____ 4. The reason the joy of winning the lottery doesn't last is that human beings are seldom satisfied with what they have.

_____ 5. Human emotions, like the human appendix, are left over from our primitive past and not really needed today.

_____ 6. Display rules are cultural expectations that govern the presentation and control of emotional expression in specific situations.

_____ 7. People all over the world rate happiness as the most intense emotion.

_____ 8. Emotions are essential to our survival.

_____ 9. There is a universal language of emotional expression that helps people understand each other.

_____ 10. Lie detector tests determine whether a statement is true or false.

Knowing the essential vocabulary... Which phrase matches the term?

	Term		Phrase
_____	1. basic emotions	a.	lottery winner's blues
_____	2. James-Lange theory	b.	universal, promote survival
_____	3. facial feedback theory	c.	physiological responses
_____	4. cognitive appraisal theory	d.	which comes first, feeling or thinking?
_____	5. mood	e.	what is a shark
_____	6. primacy question	f.	see shark, show expression of terror, feel fear
_____	7. components of emotion	g.	see shark, become physiologically aroused, feel fear
_____	8. adaptation level theory	h.	see shark, become physiologically aroused, interpret arousal as fear
_____	9. lie detector test	i.	overall emotional feeling
_____	10. big, scary fish	j.	physiological, behavioral, cognitive

Mastering the material... Which answer makes the statement true?

_____ 1. Rod Plotnik tells us about the surfer who was attacked by a shark [where does he *get* these stories?] to show that
a. emotions play a major role in our lives
b. sometimes you can feel all the emotions at once
c. sometimes survival depends on having no emotions
d. emotions (like the joy of surfing) can get in the way of common sense

_____ 2. All of the following are components of an emotion *except*
a. conscious experience
b. physiological arousal
c. overt behavior
d. genetic variation

_____ 3. All of the following are basic emotions *except*
a. intelligence
b. love
c. anger
d. hate

_____ 4. According to the ____________ theory, emotions result from specific physiological changes in the body
a. primacy
b. James-Lange
c. facial feedback
d. cognitive appraisal

_____ 5. According to the ____________ theory, emotions result from our interpretation of a situation as having positive or negative impact on our lives
a. primacy
b. James-Lange
c. facial feedback
d. cognitive appraisal

____ 6. According to the ____________ theory, emotions result from our brain's interpretation of muscle and skin movements that occur when we express an emotion

a. primacy
b. James-Lange
c. facial feedback
d. cognitive appraisal

____ 7. The answer to the primacy question, as determined by research, is that

a. thinking comes first
b. feelings come first
c. both occur at exactly the same time
d. the debate is not yet resolved

____ 8. Adaptation level theory explains why people who win big in the lottery

a. don't come forward to claim their prizes right away
b. often spend lavishly until they are right back where they started
c. don't feel much happier than anyone else after a while
d. often report that winning permanently changed them from discontented to happy persons

____ 9. Emotions do all of the following for us *except*

a. help us adapt and survive
b. allow us 100% use of our brain power
c. motivate and arouse us
d. help us express social signals

____ 10. Evidence for the universality of human emotions comes from the fact that people all over the world

a. consider happiness to be the most intense emotion
b. follow the same rules about how to show emotions
c. recognize the basic emotions
d. make up rules about how to show emotions

____ 11. Cultural rules that govern emotional expression in specific situations are called

a. display rules
b. feelings guides
c. primacy rules
d. intensity rules

____ 12. Cross-cultural research reveals that the most intense emotion is
a. happiness
b. disgust
c. anger
d. it differs from culture to culture

____ 13. Lie detector tests measure
a. whether a statement is true or false
b. how much physiological arousal the subject feels
c. whether the subject is basically honest or dishonest
d. how much character a person has

____ 14. In most courtrooms, lie detector test results are
a. admissible, because they give scientifically derived evidence
b. admissible, because the jury must hear any evidence available
c. inadmissible, because of their potential for error
d. inadmissible, because they would put lawyers out of work

____ 15. [*For Trekkies only*] This module helps us understand why we find the character of ______________ so fascinating
a. Spock
b. Uhuru
c. Kirk
d. Scotty

Answers for Chapter 9

Module 17

True-False	Matching	Multiple-Choice
1. F	1. g	1. c
2. T	2. d	2. b
3. F	3. j	3. d
4. T	4. f	4. b
5. F	5. b	5. a
6. T	6. c	6. c
7. F	7. i	7. d
8. F	8. h	8. b
9. F	9. a	9. d
10. T	10. e	10. a
		11. c
		12. b
		13. a
		14. c
		15. none

Module 18

True-False	Matching	Multiple-Choice
1. T	1. b	1. a
2. F	2. g	2. d
3. T	3. f	3. a
4. F	4. h	4. b
5. F	5. i	5. d
6. T	6. d	6. c
7. F	7. j	7. d
8. T	8. a	8. c
9. T	9. c	9. b
10. F	10. e	10. c
		11. a
		12. d
		13. b
		14. c
		15. a

Chapter 10: Child Development

The child is father to the man

One of psychology's most important contributions to modern knowledge is the idea of childhood as a separate, special phase of human life, with processes of development crucial for the rest of life. That idea seems obvious today, but not long ago most people thought of children simply as small adults, not really different in any special way, or as happy innocents enjoying a carefree period of freedom before the onset of adult concerns.

Once psychology recognized the importance of childhood, every comprehensive theory had to attempt to explain it. Not surprisingly, most of the important 'big' theories in psychology are also theories of childhood. Freud said personality forms essentially within the first five years. Erikson placed the most basic developmental tasks in the early years. Piaget said children think differently from adults. If you can master this chapter, with its heavy involvement of psychology's most famous names, you will have a good start on understanding the major theories of modern psychology.

There's more to the chapter. It also covers the basic features of childhood, from conception to school learning. In a chapter that does double duty, you need a way to cut down the new learning. First, note that there is general agreement about the several stages of childhood. There is considerable overlap in these theories, and the other research fits into these stages, too. Second, isolate the ways each major theory differs from the others. They don't disagree on everything. Concentrate on understanding the different angle each theorist takes on what is important in development.

Effective Student Tip 10

Overstudy!

My favorite myth about tests is the often-heard lament, "I studied too hard!" The idea seems to be that what you learn has only a fragile and temporary residence in your head, and studying too much disorganizes it or knocks it right back out again. A sadder myth is the belief so many students have that they are "no good at tests." No less misguided is the teeth-clenching determination to "do better next time," with no idea how to bring that about.

The truth is that in each case the student is not studying hard enough, or effectively enough. When I am able to persuade students to read the assigned chapters three or four times (they thought once was enough), the results amaze them. Almost invariably, their test grades go from D or C to B or A. Why? Because with more study, and better study, they are really mastering the material.

Determine how much studying you think will be enough for the next test. Then do more. Lots more. The single best way to improve your test scores is to overstudy the material.

Module 19: Infancy

Use this **Outline** to organize your studying. Write notes on it. Turn it into a personalized aid for effective learning.

I. Issues and approaches in child development

A. Issues

1. The famous **nature-nurture question**: which is more important?

a. Nature (inherited factors)

b. Nurture (learning and experience)

2. Is development continuous or does it occur in stages?

a. **Continuity** (gradual and progressive development)

b. **Stages** (distinct steps across the life span)

B. Methods for studying child development

1. Cross-sectional method (comparing different age groups)

2. Longitudinal method (following the same group over time)

3. Case study method (studying one person in depth over time)

II. Prenatal development

A. **Germinal period** (first 2 weeks after conception)

1. Ovulation

2. Genetics

a. Chromosomes

b. Genes

c. Amniocentesis

3. Conception

4. Zygote

B. **Embryonic period** (next 6 weeks)

1. Embryo

2. Cells divide and begin to differentiate into bone, muscle, and body organs

C. **Fetal period** (last 7 months)

1. Fetus

2. Development of vital organs

3. Harmful effects of drugs (**teratogens**)

a. Alcohol (**fetal alcohol syndrome**)

b. Tobacco

c. Cocaine, heroin

D. Birth and delivery

III. The **neonate** (newborn)

A. Sensory and perceptual responses

1. Vision

a. Visual acuity

b. Patterns

c. Faces

d. Depth perception (visual cliff research)

2. Other senses

B. Risks to the newborn

1. Malnutrition

2. Lead

C. Motor development

1. **Cephalocaudal principle** (parts closer to head develop before parts closer to feet)

2. **Proximodistal principle** (parts closer to center develop first)

3. **Maturation** (sequential development of genetic plan)

4. **Norms** for development (*average* age of new attainments)

IV. Emotional development

A. **Emotions** (Carroll Izard)

1. Expanding range of emotions

2. Interaction of biological capacity and caregiver feedback

B. **Temperament**

1. Infant temperament (Stella Chess, Alexander Thomas, Herbert Birch)

a. Easy babies (40%)

b. Slow-to-warm-up babies (15%) and difficult babies (10%)

2. Fear reactions (Jerome Kagan and Nancy Snidman)

a. Shy infants and outgoing infants

b. Partly genetic and fairly stable over time

C. **Attachment**

1. Process of attachment (Mary Ainsworth)

2. Separation anxiety

3. Kinds of attachment

a. Secure attachment

b. Insecure attachment

4. Long-term effects of quality of attachment

D. Emotional quality and parenting

1. Parenting arouses strong emotions

2. A warm emotional environment is important

3. Stressors affect parents' emotions

4. Negative emotions mean trouble

V. *Applying/Exploring:* Questions about **day care**

A. Questions about day care and child development (Allison Clarke-Stewart)

1. Does day care lead to insecure attachment?

2. Does day care lead to social problems?

3. Does day care retard intellectual development?

B. Signs of a good day care center (Sandra Scarr)

1. Ratio of caregivers to infants is 1 to 4

2. Caregivers are well trained and educated

3. Center and caregivers are stable

For psych majors only...

To win a place in the educated public's understanding, a theory needs sharp edges and distinctive, even shocking, premises. We all remember Pavlov's confused dog, Freud's obsession with sex, Piaget's surprising ideas about how children think, and Skinner's untiring lever-pressing rats.

Erik Erikson's elegant, almost poetic saga of human life lacks all that. Consequently, although psychologists respect Erikson highly, the educated public does not know his theory well. That's a shame, because it might be the most true to life theory of all.

Re-read Rod Plotnik's thoughtful discussion of Erikson in this chapter and the next. Put Erikson on your list of authors to read in the original.

Getting the general idea... Is the statement true or false?

_____ 1. The nature-nurture question asks how much development owes to inheritance and how much to learning and experience.

_____ 2. The case study method tries to learn more about normal people by carefully examining people with some disease or mental disorder.

_____ 3. The vital organs, such as the lungs and heart, develop during the germinal period.

_____ 4. The "visual cliff" is the distance after which visual acuity in newborns falls off quickly.

_____ 5. The cephalocaudal principle of motor development says that the parts closer to the head develop before the parts closer to the feet.

_____ 6. The concept of maturation is closer to "nature" than to "nurture."

_____ 7. By temperament, infants are either "easy babies" (about 60%) or "difficult babies" (about 40%).

_____ 8. Attachment is the close emotional bond that develops between infant and parent.

_____ 9. The single factor that most clearly reflects the health of the parent-child relationship is its emotional quality.

_____ 10. All the new research findings concerning day care report serious problems in emotional, social, and intellectual development.

Knowing the essential vocabulary... Which phrase matches the term?

	Term		Phrase
_____	1. nature versus...	a.	alcohol
_____	2. continuity versus...	b.	head first
_____	3. teratogen	c.	inborn timetable
_____	4. visual cliff	d.	emotional bond
_____	5. cephalocaudal principle	e.	"Dear Mom and Dad, Please send..."
_____	6. proximodistal principle	f.	nurture
_____	7. maturation	g.	depth perception
_____	8. temperament	h.	center first
_____	9. attachment	i.	easy or difficult
_____	10. disbursement	j.	stages

Mastering the material... Which answer makes the statement true?

_____ 1. Rod Plotnik recounts the remarkable adventure of Madeline, the smallest newborn ever to survive, because her story
   a. is an attention-grabber that will make us pay attention to what he says in the chapter on child development
   b. proves that miracles do happen
   c. illustrates the awesome powers of modern medical science
   d. forces us to reexamine processes we usually take for granted

_____ 2. Applying the nature-nurture question to Yani Wang, the child art prodigy, we would ask whether her special abilities
   a. are a gift of God or an accident of nature
   b. are inborn or the product of learning and experience
   c. will stay with her or fade as she gets older
   d. will be as well received in other cultures as they have been in her native China

_____ 3. If we study one individual in depth for a significant period of time, we are using the ______________ method
   a. cross-sectional
   b. longitudinal
   c. case study
   d. correlational

_____ 4. The briefest period of prenatal development is the
   a. germinal period
   b. embryonic period
   c. fetal period
   d. baby-making period [just kidding!]

_____ 5. If you believe what the textbook says about teratogens, you would tell all pregnant women to
   a. watch their weight gain very carefully
   b. get plenty of rest — even more as they approach delivery
   c. avoid alcohol entirely
   d. avoid becoming overly stressed

____ 6. The "visual cliff" is a device researchers use to test whether infants have developed
a. visual acuity
b. depth perception
c. pattern discrimination
d. space perception

____ 7. Why the head grows faster than the feet is explained by the
a. cephalocaudal principle
b. proximodistal principle
c. principle of maturation
d. principle of normal development

____ 8. Infants first use their more developed arms, and then their fingers, whose control develops later — this is the
a. cephalocaudal principle
b. proximodistal principle
c. principle of maturation
d. principle of normal development

____ 9. If you discuss the norms for infant development with new parents, be sure to emphasize the fact that
a. falling behind the norms can be a sign of serious developmental problems
b. they should consult a pediatrician the minute their child fails to meet a norm
c. there are significant differences between boys and girls in how soon infants achieve these norms
d. these norms are only averages, not fixed points after which they should worry about their child's development

____ 10. Carroll Izard has discovered that the emotional capacity of a newborn
a. is almost zero — every emotion has to be learned
b. is already complete — all the emotions are present at birth
c. consists of a few basic emotions, like interest and distress
d. consists of only two emotions, pleasure and pain

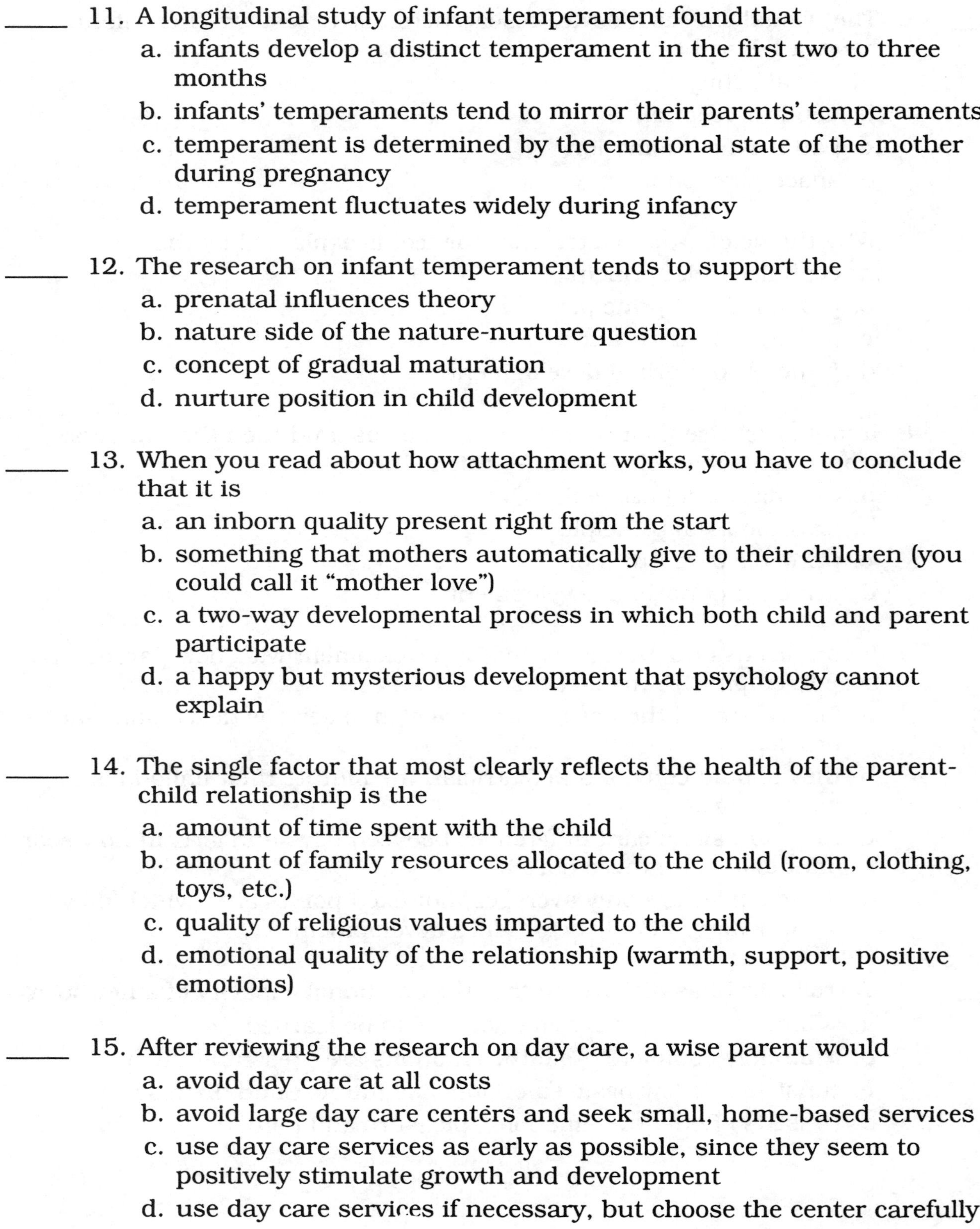

_____ 11. A longitudinal study of infant temperament found that
- a. infants develop a distinct temperament in the first two to three months
- b. infants' temperaments tend to mirror their parents' temperaments
- c. temperament is determined by the emotional state of the mother during pregnancy
- d. temperament fluctuates widely during infancy

_____ 12. The research on infant temperament tends to support the
- a. prenatal influences theory
- b. nature side of the nature-nurture question
- c. concept of gradual maturation
- d. nurture position in child development

_____ 13. When you read about how attachment works, you have to conclude that it is
- a. an inborn quality present right from the start
- b. something that mothers automatically give to their children (you could call it "mother love")
- c. a two-way developmental process in which both child and parent participate
- d. a happy but mysterious development that psychology cannot explain

_____ 14. The single factor that most clearly reflects the health of the parent-child relationship is the
- a. amount of time spent with the child
- b. amount of family resources allocated to the child (room, clothing, toys, etc.)
- c. quality of religious values imparted to the child
- d. emotional quality of the relationship (warmth, support, positive emotions)

_____ 15. After reviewing the research on day care, a wise parent would
- a. avoid day care at all costs
- b. avoid large day care centers and seek small, home-based services
- c. use day care services as early as possible, since they seem to positively stimulate growth and development
- d. use day care services if necessary, but choose the center carefully

Module 20: Childhood

Use this **Outline** to organize your studying. Write notes on it. Turn it into a personalized aid for effective learning.

I. Cognitive development (**Jean Piaget**)

A. Active involvement

1. **Assimilation** — incorporating new information into existing knowledge

2. **Accommodation** — changing existing knowledge as a result of assimilating new information

B. Stages of cognitive development

1. **Sensorimotor** (birth to age 2)

a. Relating sensory experiences to motor actions

b. **Object permanence** — objects continue to exist even when out of sight

2. **Preoperational** (2 – 7 years)

a. Use of symbols

b. Operations (mental)

c. **Egocentric thinking** — seeing world only from your own viewpoint

d. **Conservation** — amount of substance remains same even though shape changes

3. **Concrete operations** (7 – 11 years)

a. Logical, mental operations on concrete objects

b. Grasping concepts of conservation and classification

4. **Formal operations** (12 – adulthood)

a. Thinking about and solving abstract problems in a logical manner

b. Abstract ideas and hypothetical constructs

C. Evaluation of Piaget's theory

1. Support

a. Cognitive development through active involvement with environment

b. Piaget launched study of cognitive development

2. Criticisms

a. Stages not as rigid as Piaget thought

b. More emphasis today on flexible schedule and influence of social environment

II. Social development

A. Three theories of how social development takes place

1. Freud's psychosexual stages

2. Erikson's psychosocial stages

3. Bandura's social cognitive theory

B. Erik Erikson's eight **psychosocial** stages [to be continued next chapter]

1. **Trust** versus **mistrust**

a. Period: early infancy (first year)

b. Problem: how well needs for care and attention are met

2. **Autonomy** versus **shame and doubt**

a. Period: late infancy (ages 1 – 3)

b. Problem: how well needs for exploration and independence are met

3. **Initiative** versus **guilt**

a. Period: early childhood (ages 3 – 5)

b. Problem: how well need to plan and initiate new things is met

4. **Industry** versus **inferiority**

    a. Period: middle and late childhood (ages 5 – 12)

    b. Problem: how well need to be competent and effective is met

C. Three basic ideas in Erikson's theory of psychosocial development

1. Each stage presents a problem with positive and negative possible solutions

2. Each stage builds on the others

3. Social development continues throughout life

D. Vulnerability and resiliency (Emmy Werner)

1. **Vulnerability** — difficulties that put children at risk for developing psychological problems

2. **Resiliency** — factors that compensate for increased life stresses and help prevent expected problems

    a. Dispositional traits

    b. Family factors

    c. Outside emotional support

3. Implications of resiliency for theories of child development

E. Gender role development

1. Two theories of how **gender roles** are developed

    a. Social learning theory (socialization)

    b. Cognitive developmental theory (**gender schemas**)

2. Changes in gender roles

    a. **Androgyny** (Sandra Bem)

    b. Career choice

F. Gender roles around the world

1. Cross-cultural research

2. Constants in gender development across cultures

G. Gender differences — issues and discrimination (Carol Jacklin)

1. Math abilities

2. Verbal abilities

3. Play and aggression

4. Conclusions

a. Gender differences few and relatively minor

b. Little justification for existing gender stereotypes based on idea of inherited differences in abilities

III. *Applying/Exploring:* Child abuse

A. Serious problem of **child abuse**

B. Three questions about child abuse

1. Why do parents abuse their children?

a. History of having been abused themselves

b. Wide range of personal and caregiving problems

2. Are some children more likely to be abused?

a. Personal characteristics of temperament or illness

b. **Principle of bidirectionality**

3. What are the treatments for child abuse?

a. Overcoming parents' personal problems

b. Changing parent-child interactions

Getting the general idea... Is the statement true or false?

_____ 1. Piaget believed that a child's mind is like a computer — its main function is to record and store new information for later use.

_____ 2. In Piaget's first stage of cognitive development, the child relates sensory experiences to motor actions.

_____ 3. When Piaget used the word "operations," he meant behaviors such as walking and talking that accomplish important tasks for the child.

_____ 4. In Erikson's scheme, each stage of life contains a "test" that, if failed, prevents you from entering the next stage.

_____ 5. Modifying Freud, Erikson argued that psychological development continues all through life.

_____ 6. Studies of "resilient" children tend to support Erikson's idea that later positive experiences can compensate for early trauma.

_____ 7. Sandra Bem proposed the concept of androgyny to explain why some boys are "sissies" and some girls are "tomboys."

_____ 8. Cross-cultural studies indicate that knowledge of gender roles develops in a similar way at a similar time in many different countries.

_____ 9. Studies on gender differences come down to this: inherited gender differences are few, relatively minor, and do not support the common gender stereotypes.

_____ 10. Ninety percent of abusive parents were themselves abused children.

Knowing the essential vocabulary... Which phrase matches the term?

	Term		Phrase
_____	1. assimilation	a.	your gum (wadded up) is not less
_____	2. accommodation	b.	interacting with other people
_____	3. object permanence	c.	incorporating new information
_____	4. conservation	d.	explaining how child abuse happens
_____	5. psychosocial	e.	if your Honey is at a different school
_____	6. resiliency	f.	your Honey (gone to class) still exists
_____	7. gender roles	g.	why not have the best of both?
_____	8. androgyny	h.	changing, revising existing knowledge
_____	9. bidirectionality	i.	inoculation against stress
_____	10. bicollegiality	j.	what boys do and what girls do

Mastering the material... Which answer makes the statement true?

_____ 1. The essence of Piaget's theory of cognitive development is that
- a. through thousands and thousands of mistakes, the child gradually builds a factual picture of the world
- b. a child's picture of the world is slowly, gradually shaped by a steady succession of learning experiences
- c. each stage is characterized by a distinctly different way of understanding the world
- d. the mind of a child is like the mind of an adult — there just isn't as much information in it

_____ 2. When new information forces a child to revise some idea about the world, we see the process of _____________ in action
- a. assimilation
- b. accommodation
- c. conservation
- d. permeation

_____ 3. The concept of object permanence develops during the _____________ stage
- a. sensorimotor
- b. preoperational
- c. concrete operations
- d. formal operations

_____ 4. Watching juice poured from a short, wide glass into a tall, narrow glass, the child cries, "I want [the tall] glass!" thus illustrating the problem of
- a. object permanence
- b. egocentric thinking
- c. classification
- d. conservation

_____ 5. The aspect of Piaget's theory that has received the greatest criticism is
- a. his belief that children are active participants in their cognitive development
- b. his emphasis on inherited abilities
- c. the rigidity of his stages
- d. the absence of stages of adult cognitive development

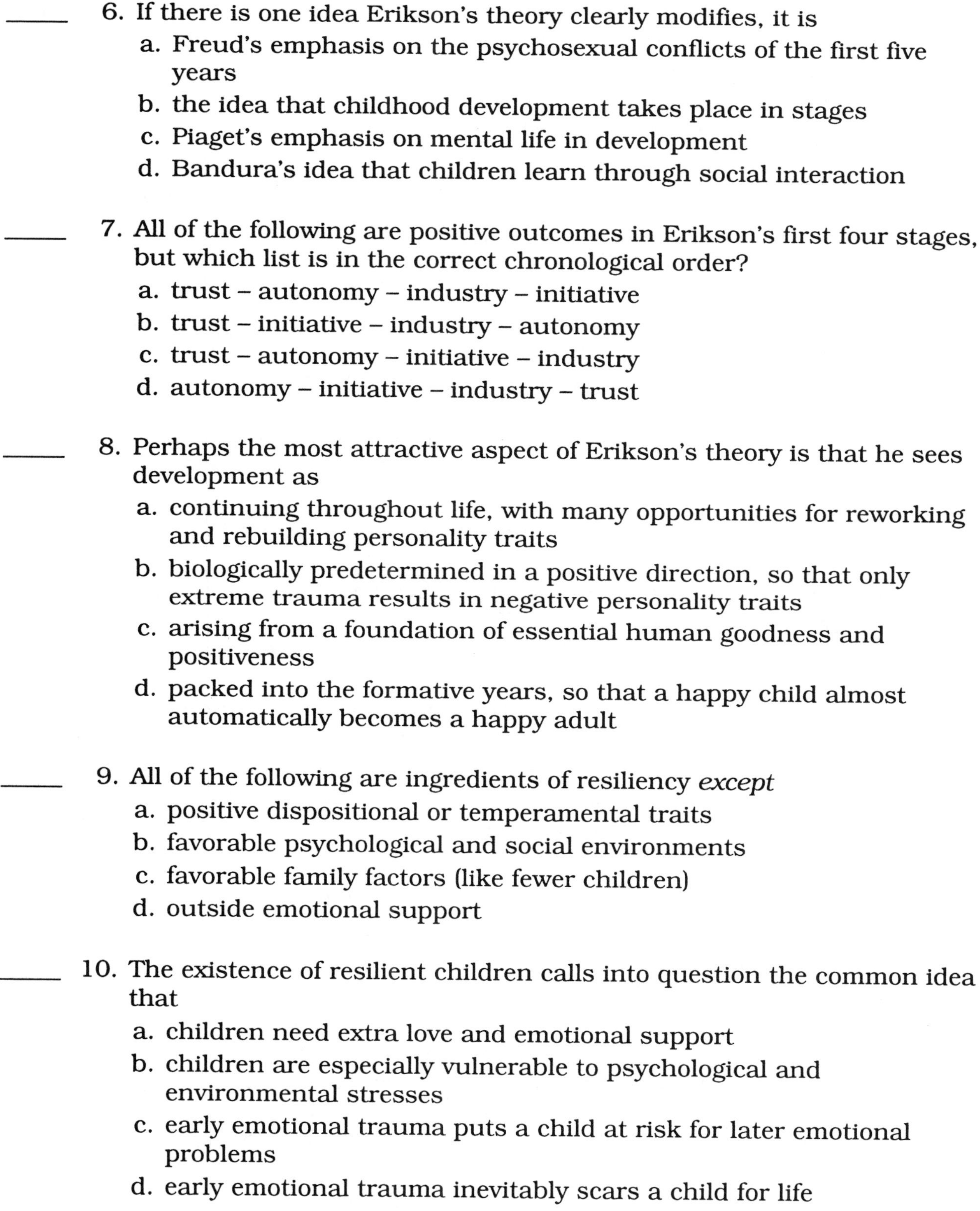

_____ 6. If there is one idea Erikson's theory clearly modifies, it is
a. Freud's emphasis on the psychosexual conflicts of the first five years
b. the idea that childhood development takes place in stages
c. Piaget's emphasis on mental life in development
d. Bandura's idea that children learn through social interaction

_____ 7. All of the following are positive outcomes in Erikson's first four stages, but which list is in the correct chronological order?
a. trust – autonomy – industry – initiative
b. trust – initiative – industry – autonomy
c. trust – autonomy – initiative – industry
d. autonomy – initiative – industry – trust

_____ 8. Perhaps the most attractive aspect of Erikson's theory is that he sees development as
a. continuing throughout life, with many opportunities for reworking and rebuilding personality traits
b. biologically predetermined in a positive direction, so that only extreme trauma results in negative personality traits
c. arising from a foundation of essential human goodness and positiveness
d. packed into the formative years, so that a happy child almost automatically becomes a happy adult

_____ 9. All of the following are ingredients of resiliency *except*
a. positive dispositional or temperamental traits
b. favorable psychological and social environments
c. favorable family factors (like fewer children)
d. outside emotional support

_____ 10. The existence of resilient children calls into question the common idea that
a. children need extra love and emotional support
b. children are especially vulnerable to psychological and environmental stresses
c. early emotional trauma puts a child at risk for later emotional problems
d. early emotional trauma inevitably scars a child for life

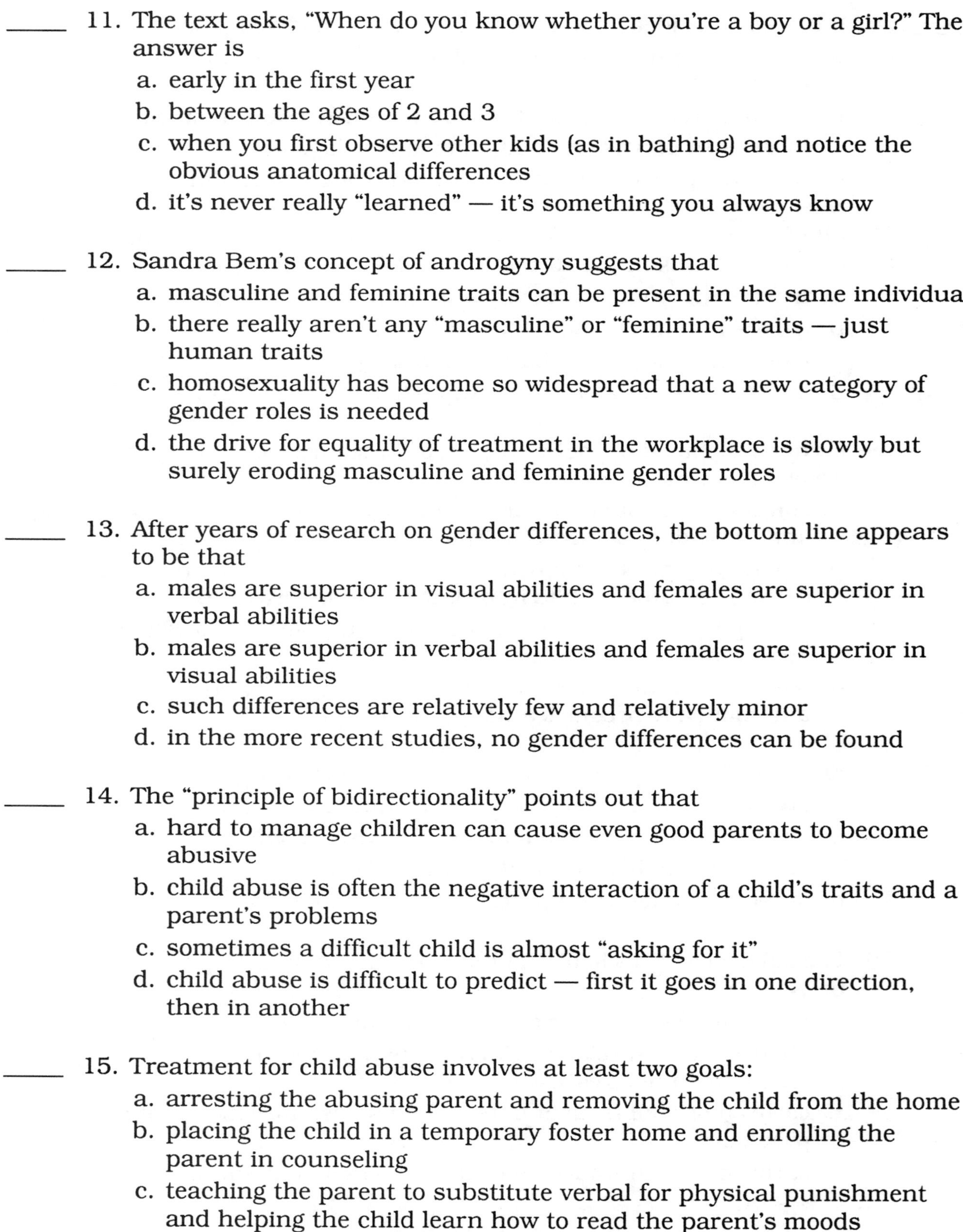

_____ 11. The text asks, "When do you know whether you're a boy or a girl?" The answer is

a. early in the first year
b. between the ages of 2 and 3
c. when you first observe other kids (as in bathing) and notice the obvious anatomical differences
d. it's never really "learned" — it's something you always know

_____ 12. Sandra Bem's concept of androgyny suggests that

a. masculine and feminine traits can be present in the same individual
b. there really aren't any "masculine" or "feminine" traits — just human traits
c. homosexuality has become so widespread that a new category of gender roles is needed
d. the drive for equality of treatment in the workplace is slowly but surely eroding masculine and feminine gender roles

_____ 13. After years of research on gender differences, the bottom line appears to be that

a. males are superior in visual abilities and females are superior in verbal abilities
b. males are superior in verbal abilities and females are superior in visual abilities
c. such differences are relatively few and relatively minor
d. in the more recent studies, no gender differences can be found

_____ 14. The "principle of bidirectionality" points out that

a. hard to manage children can cause even good parents to become abusive
b. child abuse is often the negative interaction of a child's traits and a parent's problems
c. sometimes a difficult child is almost "asking for it"
d. child abuse is difficult to predict — first it goes in one direction, then in another

_____ 15. Treatment for child abuse involves at least two goals:

a. arresting the abusing parent and removing the child from the home
b. placing the child in a temporary foster home and enrolling the parent in counseling
c. teaching the parent to substitute verbal for physical punishment and helping the child learn how to read the parent's moods
d. overcoming the parent's personal problems and changing parent-child interactions

Answers for Chapter 10

Module 19

True-False	Matching	Multiple-Choice
1. T	1. f	1. d
2. F	2. j	2. b
3. F	3. a	3. c
4. F	4. g	4. a
5. T	5. b	5. c
6. T	6. h	6. b
7. F	7. c	7. a
8. T	8. i	8. b
9. T	9. d	9. d
10. F	10. e	10. c
		11. a
		12. b
		13. c
		14. d
		15. d

Module 20

True-False	Matching	Multiple-Choice
1. F	1. c	1. c
2. T	2. h	2. b
3. F	3. f	3. a
4. F	4. a	4. d
5. T	5. b	5. c
6. T	6. i	6. a
7. F	7. j	7. c
8. T	8. g	8. a
9. T	9. d	9. b
10. F	10. e	10. d
		11. b
		12. a
		13. c
		14. b
		15. d

Chapter 11: Adolescence and Adulthood

All about you

If there is one chapter in the textbook that clearly is about *you*, this is it. You've just been an adolescent and now you're an adult. Therefore, it will be the hardest chapter to learn.

Say what?

When studying something like the brain or memory or language, even though it's all right on top of our shoulders, it seems removed from our everyday knowledge. In a way, that makes it easier to objectify, and hence to learn.

The facts and theories of adolescence and adulthood, on the other hand, are so close to our everyday experience that it is difficult to get sufficient distance to allow getting a handle on them. As you read, you say "yes..., yes..., yes...," but later it's hard to remember what ought to stand out as important to learn.

To make matters more difficult, there is only one grand theory to cling to in this area: Erik Erikson's eight stages of life. Even then, only half of Erikson's theory applies. As for the other theories discussed in the chapter, most are too descriptive, too narrow, or too new to have won universal acceptance by psychologists.

How to learn less

I suggest a three-step process in studying this material. First, give yourself credit for what you have learned from your own experience. Don't expect every idea in the chapter to be new to you. Second, recognize that many of the new ideas in the chapter may be interesting, but have not yet been accepted as permanent contributions to knowledge. Find out from your professor what to master. Third, have one simple question in mind as you read and study: is this idea helpful? In other words, does what you are reading add to your knowledge, and thus deepen your understanding of adolescence and adulthood? Retain the facts and ideas that do.

Effective Student Tip 11

How to Beat Test Anxiety

Remember the dogs who learned to be helpless when they couldn't escape shocks? If we could ask them, they might tell us 'test anxiety' prevented them from jumping over to the safe side.

Sometimes school can be like the shock box. Too many painful defeats, and you learn to accept failure as a normal part of life. You don't like it, but you have no experience of escaping it. So don't be too quick to say you are no good at tests. You may have learned to think so, but you can't really know until you take a test *for which you have prepared effectively.*

Scratch the surface of most test anxiety and you find ineffective techniques. The first thing to do is stop blaming yourself. Next, discard the idea that you simply have to try harder. Finally, dissect your weaknesses (note-taking, studying, test-taking, etc.) and replace them with strategies and skills that bring success (start with tip #10).

You will begin to feel effective when you begin to be effective. As your feeling of effectiveness increases, your ability to work out winning strategies will also increase. Effectiveness is the basis for further effectiveness. You may still experience some jitters (phobic effects linger), but who cares? Test anxiety will no longer rule your life.

Module 21: Adolescence

Use this **Outline** to organize your studying. Write notes on it. Turn it into a personalized aid for effective learning.

I. Biological change: **puberty**

A. Development of female sexual maturity

1. **Menarche**

a. Hypothalamus stimulates pituitary to produce hormones

b. **Estrogen**

2. Female secondary sexual characteristics

3. Surge in physical growth

4. Early versus late maturing girls

B. Development of male sexual maturity

1. Growth of genital organs and production of sperm

a. Hypothalamus stimulates pituitary to produce hormones

b. **Testosterone**

2. Male secondary sexual characteristics

3. Surge in physical growth

4. Early- versus late-maturing boys

C. Sexual behavior

1. Intercourse

2. Sex education

II. Personality and social development

A. Identity or self

1. Values, goals, traits, interests, and motivations

2. Psychosocial stage (Erikson)

a. **Identity** versus...

b. **Role confusion**

B. **Self-esteem**

1. Four patterns in development of self-esteem

a. Maintain or increase strong self-esteem

b. Continue chronically low self-esteem

c. Dramatic reversal in self-esteem (usually down)

d. Lowering of girls' self-esteem

2. Effects of positive or negative identity and self-esteem

III. Cognitive changes

A. Adolescent thinking — Piaget's last stage of cognitive development

B. **Formal operations**

1. Ability to take another person's viewpoint

2. Continued **adolescent egocentric thinking**

3. Thinking abstractly

4. Planning for the future

IV. Moral development (**Lawrence Kohlberg**)

A. Theory of **moral reasoning** based on **moral dilemma research**

1. Preconventional level

a. Stage 1: obedience and fear of punishment

b. Stage 2: recognition of just punishment

2. Conventional level

a. Stage 3: conformity to group standards

b. Stage 4: recognition of needs of society

3. Postconventional level

a. Stage 5: balance between human rights and laws of society

b. Stage 6: higher moral laws [this stage has been dropped]

B. Questions and criticisms of Kohlberg's theory

1. Does everyone go through all five stages in the same order?

a. Kohlberg assumed fixed order

b. Supported by further research

2. How much does moral reasoning reflect actual moral behavior?

3. Are there gender differences in moral reasoning? (Carol Gilligan)

a. **Care orientation** (females)

b. **Justice orientation** (males)

V. Styles of parenting

A. Three styles of parenting (Diana Baumrind)

1. **Authoritarian**

a. Obedience and punishment

b. Tendency toward hostile boys and dependent and submissive girls

2. **Authoritative**

a. Rational, intelligent direction; supportive, loving, committed

b. Tendency toward competent, well-balanced children

3. **Permissive**

a. Less controlling, nonpunishing, accepting

b. Less achievement minded; less socially assertive girls

B. Parenting styles have distinct influences on development

VI. *Applying/Exploring:* **Teenage suicide**

A. Rising rates of teenage suicide

B. Factors related to teenage suicide

1. Psychological problems

a. Depression, feelings of helplessness, drug-related problems

b. School failure, social isolation and withdrawal, problems at home

2. Precipitators

3. Expressed wish to die

C. Preventing teenage suicide

1. Recognizing youths at risk

2. Four steps when counselor sees imminent danger: help youth...

    a. Promise not to engage in suicidal behavior

    b. Focus on strengths and good things

    c. Recognize intensity of feelings

    d. Make detailed plan for seeking help when negative feelings intensify

Now take the
Self-Tests
to check your understanding and mastery of this module.

Getting the general idea... Is the statement true or false?

_____ 1. New research shows that adolescence is a period of great psychological turmoil and severe emotional stress.

_____ 2. Girls normally experience the physical changes of puberty about two years earlier than boys.

_____ 3. For obvious reasons, early maturing girls are more confident and outgoing than late maturing girls.

_____ 4. Sexually active adolescents seem to have gotten the message, because almost all of them now use contraceptives.

_____ 5. Erik Erikson saw the key developmental issue of adolescence as the acquisition of a positive sense of identity.

_____ 6. Girls tend to experience increases in self-esteem during adolescence.

_____ 7. Jean Piaget places adolescent cognitive development in the stage he called concrete operations.

_____ 8. According to Lawrence Kohlberg, the typical adolescent resolves moral dilemmas by asking, "What are the chances I'll get caught?"

_____ 9. The good news (too late for you) is that the happiest, best adjusted adolescents come from families using the permissive style of parenting.

_____ 10. The surprise and shock felt by family and friends when an adolescent commits suicide are clues that for too long the victim's problems were denied, neglected, or not recognized.

Knowing the essential vocabulary... Which phrase matches the term?

	Term		Phrase
_____	1. menarche	a.	men
_____	2. estrogen	b.	Erik Erikson
_____	3. testosterone	c.	can change during adolescence
_____	4. identity	d.	women
_____	5. self-esteem	e.	in love
_____	6. formal operations	f.	guns
_____	7. moral reasoning	g.	first menstrual cycle
_____	8. authoritative	h.	Jean Piaget
_____	9. suicide	i.	Lawrence Kohlberg
_____	10. just a teenager	j.	parenting style

Mastering the material... Which answer makes the statement true?

____ 1. Experts now believe that adolescence is *not* a period of
   a. great psychological turmoil and emotional stress
   b. considerable biological, cognitive, and social changes
   c. searching for personal identity
   d. dramatic positive or negative changes in self-esteem

____ 2. When you compare the development of sexual maturity in girls and boys during puberty, you find that the changes are
   a. radically different in girls and boys
   b. parallel in girls and boys
   c. essentially the same, but occur about two years earlier in girls
   d. somewhat similar, except that the difference between a boy and a man is far greater than the difference between a girl and a woman

____ 3. In terms of enjoying a psychological advantage in adjustment, the best thing to be is
   a. an early-maturing girl
   b. a late-maturing girl
   c. an early-maturing boy
   d. a late-maturing boy

____ 4. And the worst thing to be is
   a. an early-maturing girl
   b. a late-maturing girl
   c. an early-maturing boy
   d. a late-maturing boy

____ 5. Are adolescents getting the sex information they need? Are they practicing safe sex? The answers to these two questions seem to be
   a. yes and yes
   b. more information from parents and increasing use of contraceptives
   c. more information from schools and far greater use of contraceptives
   d. no and no

____ 6. In Erikson's psychosocial stage theory, an adolescent who does not develop a positive sense of identity is likely to suffer from
a. isolation
b. stagnation
c. a sense of inferiority
d. role confusion

____ 7. A disturbing finding in research on adolescent self-esteem is that
a. early-maturing boys suffer lowered self-esteem
b. adolescent girls are more likely to experience lowered self-esteem
c. adolescent self-esteem is based almost entirely on grades in school
d. adolescents do not seem to be concerned about self-esteem

____ 8. The essential difference between Piaget's last stage of cognitive development and the earlier ones is
a. the ability to perform concrete operations
b. the ability to think calmly and clearly without letting feelings predominate
c. increased capacity for abstract thought
d. decreased interest in humor and playfulness

____ 9. Adolescent egocentric thinking is the belief that
a. the demands of parents and society are less important than what the adolescent wants
b. everyone is as totally preoccupied with the adolescent's appearance, thoughts, and feelings as the adolescent is
c. "I am smarter and more attractive than everyone else"
d. "If I want it and need it, why shouldn't I have it?"

____ 10. Lawrence Kohlberg based his theory of moral development on research into
a. the behaviors that children of different ages listed as "good" or "bad"
b. stories children made up when asked to illustrate good and bad behavior
c. the correlation between how children rated their own behavior and how their teachers rated it
d. the reasoning children used to solve problems that posed moral dilemmas

_____ 11. The concepts of care orientation and justice orientation have been used to
- a. investigate possible gender differences in moral reasoning
- b. explain why older children have a broader idea of morality than younger children do
- c. explain why Kohlberg's sixth stage had to be abandoned
- d. investigate possible age differences in moral reasoning

_____ 12. All of the following are parenting styles *except*
- a. authoritarian
- b. authoritative
- c. permissive
- d. protective

_____ 13. Your new friend seems to be competent, independent, and achievement oriented; you guess that she had ______________ parents
- a. authoritarian
- b. authoritative
- c. permissive
- d. protective

_____ 14. When boys commit suicide, it is most commonly by
- a. pills
- b. hanging
- c. guns
- d. asphyxiation

_____ 15. When a young person commits suicide, our typical reaction is an anguished, "Why? Why?" ... but the truth is that
- a. nothing can stop a person who has decided to commit suicide
- b. there probably were signs of psychological problems and behavioral symptoms long before
- c. psychology has no answer to the riddle of why adolescents, with their whole lives before them, sometimes take their own lives
- d. adolescents who are contemplating suicide go to great lengths to disguise their intentions

A special Rock 'n Roll quiz on adolescence

Teenagers have always been aware of living in an emotional pressure cooker, and the music they listen to reflects their concerns. Can you match these worries of adolescence with the Golden Oldies that expressed them so memorably?

_____	1. masculinity	a. Little Sweet Sixteen
_____	2. femininity	b. Get a Job
_____	3. androgyny	c. Under the Boardwalk
_____	4. vulnerability	d. Going to the Chapel
_____	5. chastity	e. Fifty Ways to Leave Your Lover
_____	6. intimacy	f. Love Potion Number Nine
_____	7. romantic love	g. Lola
_____	8. career	h. Big Girls Don't Cry
_____	9. marriage	i. Where Did My Baby Go?
_____	10. commitment *(not!)*	j. Walk Like a Man

How about making up a quiz of your own? You could try one based on current hits.

Module 22: Adulthood

I. Consistency versus change

   A. Research methods

      1. **Longitudinal** studies

      2. **Cross-sectional** studies

   B. Variables in consistency and change

      1. Cognition

      2. Personality traits

      3. Mental health

      4. Major concerns and success

II. Physical changes

   A. Normal aging

      1. **Wear and tear theory**

      2. **Biological limit theory**

   B. Pathological aging

      1. Alzheimer's disease

      2. Progeria

   C. Bodily changes

      1. Early adulthood

      2. Middle adulthood

      3. Late adulthood

      4. Very late adulthood

Use this

Outline

to organize your studying. Write notes on it. Turn it into a personalized aid for effective learning.

D. Ways to slow aging

1. Chronological age

2. Functional age

3. Quality of life

E. Life expectancy

III. Cognitive changes

A. Decline in cognitive processes

1. Reaction time

2. Perceptual speed

3. Memory

B. Growth in cognitive processes

1. Memorization versus interpretation

2. Exercise and memory

IV. Stages of adulthood

A. **Psychosocial** stages of adulthood (Erik Erikson)

1. Stage 6 (young adult)

a. **Intimacy** versus...

b. **Isolation**

2. Stage 7 (middle adult)

a. **Generativity** versus...

b. **Stagnation**

3. Stage 8 (late adult)

a. **Integrity** versus...

b. **Despair**

B. **Real-life** stages of adulthood (Daniel Levinson)

1. Early adult transition (17–22)

2. Entering the adult world (22–28)

3. Age thirty transition (28–33)

4. Settling down (33–40)

5. Midlife transition (early forties)

6. Entering middle adulthood (middle forties)

C. Do stage theories explain adulthood?

1. Yes — they bring out how well we handle the predictable problems of predictable stages

2. No — average behavior descriptive of a stage does not explain actual behavior of individuals

V. Personality development

A. Gender roles

1. Traditional view of gender roles

a. **Masculinity** and **femininity** as opposites

b. Stability of gender roles over time

2. Contemporary view of gender roles

a. Masculinity and femininity as independent traits

b. Psychological **androgyny** (Sandra Bem)

3. Gender roles and mental health

a. Advantages of masculine traits

b. Advantages of feminine traits

c. Advantages of androgynous traits

VI. Social development: relationships

A. **Triangular theory of love** (Robert Sternberg)

1. Three components of love

a. Passion

b. Intimacy

c. Commitment

2. Goal for most people is **complete love**

B. Questions about love

1. Is there love at first sight (**infatuated love**)?

2. Why do people get married after being in love for a very short time (**Hollywood love**)?

3. Why doesn't **romantic love** last?

4. Can there be love without sex (**companionate love**)?

C. Marriage

1. Selecting a marriage partner

2. Success versus failure in marriage

a. Conflict resolution

b. Communication patterns

c. Sharing experiences

D. Cultural differences in preferences for partners

1. Desirable traits

2. Cultural differences in ranking of desirable traits

VII. Sexual behavior in middle and late adulthood

A. Women: **menopause**

1. Physical symptoms

2. Psychological symptoms

B. Men: sexual responsiveness

VIII. Social development: careers

A. Importance of job satisfaction

1. Men

2. Women

B. Difficulties facing women in the work force

1. Job and pay discrimination

2. Sexual harassment

IX. *Applying/Exploring:* Views on death

A. Five **stages of death and dying** (Elisabeth Kübler-Ross)

1. Denial

2. Anger

3. Bargaining

4. Depression

5. Acceptance

B. Dying with dignity

1. **Hospice**

2. Assisted suicide

C. Death and moral rights

Now take the **Self-Tests** to check your understanding and mastery of this module.

Getting the general idea... Is the statement true or false?

_____ 1. Gerontologists have abandoned the 30-year-old "wear and tear" theory of aging and have adopted the newer "biological limit" theory.

_____ 2. Enjoy it while you can! The sad fact is that *all* cognitive abilities eventually decline with age.

_____ 3. According to Erikson, the main task of young adulthood is to find intimacy by developing loving relationships.

_____ 4. Daniel Levinson's explanation of adulthood focuses on how adults deal with, and solve, real-life problems.

_____ 5. In the last two decades there has been a great revolution in how Americans view gender roles.

_____ 6. Robert Sternberg's triangular theory of love explains why romantic love doesn't last — it has passion and intimacy, but it lacks commitment.

_____ 7. Can there be love without sex? Sure — combine commitment and intimacy and leave out passion and you've got companionate love.

_____ 8. Regardless of culture, young adults all over the world ranked traits desirable in a potential mate in almost exactly the same way.

_____ 9. Most women report a kind of relief after menopause — at least they don't have to have sex anymore.

_____ 10. Elisabeth Kübler-Ross described dying as a series of stages, running from initial denial to final acceptance.

Knowing the essential vocabulary... Which phrase matches the term?

	Term		Phrase
_____	1. progeria	a.	psychosocial task of middle adulthood
_____	2. functional age	b.	men care more about it than women
_____	3. generativity	c.	female hormones
_____	4. gender roles	d.	please *don't* try to act your age
_____	5. androgyny	e.	testosterone
_____	6. complete love	f.	male hormone
_____	7. chastity	g.	what little girls and boys are made of
_____	8. menopause	h.	pathological aging
_____	9. testosterone	i.	passion, intimacy, and commitment
_____	10. Sylvester Stallone	j.	the best of both worlds

Mastering the material... Which answer makes the statement true?

_____ 1. Rod Plotnik tells the story of Susan, the 40-year-old former prom queen, to make the point that
   a. there is no way to predict what problems adults will encounter
   b. adulthood, for most people, is a steadily downhill process
   c. having too much, too soon, can lead to tragedy
   d. adulthood is a complicated period with many ups and downs

_____ 2. Our bodies age because of naturally occurring problems or breakdowns in the body's cells — so says the _____________ theory
   a. wear and tear
   b. functional aging
   c. biological limit
   d. chronological aging

_____ 3. All of the following cognitive abilities decrease with aging *except*
   a. reaction time
   b. perceptual speed
   c. memorization
   d. interpretation

_____ 4. In Erik Erikson's sixth stage of psychosocial development, the young adult faces the challenge of
   a. identity versus role confusion
   b. intimacy versus isolation
   c. generativity versus stagnation
   d. integrity versus despair

_____ 5. What we need in late adulthood, says Erikson, is
   a. recognition, respect, and honor from our family and colleagues
   b. a sense of pride in our acquisitions and our standing in the community
   c. a sense of contentment about how we lived and what we accomplished
   d. mainly good health — without it there is despair

_____ 6. All of the following are questions that come up in Daniel Levinson's "real-life stages" *except*
   a. When should I move away from home?
   b. Should I stick with my present career?
   c. Am I doing enough to help the next generation?
   d. What do I do now that it's too late to change?

_____ 7. All of the following TV shows portray traditional gender roles *except*
   a. Growing Pains
   b. The Cosby Show
   c. Family Ties
   d. Who's the Boss?

_____ 8. Sandra Bem developed the concept of androgyny to make the point that
   a. there really are *three* sexes: men, women, and people who are homosexual or bisexual
   b. preferred masculine and feminine traits can both be present in the same individual
   c. regardless of whether you are born male or female, social pressures can be strong enough to change your sexual orientation
   d. the contemporary blurring of gender lines constitutes a threat to the traditional family, and hence to society itself

_____ 9. What is this thing called love? According to Robert Sternberg's triangular theory, love is a combination of
   a. romantic love, respect, and companionship
   b. romance, sharing, and loyalty
   c. infatuated love plus companionate love
   d. passion, intimacy, and commitment

_____ 10. Sternberg can offer interesting insight into questions like, "Is there love at first sight?" because his theory
   a. does not limit our understanding of love to a single, all-or-nothing quality
   b. takes into account the fact that love never lasts very long
   c. explains why love is such a powerful emotion
   d. integrates both the male and female experience of love into a unified theory of human attraction

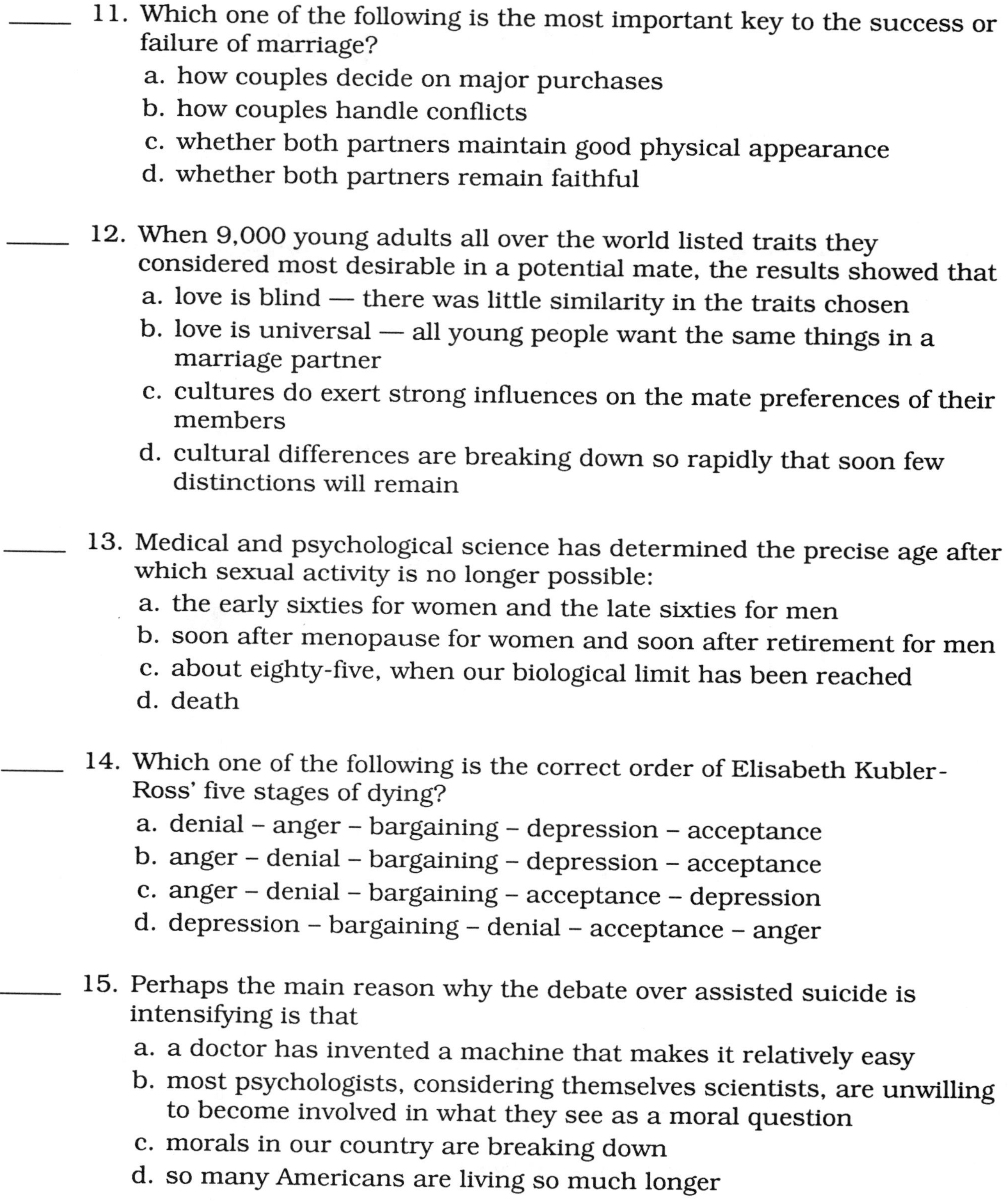

_____ 11. Which one of the following is the most important key to the success or failure of marriage?

a. how couples decide on major purchases
b. how couples handle conflicts
c. whether both partners maintain good physical appearance
d. whether both partners remain faithful

_____ 12. When 9,000 young adults all over the world listed traits they considered most desirable in a potential mate, the results showed that

a. love is blind — there was little similarity in the traits chosen
b. love is universal — all young people want the same things in a marriage partner
c. cultures do exert strong influences on the mate preferences of their members
d. cultural differences are breaking down so rapidly that soon few distinctions will remain

_____ 13. Medical and psychological science has determined the precise age after which sexual activity is no longer possible:

a. the early sixties for women and the late sixties for men
b. soon after menopause for women and soon after retirement for men
c. about eighty-five, when our biological limit has been reached
d. death

_____ 14. Which one of the following is the correct order of Elisabeth Kubler-Ross' five stages of dying?

a. denial – anger – bargaining – depression – acceptance
b. anger – denial – bargaining – depression – acceptance
c. anger – denial – bargaining – acceptance – depression
d. depression – bargaining – denial – acceptance – anger

_____ 15. Perhaps the main reason why the debate over assisted suicide is intensifying is that

a. a doctor has invented a machine that makes it relatively easy
b. most psychologists, considering themselves scientists, are unwilling to become involved in what they see as a moral question
c. morals in our country are breaking down
d. so many Americans are living so much longer

Answers for Chapter 11

Module 21

True-False		Matching		Multiple-Choice	
1.	F	1.	g	1.	a
2.	T	2.	d	2.	c
3.	F	3.	a	3.	c
4.	F	4.	b	4.	a
5.	T	5.	c	5.	d
6.	F	6.	h	6.	d
7.	F	7.	i	7.	b
8.	F	8.	j	8.	c
9.	F	9.	f	9.	b
10.	T	10.	e	10.	d
				11.	a
				12.	d
				13.	b
				14.	c
				15.	b

Module 22

True-False		Matching		Multiple-Choice	
1.	F	1.	h	1.	d
2.	F	2.	d	2.	a
3.	T	3.	a	3.	d
4.	T	4.	g	4.	b
5.	F	5.	j	5.	c
6.	T	6.	i	6.	c
7.	T	7.	b	7.	d
8.	F	8.	c	8.	b
9.	F	9.	f	9.	d
10.	T	10.	e	10.	a
				11.	b
				12.	c
				13.	d
				14.	a
				15.	d

A special Rock 'n Roll quiz on adolescence

1. j 2. h 3. g 4. i 5. a 6. c 7. f 8. b 9. d 10. e

Chapter 12: Personality

Could this be the deepest chapter of all?

Personality theories tackle the big questions in psychology, the questions we think about when we try to understand who we are and what meaning and purpose our lives have. We feel that we are unique individuals, but are we essentially like everyone else? We know we are growing and developing, but are we also somehow very much the same from year to year? We would like to change some things about ourselves, but why does that seem so difficult to do?

A theory of personality is necessarily comprehensive. The better it is, the more of our questions about ourselves it answers. As you study, pay attention to each theory's basic assumptions about human nature. Do you agree with them? To what extent can you see yourself in each theory? Does it describe you and explain your life?

I've said it before, but it's especially true about this chapter: challenge every new idea you meet. When Freud says you have inborn aggressive tendencies or when Rogers says humans are fundamentally good, measure the idea against your own beliefs and experiences. Is that idea true? Does that theory explain my own experience?

Finally, you might think about your own theory of personality. You do have one, even though you probably haven't thought it through. Anyone who studies psychology inevitably comes to have some sort of theory of personality — a global view of how all the facts and ideas in psychology fit together, and how they apply to everyday life. Reflecting on your own ideas about human nature will help you understand psychology's famous theories of personality.

Effective Student Tip 12

Manage Your Grade

True, we professors set the course standards and assign the final grades. Since most professors stick to the rules once they are established, however, *you* have almost total control over what that grade will be. The trick is to take a management attitude toward your grades.

Taking charge and managing your grade involves six steps: (1) Understand your inner motivation concerning grades (to guard against self-sabotage). (2) Understand the grading system in the course. (3) Keep accurate records of your scores and grades. (4) Project your final grade from your current performance. (5) Determine what immediate steps you must take. (6) Make adjustments necessary for effective pursuit of your goal.

Don't underestimate the importance of grades to your mental health. Rightly or wrongly, we interpret grades, like earnings, as powerful messages about our effectiveness.

You can passively allow your grades to happen to you, as many students do, or you can take charge and make them what you want.

Module 23: Freudian and Humanistic Theories

Use this

Outline

to organize your studying. Write notes on it. Turn it into a personalized aid for effective learning.

I. **Psychodynamic** theory of **Sigmund Freud**

A. Layers of the mind

1. Conscious

2. Unconscious

B. Understanding **unconscious motivation**

1. **Free association**

2. Dream interpretation

3. "Freudian slips"

C. Divisions of the mind

1. **Id**

2. **Ego**

3. **Superego**

D. Anxiety and **defense mechanisms** of the ego

1. **Rationalization**

2. Denial

3. **Repression**

4. **Projection**

5. **Reaction formation**

6. Displacement

7. **Sublimation**

E. **Psychosexual stages** of childhood development

1. Oral stage

2. Anal stage

3. Phallic stage and **Oedipus complex**

4. Latency period

5. Genital stage

F. Importance of childhood in personality development

1. **Fixation**

2. First five years

G. Psychoanalysis since Freud

1. Neo-Freudians

    a. **Carl Jung** (collective unconscious)

    b. **Alfred Adler** (social urges)

    c. **Karen Horney** (social interactions)

    d. **Erik Erikson** (psychosocial stages of development)

2. Freudian theory today

    a. Difficult to test scientifically

    b. Are the first five years the most important?

    c. Is there evidence for the unconscious?

H. Exploring the unconscious

1. **Projective tests**

    a. **Rorschach Inkblot Test**

    b. **Thematic Apperception Test (TAT)**

   2. Advantages and disadvantages of projective tests
      a. Reliability
      b. Validity

II. **Humanistic** theories of Abraham Maslow and Carl Rogers

   A. Features of humanistic theories of personality
      1. **Phenomenological perspective** (perception becomes reality)
      2. **Holistic view** (unique, total entity functioning as a unit)
      3. **Self-actualization** (tendency to reach true potentials)

   B. **Abraham Maslow**
      1. **Hierarchy of needs** (five levels)
         a. Deficiency needs
         b. Growth needs
      2. **Self-actualization** (characteristics of self-actualized individuals)

   C. **Carl Rogers**
      1. **Self theory** (self-concept)
         a. Positive or negative self-concept
         b. **Real self** and **ideal self**
      2. **Unconditional positive regard**
      3. Self-actualization

   D. Evaluation of humanistic theories: three contributions
      1. Basic goodness of human nature
      2. Need to study whole person
      3. Personal growth and self-actualization

E. Personal values and achievement: the boat people

1. Primary values

2. Academic success

III. *Applying/Exploring:* **Shyness**

A. Characteristics of shy people

B. Explanations of shyness

1. **Psychodynamic approach**

a. Unconscious fears and anxiety

b. Unresolved conflicts

2. **Cognitive-behavioral approach**

a. Observable, measurable components

b. Relationship between genetic, emotional, and behavioral influences

Now take the **Self-Tests** to check your understanding and mastery of this module.

Getting the general idea... Is the statement true or false?

_____ 1. Freud's famous personality theory is provocative, but hard to test scientifically.

_____ 2. Freud's key concept is the idea of conscious processes — how we understand reality.

_____ 3. Because almost all of Freud's main followers broke with him, today his ideas have little influence.

_____ 4. Free association is necessary because we cannot know the unconscious directly.

_____ 5. For Freud, most personality development takes place during the first five or six years of life.

_____ 6. Maslow and Rogers are pessimistic about the degree to which personality can change.

_____ 7. Self-actualization means honestly recognizing your actual weaknesses.

_____ 8. The hierarchy of needs helps explain why children who come to school hungry don't learn well.

_____ 9. Rogers believes that a child who receives only unconditional positive regard will grow up spoiled and unrealistic about life.

_____ 10. Children of the Indochinese "boat people" did well in school because of personal and cultural values.

Knowing the essential vocabulary... Which phrase matches the term?

	Term		Phrase
_____	1. unconscious forces	a.	be all that you can be
_____	2. free association	b.	these questions are too tricky
_____	3. ego	c.	reality principle
_____	4. rationalization	d.	love of learning
_____	5. Oedipus complex	e.	love of wheels
_____	6. hierarchy of needs	f.	Mommy loves you... when you're good
_____	7. self-actualization	g.	no, no... I don't love Mommy!
_____	8. conditional positive regard	h.	relax and say whatever comes to mind
_____	9. the boat people	i.	id
_____	10. the car people	j.	eat pizza first, then you can study

Mastering the material... Which answer makes the statement true?

_____ 1. In psychology, the term "personality" means
   a. a fixed way of responding to other people that is based on our inherited emotional makeup
   b. a combination of lasting and distinctive behaviors, thoughts, and emotions that typify how we react to other people and situations
   c. favorable and unfavorable personal characteristics
   d. how interesting and attractive we are to other people

_____ 2. According to Freud's psychodynamic theory of personality, the unconscious contains
   a. everything we are aware of at a given moment
   b. feelings and thoughts we remember from long ago
   c. material that can easily be brought to awareness
   d. repressed memories and emotions

_____ 3. Saying whatever comes to mind, even if it seems senseless, painful, or embarrassing, is part of the Freudian technique known as
   a. a defense mechanism
   b. a Freudian slip
   c. free association
   d. projection

_____ 4. The ability to create feelings of guilt gives the _______________ its power
   a. superego
   b. ego
   c. id
   d. unconscious

_____ 5. A student who blames poor test performance on "tricky questions" — rather than admit to poor preparation — is using the defense mechanism of
   a. compensation
   b. denial
   c. projection
   d. rationalization

____ 6. The defense mechanism in which unacceptable wishes are turned into their opposites is known as
   a. projection
   b. reaction-formation
   c. compensation
   d. rationalization

____ 7. Which of the following shows the correct order of Freud's psychosexual stages?
   a. oral – anal – phallic – genital
   b. anal – phallic – oral – genital
   c. genital – phallic – oral – anal
   d. anal – oral – phallic – genital

____ 8. Because they use ______________ , projective tests often bring out unconscious material
   a. pictures of people
   b. simple materials
   c. ambiguous stimuli
   d. computer analysis

____ 9. Unlike psychodynamic theories, humanistic theories of personality emphasize
   a. the continual operation of contradictory forces buried deep in our unconscious minds
   b. our capacity for personal growth, the development of our potential, and freedom to choose our destinies
   c. how difficult it is — even with therapy — to change personality significantly
   d. the importance of perceptions and beliefs

____ 10. At the first level of Maslow's hierarchy, we find ______________ needs
   a. self-actualization
   b. esteem
   c. love and belongingness
   d. physiological

_____ 11. By self-actualization, Maslow meant
a. reaching our full potential
b. having our deficiency needs satisfied
c. being loved and loving someone in return
d. gaining recognition and status in society

_____ 12. Rogers says the main reason so many people are unhappy is that
a. happiness is only possible when we become self-actualized
b. happiness is only an illusion
c. we have two selves — a real self and an ideal self
d. we have two selves — a positive self and a negative self

_____ 13. The story of the Indochinese "boat people" illustrates the basic assumption of _______________ psychology that all humans possess _______________
a. humanistic ... a hierarchy of needs
b. humanistic ... a tendency toward self-fulfillment
c. psychodynamic ... a fierce determination to survive
d. psychodynamic ... a tendency toward love as well as toward aggression

_____ 14. The old warning, "Of course Mommy loves you... when you're good!" is an example of Rogers' concept of
a. self-actualization
b. self-esteem needs
c. conditional positive regard
d. unconditional positive regard

_____ 15. It is a basic assumption of humanistic theories that humans are
a. basically good
b. basically evil
c. neither good nor evil, but simply reflections of their environment
d. either good or evil, depending on what they inherit from their parents

Module 24: Social-Learning and Trait Theories

Use this **Outline** to organize your studying. Write notes on it. Turn it into a personalized aid for effective learning.

I. **Social-learning** theories

  A. Social-cognitive theory (**Albert Bandura**)

    1. Language and information processing

    2. **Observational learning**

    3. Purposeful behavior

    4. Self-analysis

  B. Three *beliefs* that influence *behavior*

    1. Locus of control (Julian Rotter)

      a. **Internal** locus of control

      b. **External** locus of control

    2. **Self-efficacy**

    3. **Delay of gratification** (Walter Mischel)

  C. Evaluation of social-learning theory

    1. Objective measurement

    2. Specific learning and cognitive processes

    3. Successful programs for changing behavior and personality

II. **Trait** theories of Allport and Cattell

A. Concept of **trait** (relatively stable and enduring tendency to behave in a particular way)

B. Search for basic traits of human personalty

1. Comprehensive list of 18,000 terms yielding 4,500 traits (**Gordon Allport**)

2. **Factor analysis** reduction of list to 35 basic traits (**Raymond Cattell**)

3. **Five-factor model** (Big Five)

a. Openness to experience

b. Conscientiousness

c. Extraversion

d. Agreeableness

e. Neuroticism

C. Hierarchy of traits (Hans Eysenck)

D. Consistency of traits across **situations** (Mischel)

1. Person-situation dilemma

2. Personality change before and after age 30

E. Genetic influences on traits

1. **Behavioral genetics**

a. Twin studies

b. **Heritability**

2. Up to 50% of personality may be inherited

F. Evaluation of trait theory

1. Comprehensive list of traits

2. Consistency across situations

3. Influence of genetic factors

III. *Applying/Exploring:* Measuring traits

A. Popular, non-scientific methods

1. Horoscopes

a. Reliability and validity

b. **Barnum principle**

2. **Graphology**

B. Personality tests

1. Projective tests

2. Self-report inventories

a. Structured formats including objective questions

b. **Minnesota Multiphasic Personality Inventory (MMPI)**

Now take the
Self-Tests
to check your understanding and mastery of this module.

Getting the general idea... Is the statement true or false?

_____ 1. Social-learning theory combines reinforcement theory with ideas about how we think.

_____ 2. Gordon Allport and Raymond Cattell were early pioneers of social-learning theory.

_____ 3. One of the key ideas of social-learning theory is observational learning.

_____ 4. College students who think they "can't beat the system" ought to study the concept of locus of control.

_____ 5. The most important measure of self-efficacy is the ability to delay gratification.

_____ 6. A trait is a personal quirk — something that makes you different from everyone else in the world.

_____ 7. After a long search, researchers now believe that there are as many as 4,500 different personality traits.

_____ 8. One problem with the concept of traits is that they are not always consistent across situations.

_____ 9. Most changes in personality occur before the age of thirty.

_____ 10. Genetic influences can determine physical factors (like height), but not psychological factors like personality.

Knowing the essential vocabulary... Which phrase matches the term?

	Term		Phrase
_____	1. observational learning	a.	I really believe I can be an "A" student
_____	2. external locus of control	b.	end result of a long search
_____	3. internal locus of control	c.	from single acts to abstract categories
_____	4. self-efficacy	d.	a movie now or good grades later?
_____	5. delay of gratification	e.	who takes the bill on a first date?
_____	6. traits	f.	will you still love me tomorrow?
_____	7. five-factor model	g.	imitation
_____	8. hierarchy of traits	h.	why women may make better cops
_____	9. person-situation dilemma	i.	if I study it once more I'll do better
_____	10. person-payment dilemma	j.	if I don't know it now I'll never know it

Mastering the material... Which answer makes the statement true?

_____ 1. Rod Plotnik's point in telling the story of actor Charles Dutton, star of the television series "Roc," is that
  a. no matter how unsatisfactory your personality is now, you *can* change if you try
  b. no one should ever give up — you can make it if you want it badly enough
  c. beliefs and ideas play a large part in personality
  d. behaviors, both good and bad, are the main component of personality

_____ 2. One of the key concepts in Bandura's social-learning theory is
  a. need for social approval
  b. observational learning
  c. self-actualization
  d. unconscious conflict

_____ 3. The only statement below that shows *internal* locus of control is
  a. often exam questions are so unrelated to course work that studying is useless
  b. no matter how hard you try, some people just don't like you
  c. it is not always wise to plan too far ahead, because many things just turn out to be a matter of good or bad fortune
  d. when I make plans, I am almost certain I can make them work

_____ 4. According to Bandura, all of the following are keys to determining our sense of self-efficacy *except*
  a. successes and failures we have experienced in the past
  b. comparing ourselves to others
  c. what others say about our capabilities
  d. the power of our conscience to make us feel guilty

_____ 5. Walter Mischel used children and marshmallows in his study of
  a. delay of gratification
  b. locus of control
  c. observational learning
  d. traits

_____ 6. One of the major contributions of social-learning theory to understanding personality is
   a. going beyond symptoms to the deeper emotional or unconscious causes of problems
   b. the development of successful programs for changing behavior and personality
   c. explaining the emotional and genetic causes of behavior
   d. offering a complete theory of personality and human nature

_____ 7. Do women make better cops? Evidence suggests that the answer is
   a. yes, at least for now, because women have a greater determination to succeed
   b. no, because women in our society tend to have a lower sense of self-efficacy
   c. yes, because personality traits shared by many women are useful in police work
   d. no, because the performance of male and female officers is about the same

_____ 8. A trait is a
   a. relatively stable and enduring tendency to behave in a particular way
   b. personal idiosyncrasy that distinguishes us from all others
   c. behavioral tendency that is genetically determined
   d. specific belief about the world that influences our personality

_____ 9. For years, research in personality has tried to identify the
   a. single trait that all humans share
   b. particular traits that make up a healthy personality
   c. most complete list of terms that deal with personality differences
   d. fewest number of traits that cover the largest range of human behaviors

_____ 10. When we need to form an idea about another person, we seek information about
   a. their highly specific traits, like what jokes they laugh at
   b. their broadly general traits, like whether they are introverts or extroverts
   c. their middle-level traits, like whether they are fun loving or not
   d. their lower-order traits, like what they have done wrong recently

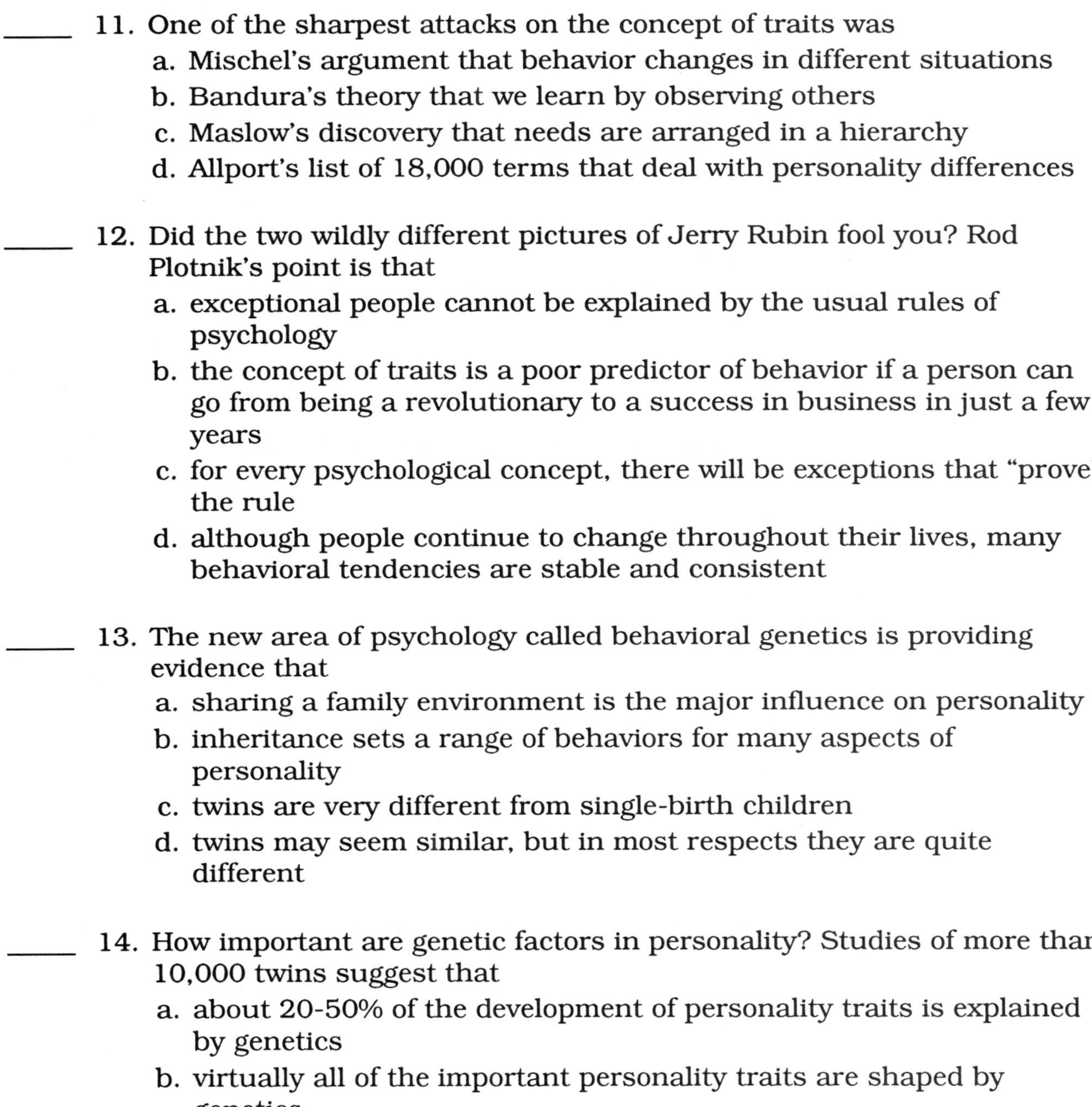

_____ 11. One of the sharpest attacks on the concept of traits was
a. Mischel's argument that behavior changes in different situations
b. Bandura's theory that we learn by observing others
c. Maslow's discovery that needs are arranged in a hierarchy
d. Allport's list of 18,000 terms that deal with personality differences

_____ 12. Did the two wildly different pictures of Jerry Rubin fool you? Rod Plotnik's point is that
a. exceptional people cannot be explained by the usual rules of psychology
b. the concept of traits is a poor predictor of behavior if a person can go from being a revolutionary to a success in business in just a few years
c. for every psychological concept, there will be exceptions that "prove" the rule
d. although people continue to change throughout their lives, many behavioral tendencies are stable and consistent

_____ 13. The new area of psychology called behavioral genetics is providing evidence that
a. sharing a family environment is the major influence on personality
b. inheritance sets a range of behaviors for many aspects of personality
c. twins are very different from single-birth children
d. twins may seem similar, but in most respects they are quite different

_____ 14. How important are genetic factors in personality? Studies of more than 10,000 twins suggest that
a. about 20-50% of the development of personality traits is explained by genetics
b. virtually all of the important personality traits are shaped by genetics
c. while genetic influences are apparent, family environment is still the root of all the important features of personality
d. the range of behaviors set by genetic influences is about 50-80%

_____ 15. Which one of the following is *not* a criticism of trait theory?
   a. traits measured in one situation do not necessarily predict behavior in different situations
   b. data from questionnaires may paint too simplistic a picture of human personality
   c. there may be as few as five major traits that describe personality differences
   d. inherited factors should not be exaggerated, because most of the explanation for traits is due to environmental factors

For psych majors only...a quiz on the famous psychologists

Not only is this chapter the most philosophical, it also discusses many famous psychologists, whose names a psych major should know. Can you match these important pioneers to the phrase that fits their work or ideas?

_____	1. Sigmund Freud	a.	delay of gratification
_____	2. Carl Jung	b.	personality traits
_____	3. Karen Horney	c.	observational learning
_____	4. Abraham Maslow	d.	unconditional positive regard
_____	5. Carl Rogers	e.	don't trust anyone over thirty
_____	6. Albert Bandura	f.	locus of control
_____	7. Walter Mischel	g.	"penis envy" is nonsense
_____	8. Gordon Allport	h.	hierarchy of needs
_____	9. Julian Rotter	i.	collective unconscious
_____	10. Jerry Rubin*	j.	unconscious motivation

**Not!*

Answers for Chapter 12

Module 23

True-False		Matching		Multiple-Choice	
1.	T	1.	i	1.	b
2.	F	2.	h	2.	d
3.	F	3.	c	3.	c
4.	T	4.	b	4.	a
5.	T	5.	g	5.	d
6.	F	6.	j	6.	b
7.	F	7.	a	7.	a
8.	T	8.	f	8.	c
9.	F	9.	d	9.	b
10.	T	10.	e	10.	d
				11.	a
				12.	c
				13.	b
				14.	c
				15.	a

Module 24

True-False		Matching		Multiple-Choice	
1.	T	1.	g	1.	c
2.	F	2.	j	2.	b
3.	T	3.	i	3.	d
4.	T	4.	a	4.	d
5.	F	5.	d	5.	a
6.	F	6.	h	6.	b
7.	F	7.	b	7.	c
8.	T	8.	c	8.	a
9.	T	9.	f	9.	d
10.	F	10.	e	10.	c
				11.	a
				12.	d
				13.	b
				14.	a
				15.	c

For psych majors only...a quiz on the famous psychologists

1. j 2. i 3. g 4. h 5. d 6. c 7. a 8. b 9. f 10. e

Chapter 13: Stress and Health

This chapter could save your life!

O.K., maybe I'm exaggerating. Then again, maybe not. Remember Rod Plotnik's discussion of the relationship between illness and stress? Go back and check the percentage of illness doctors estimate results from stress. The figure is startling.

It is becoming clear that stress is one of the greatest health hazards we face. We all feel it. Sometimes it seems that modern life not only is more stressful than 'the good old days' were, but that the number of our daily stressors continues to increase.

Does it have to be this way?

Ironically, considering its prevalence, stress is the one health hazard that is not inevitable — at least not in theory. Old age, eventually, is going to get each of us. Accidents will happen. We can't eliminate all disease. You won't solve the problem of pollution all by yourself. Yet you are not doomed to be ravaged by stress.

What can you do about it? First, you can adopt a positive attitude and a healthy life style that will tend to protect you against stress. Second, you can learn how to manage the stress you can't escape. Chapter 13 explains how both of these safeguards work.

Never mind the grade on the test... Study this chapter to learn how to live a long and healthy life!

Effective Student Tip 13

What 'Boring' Really Means

Students often complain that they aren't doing well because their classes and schoolwork are boring. I could suggest that *they* are interesting persons, and therefore have a duty to help make their classes interesting. It would be more realistic, however, to advise them to reconsider what boring really means.

Most students think certain people (not themselves) or certain activities are boring, but that is incorrect. Psychologically, boredom means being trapped, not being able to engage in an activity that is good for you. The next time you feel bored, ask yourself if there is anything taking place that allows you to grow and to express what is uniquely you. I'll bet you'll discover that 'boring' means not being able to exercise your urge to be effective.

Nothing is intrinsically boring. Every experienced teacher I've known had something worthwhile to say. Give me any example of activity or knowledge you might consider boring and I'll find someone, somewhere, whose great passion in life is pursuing exactly that activity or acquiring precisely that knowledge. Your schoolwork isn't boring, but perhaps you haven't yet found a way to connect it to the passions in *your* life.

Module 25: Responding to Stress

Use this

Outline

to organize your studying. Write notes on it. Turn it into a personalized aid for effective learning.

I. **Stress** — how it is defined in psychology

II. **Appraisal** — how we think about stress

A. **Primary appraisal** — we decide that a situation is stressful if it...

1. Will do us harm or cause us loss (**harm/loss**)

2. Threatens us with harm or loss (**threat**)

3. Challenges us to positive action (**challenge**)

B. **Secondary appraisal** — we decide how we can cope with the situation

III. Physiological arousal — how our body reacts to stress

A. Six steps from feeling stress to **fight or flight**

1. Appraise a situation as threatening

2. Hypothalamus activates autonomic nervous system

3. Pituitary gland stimulates adrenal cortex

4. Sympathetic division of nervous system produces arousal

5. Adrenal medulla mobilizes energy

6. Adrenal cortex regulates energy

B. **General Adaptation Syndrome** (Hans Selye)

1. Alarm stage — body activates fight or flight and becomes aroused

2. Resistance stage — body continues to use up energy reacting to stress

3. Exhaustion stage — body breaks down under long-term, continuous stress

C. **Psychosomatic** symptoms

1. Genetic predispositions and life-style factors create weakened organs

2. Stress attacks weaker organs

D. Stress and the immune system

1. **Psychoneuroimmunology**

2. Conditioning the immune system to resist stress

IV. An example from another culture

A. Body temperature of Tibetan monks

B. Importance of meditation or relaxation

V. *Applying/Exploring:* **Stress management** (part one)

A. Importance of relaxation

B. Learning to relax

1. **Biofeedback**

2. **Progressive relaxation**

3. **Meditation**

Now take the
Self-Tests
to check your understanding and mastery of this module.

Getting the general idea... Is the statement true or false?

_____ 1. Stress depends partly on how we evaluate a situation.

_____ 2. To "appraise" something means to feel very positive about it.

_____ 3. Our feelings about a situation influence how stressful it will be for us.

_____ 4. Stress means facing a problem no one could solve.

_____ 5. The fight or flight response goes back to the earliest days of the human species.

_____ 6. The "general adaptation syndrome" is a technique for warding off stress.

_____ 7. Psychosomatic symptoms are psychological signs that stress is damaging our ability to think clearly.

_____ 8. You are more likely to become ill soon after final exams than just before them.

_____ 9. Some Tibetan monks have developed a type of yoga that allows them to levitate their bodies several inches off the ground.

_____ 10. One of the main ingredients of a stress management program is learning how to relax.

Knowing the essential vocabulary... Which phrase matches the term?

	Term		Phrase
_____	1. stress	a.	provides energy for action
_____	2. primary appraisal	b.	activation of fight or flight response
_____	3. fight or flight response	c.	our primitive response to stress
_____	4. adrenal medulla	d.	ridding oneself of anxious thoughts
_____	5. psychosomatic symptom	e.	"Rod..., Rod..."
_____	6. alarm stage	f.	power of meditation
_____	7. psychoneuroimmunology	g.	strains our psychological resources
_____	8. Tibetan monks	h.	mental powers against disease
_____	9. relaxation response	i.	bodily ailment, psychological cause
_____	10. nurse's syringe	j.	initial evaluation of a situation

Mastering the material... Which answer makes the statement true?

_____ 1. Rod Plotnik gives us a new idea about stress — the observation that
   a. stress results from situations hardly anyone could stand
   b. stress depends greatly on how we think about a situation
   c. men are just as likely to experience stress as women
   d. simple medical procedures can be very stressful

_____ 2. All of the following are types of primary appraisal *except*
   a. harm/loss
   b. threat
   c. challenge
   d. advantage/resource

_____ 3. When Richard Lazarus showed a film about a bloody accident, the subjects who experienced the greatest stress were those who had been told to
   a. look away if they began to feel faint
   b. appraise the situation objectively
   c. appraise the situation by identifying with the victim
   d. remind themselves "it's only a movie"

_____ 4. Rod Plotnik lists people's reactions to a number of common stressors in order to illustrate the point that
   a. modern life has become almost unbearably stressful
   b. not everyone appraises these situations the same way
   c. there is a core of common experiences that everyone considers stressful
   d. the one thing everybody hates is waiting

_____ 5. Secondary appraisal means
   a. deciding what we can do to manage, cope, or deal with the situation
   b. our subjective evaluation of a situation to decide if we can deal with it
   c. the extent to which we appraise a situation as stressful after we have taken time to think about it objectively
   d. the extent to which we find a situation stressful the second time we encounter it

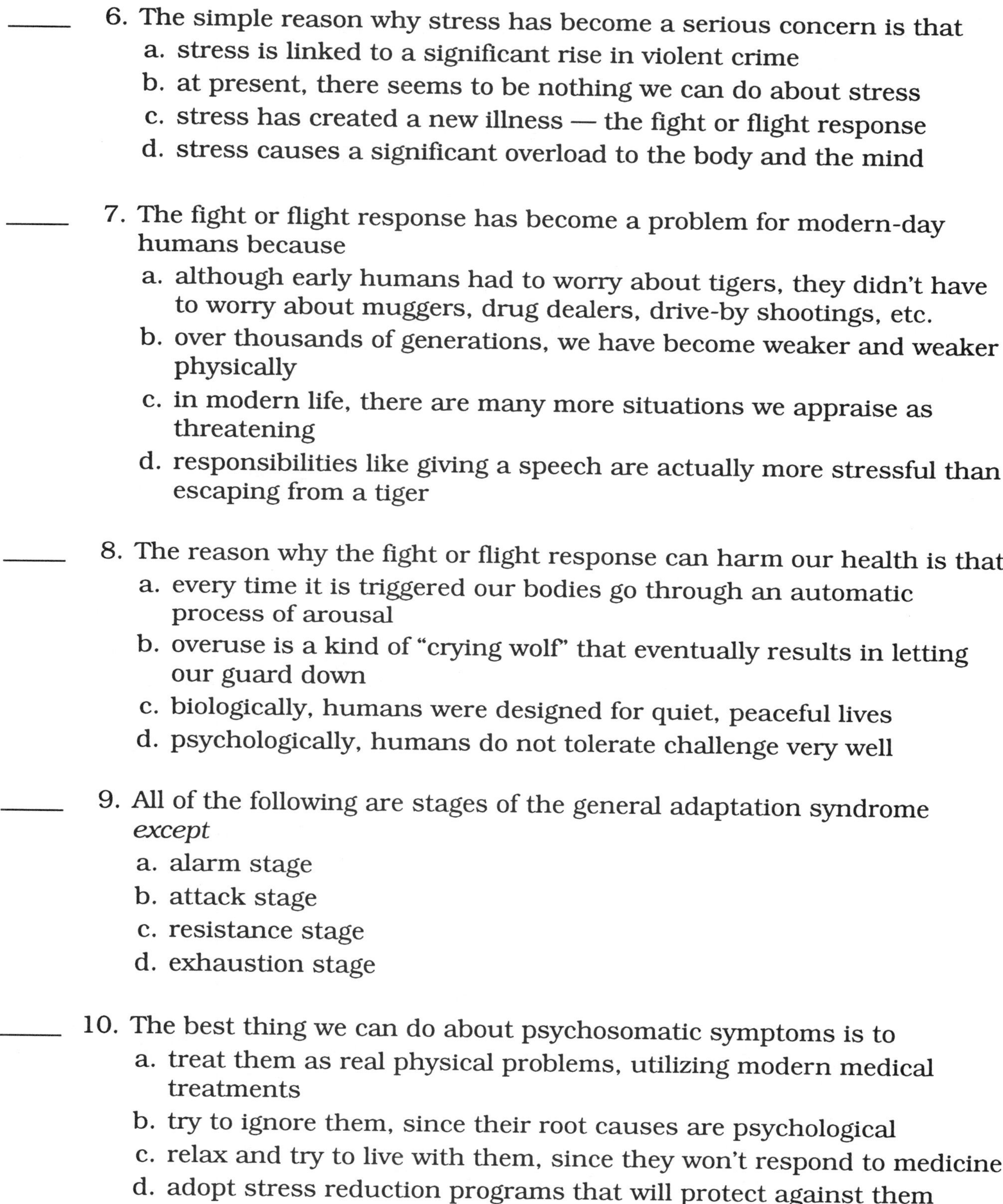

____ 6. The simple reason why stress has become a serious concern is that
   a. stress is linked to a significant rise in violent crime
   b. at present, there seems to be nothing we can do about stress
   c. stress has created a new illness — the fight or flight response
   d. stress causes a significant overload to the body and the mind

____ 7. The fight or flight response has become a problem for modern-day humans because
   a. although early humans had to worry about tigers, they didn't have to worry about muggers, drug dealers, drive-by shootings, etc.
   b. over thousands of generations, we have become weaker and weaker physically
   c. in modern life, there are many more situations we appraise as threatening
   d. responsibilities like giving a speech are actually more stressful than escaping from a tiger

____ 8. The reason why the fight or flight response can harm our health is that
   a. every time it is triggered our bodies go through an automatic process of arousal
   b. overuse is a kind of "crying wolf" that eventually results in letting our guard down
   c. biologically, humans were designed for quiet, peaceful lives
   d. psychologically, humans do not tolerate challenge very well

____ 9. All of the following are stages of the general adaptation syndrome *except*
   a. alarm stage
   b. attack stage
   c. resistance stage
   d. exhaustion stage

____ 10. The best thing we can do about psychosomatic symptoms is to
   a. treat them as real physical problems, utilizing modern medical treatments
   b. try to ignore them, since their root causes are psychological
   c. relax and try to live with them, since they won't respond to medicine
   d. adopt stress reduction programs that will protect against them

_____ 11. "Psychoneuroimmunology" means the study of
a. the manner in which psychological factors create physical symptoms
b. how disease can make a person psychotic or neurotic
c. the interaction of physical and psychological factors in health
d. this is a trick question — that is a made-up word

_____ 12. The startling fact that people can have allergic reactions to plastic flowers suggests that
a. a so-called disease is really just something in your mind
b. people could be conditioned to increase their immune response in order to guard against disease
c. allergies are psychosomatic symptoms rather than real physical problems
d. people with allergies are really faking illness to get attention

_____ 13. If Tibetan monks can raise their body temperature through meditation, then perhaps
a. Western medicine should pay more attention to psychological factors
b. Western medicine — not Asian — represents the real medical fakery
c. every culture has a form of medicine that is best for its own members
d. every culture develops some phenomena that can't be fully explained

_____ 14. The relaxation technique that involves learning to increase or decrease physiological signals from the body is called
a. the relaxation response
b. progressive relaxation
c. biofeedback
d. Transcendental Meditation (TM)

_____ 15. The relaxation technique that has proven most effective in reducing mild anxiety is
a. biofeedback
b. progressive relaxation
c. Transcendental Meditation (TM)
d. all three techniques are about equally effective

Module 26: Coping with Stress

I. Coping

   A. **Problem-focused coping** (working on the problem itself)

   B. **Emotion-focused coping** (working on our thoughts and feelings)

II. Kinds of problems that cause stress

   A. **Major life events** and their effect on health

   B. A ton of **daily hassles** and maybe a few **uplifts**

   C. Situational stressors

      1. **Frustration**

      2. Burnout

   D. Three common types of **conflict** diagrammed

      1. Approach/avoidance

      2. Approach/approach

      3. Avoidance/avoidance

   E. **Cultural stress** (when two cultures clash)

   F. **Anxiety** (the stress of fear)

      1. How anxiety can be learned (and unlearned)

         a. **Classical conditioning** (anxiety paired with neutral event)

         b. **Observational learning** (seeing an anxiety-provoking event)

      2. How we deal with hidden anxiety

         a. Freud's concept of **unconscious conflict**

         b. Reducing anxiety through the use of **defense mechanisms**

Use this

Outline

to organize your studying. Write notes on it. Turn it into a personalized aid for effective learning.

III. Personality factors that affect how we deal with stress

   A. **Hardiness** (the right combination of attitudes)

   B. Locus of control

      1. **Internal locus of control**

      2. External locus of control

   C. **Type A** personality (and heart attacks)

      1. Does personality really affect stress?

      2. Revised definition of Type A behavior

   D. The **disease-prone personality**

IV. Social factors in stress

   A. **Social support**

   B. How social support helps us cope with stress

V. *Applying/Exploring:* **Stress management** (part two)

   A. Stress management programs

   B. Steps to take

      1. Self-observation (observing and recording behaviors)

      2. Appraisal (replacing threat appraisals with challenge appraisals)

      3. Coping (techniques for positive coping)

      4. Unavoidable situations (defeating anticipatory stress)

      5. Success (stick to the program and practice)

Now take the **Self-Tests** to check your understanding and mastery of this module.

Getting the general idea... Is the statement true or false?

_____ 1. "Coping" means a desperate struggle just to get by.

_____ 2. Research shows that small daily hassles are far more stressful than major life events.

_____ 3. The way we respond to frustration influences our levels of stress.

_____ 4. Burnout is a relatively frequent cause of students dropping out of college.

_____ 5. Conflict means the inevitable run-ins that occur when you have to work with someone else.

_____ 6. Anxiety has both emotional and physiological effects on us.

_____ 7. Research has shown that Freud was right, and the learning approaches therefore wrong, about the cause and treatment of anxiety.

_____ 8. Your personality can influence how well you deal with stress.

_____ 9. One of the best prescriptions for successfully handling stress is to have many relationships that confer social support.

_____ 10. The key idea in stress management programs is that it is better to think positive thoughts and not pay so much attention to our problems.

Knowing the essential vocabulary... Which phrase matches the term?

	Term		Phrase
_____	1. problem-focused coping	a.	death of spouse, divorce, separation
_____	2. emotion-focused coping	b.	uneasiness and apprehension
_____	3. major life event	c.	rationalization, denial, repression
_____	4. daily hassles	d.	study for exam or write term paper?
_____	5. avoidance/avoidance	e.	kick back, relax, and forget the test!
_____	6. anxiety	f.	taking action to solve a problem
_____	7. defense mechanisms	g.	competitive, aggressive, and hostile
_____	8. hardiness	h.	control, commitment, and challenge
_____	9. Type A	i.	stuck in traffic, noise, running late
_____	10. Type F	j.	dealing with feelings about a problem

Mastering the material... Which answer makes the statement true?

_____ 1. Rod Plotnik used the example of Sandra, a welfare mother in college, to show that
- a. when we stereotype someone we are often wrong
- b. "reach-out" programs often justify their cost to the taxpayer
- c. it is possible to cope with extreme demands on our resources
- d. it is possible to cope with anything if you have the "I can" spirit

_____ 2. Sandra is using problem-focused coping when she
- a. studies with a friend
- b. reminds herself how much time she spends reading to her son
- c. puts herself down for having to go on welfare
- d. feels uncomfortable around students from wealthy families

_____ 3. Sandra is using emotion-focused coping when she
- a. studies with a friend
- b. reminds herself how much time she spends reading to her son
- c. puts herself down for having to go on welfare
- d. feels uncomfortable around students from wealthy families

_____ 4. The total score on the Social Readjustment Rating Scale
- a. subtracts positive life events from negative life changes
- b. gives a precise cut-off point for becoming an ill or staying well
- c. reflects how well you cope with stress
- d. reflects how many major life changes you have experienced in the past year

_____ 5. Researchers now pay just as much attention to small daily hassles as to major life events because
- a. hassles turn out to be more stressful than major life events
- b. hassles are good predictors of psychological symptoms and stress
- c. major life events are difficult to measure
- d. major life events are too infrequent to relate to stress

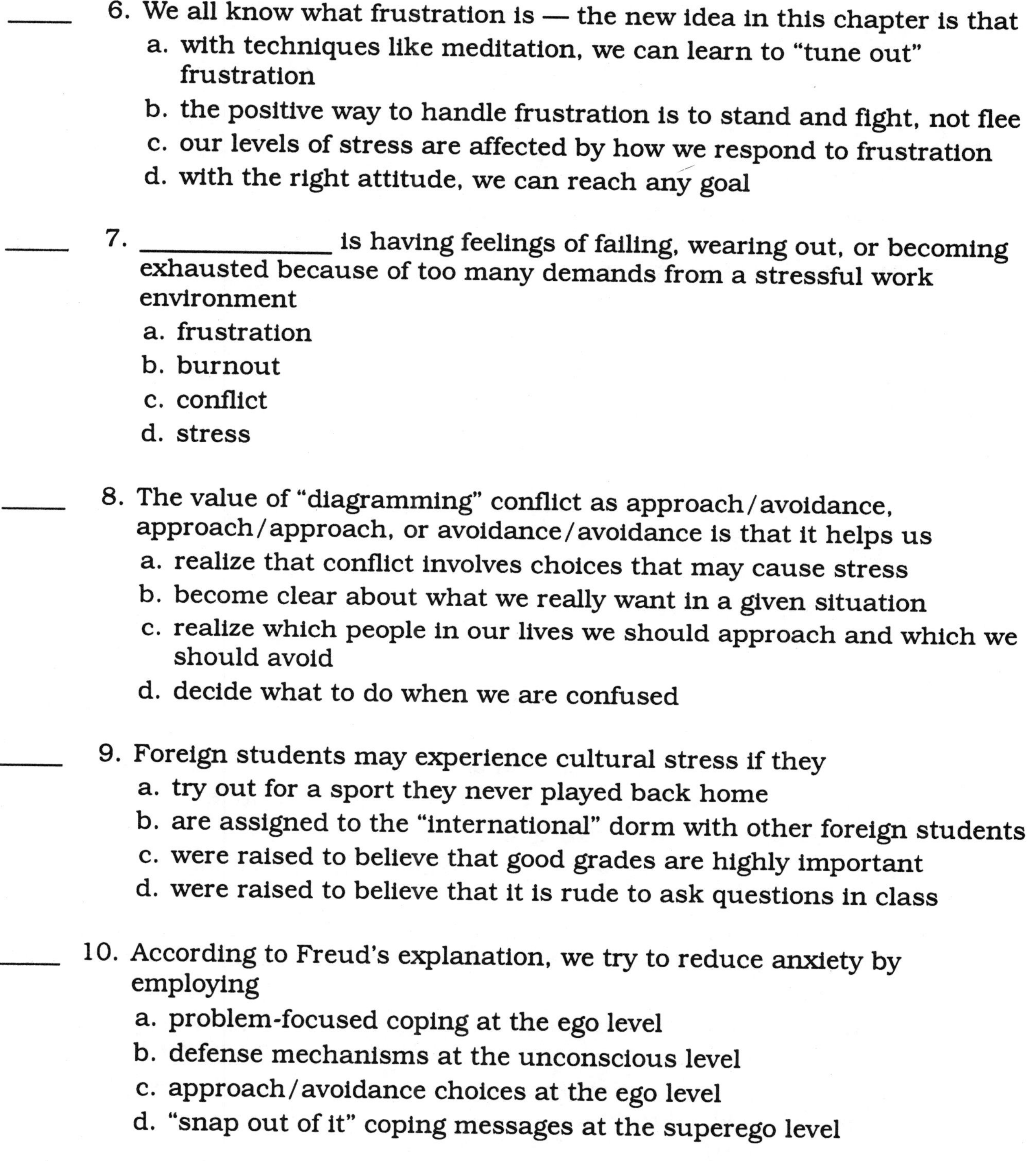

_____ 6. We all know what frustration is — the new idea in this chapter is that

a. with techniques like meditation, we can learn to "tune out" frustration
b. the positive way to handle frustration is to stand and fight, not flee
c. our levels of stress are affected by how we respond to frustration
d. with the right attitude, we can reach any goal

_____ 7. _____________ is having feelings of failing, wearing out, or becoming exhausted because of too many demands from a stressful work environment

a. frustration
b. burnout
c. conflict
d. stress

_____ 8. The value of "diagramming" conflict as approach/avoidance, approach/approach, or avoidance/avoidance is that it helps us

a. realize that conflict involves choices that may cause stress
b. become clear about what we really want in a given situation
c. realize which people in our lives we should approach and which we should avoid
d. decide what to do when we are confused

_____ 9. Foreign students may experience cultural stress if they

a. try out for a sport they never played back home
b. are assigned to the "international" dorm with other foreign students
c. were raised to believe that good grades are highly important
d. were raised to believe that it is rude to ask questions in class

_____ 10. According to Freud's explanation, we try to reduce anxiety by employing

a. problem-focused coping at the ego level
b. defense mechanisms at the unconscious level
c. approach/avoidance choices at the ego level
d. "snap out of it" coping messages at the superego level

_____ 11. The career of famous heart surgeon Dr. Michael DeBakey illustrates the point that
a. personality factors help explain how we react to stress
b. people who are highly competitive handle stress better
c. for every psychological concept (like stress), there is an exception that proves the rule
d. once you have conquered stress you can do anything

_____ 12. Which one of the following is *not* an ingredient of hardiness?
a. control
b. commitment
c. contentment
d. challenge

_____ 13. The famous "Type A" research studies attempted to relate certain behaviors to
a. hardy personality
b. locus of control
c. increased risk of cancer
d. increased risk of heart attack

_____ 14. The concept of the disease-prone personality relates being at risk for certain diseases to
a. traits like anxiety, anger, and depression
b. "risky" behaviors like smoking and substance abuse
c. being abrasive and hard to like
d. traits like risk-taking, competitiveness, and perfectionism

_____ 15. People in Roseto, Pennsylvania didn't follow healthy life styles, but they had lower rates of heart attacks, ulcers, and emotional problems because
a. the steep Pennsylvania hills forced them to exercise whether they wanted to or not
b. being the home of the University of Pennsylvania, the town had superb medical facilities
c. families in this small town were all related to each other, which had built up a good genetic background over many generations
d. relationships with family and neighbors were extremely close and mutually supportive

Answers for Chapter 13

Module 25

True-False		Matching		Multiple-Choice	
1.	T	1.	g	1.	b
2.	F	2.	j	2.	d
3.	T	3.	c	3.	c
4.	F	4.	a	4.	b
5.	T	5.	i	5.	a
6.	F	6.	b	6.	d
7.	F	7.	h	7.	c
8.	T	8.	f	8.	a
9.	F	9.	d	9.	b
10.	T	10.	e	10.	d
				11.	c
				12.	b
				13.	a
				14.	c
				15.	d

Module 26

True-False		Matching		Multiple-Choice	
1.	F	1.	f	1.	c
2.	F	2.	j	2.	a
3.	T	3.	a	3.	b
4.	T	4.	i	4.	d
5.	F	5.	d	5.	b
6.	T	6.	b	6.	c
7.	F	7.	c	7.	b
8.	T	8.	h	8.	a
9.	T	9.	g	9.	d
10.	F	10.	e	10.	b
				11.	a
				12.	c
				13.	d
				14.	a
				15.	d

Chapter 14: Disorders

The story of a troubled person

One of the most perplexing and controversial problems of psychology is how to understand and treat human anguish and suffering. The great danger is that we may classify, label, and prescribe, but without really understanding. Modern psychology has come a long way from the unthinking and often cruel 'treatment' in use not so long ago, but we are still far from having a reliable science of diagnosis and therapy.

I want to suggest an exercise that may help you think about the complexity of emotional disturbance, and show you that your own psychological sensitivity and insight into human suffering may be greater than you realize. The exercise is to write a brief paper about a troubled person you know. [You may simply write this paper in your mind, but if you do put it on paper it might fit an assignment in psychology or English composition.]

Write about someone you know fairly well (a relative, friend, classmate, or coworker) who seems unable to enjoy the normal human satisfactions of love and work (Freud's definition of emotional disturbance). The reasons for the troubled person's distress could be anything from the psychological problems of severe depression or schizophrenia to the social problems of alcoholism or the trauma of child abuse. What you already know about the person is enough for this exercise.

How clear a picture of your troubled person can you draw? Include a description of personality, tell the life history briefly, and offer suggestions for treatment.

Your conclusion should reinforce two points: (1) your theory about why the person became troubled, and (2) what the story of this troubled person teaches us about human behavior — what lessons it has for our own lives.

You could use this exercise as an opportunity to think and write about your own life and problems. Even though you probably aren't a troubled person, you may have private doubts and worries or painful experiences you would benefit from exploring.

Effective Student Tip 14

What the Professor Wants

Professors love compliments and admiring students. They're human, after all. That isn't what they really want, though.

Every professor wants to be an effective teacher. What your professor wants from you personally is that you really do *learn.* The best thing you can do for your professor is also the best thing you can do for yourself: learn, achieve your goals, and be successful.

Professors sometimes deceive themselves and each other by saying, "If I can help just one student, it's all worth while...," but they don't really believe it. Deep down, they wish *every one* of their students would learn and progress. Then they would know what they are doing is right, which would satisfy their own urge to be effective.

Like you, your professor wants to be effective, but because the measure of that effectiveness is your learning, only you can bring it about. Does it occur to you that you and the professor really need each other? Both of you want to be effective in life, and you can help each other achieve that effectiveness. Don't underestimate your power. The professor's fate is in your hands!

Module 27: Disorders I

Use this **Outline** to organize your studying. Write notes on it. Turn it into a personalized aid for effective learning.

I. Issues in abnormal psychology

A. Approaches to understanding psychological disorders

1. **Medical model**

2. **Psychoanalytic**

3. **Cognitive-behavioral**

B. Defining abnormal behavior

1. **Statistical frequency**

2. **Deviation from social norms**

3. **Maladaptive behavior**

C. Overview of mental disorders

1. Classifying mental disorders

a. Clinical interviews

b. Psychological tests

c. Neurological examinations

2. Why psychiatrists sometimes disagree

3. *Diagnostic and Statistical Manual of Mental Disorders (DSM)*

a. How *DSM* works (five axes)

b. Major categories

4. A research portrait of mental disorders in the United States

II. Common, less serious psychological troubles

A. **Anxiety** disorders

1. Generalized anxiety disorder

2. **Panic** disorder

3. **Phobia**

a. Simple phobias

b. Social phobias

c. Agoraphobia

4. **Obsessive-compulsive** disorder

a. Obsessions

b. Compulsions

B. **Somatoform** disorders

1. **Conversion** disorder

2. **Somatization** disorder

III. Cultural diversity: *taijin kyofusho (TKS)*

IV. *Applying/Exploring:* Treating phobias

A. Behavioral treatment: exposure

B. Drug treatment

C. Cognitive-behavioral treatment

Getting the general idea... Is the statement true or false?

_____ 1. Psychiatrists agree that Jeffrey Dahmer is insane.

_____ 2. Psychiatry has nothing as precise as a blood test with which to determine mental disorders.

_____ 3. John Hinckley shot President Reagan to dramatize the Republican Party's failure to do anything about gun control.

_____ 4. When psychiatrists make diagnoses, they turn to the *DSM*.

_____ 5. Nearly three-fourths of all Americans report having had at least one mental disorder during their lifetimes.

_____ 6. For some unknown reason, panic disorder is much more common among men than women.

_____ 7. Don't worry about your phobias; they usually disappear in a few months.

_____ 8. Problems of anxiety can show themselves in many different ways.

_____ 9. Culture has a powerful influence on the development of mental disorders.

_____ 10. Research has shown that drug treatment offers the best hope for getting rid of phobias.

Knowing the essential vocabulary... Which phrase matches the term?

	Term		Phrase
_____	1. legal insanity	a.	behavior that hurts yourself
_____	2. medical model	b.	classification of mental disorders
_____	3. maladaptive	c.	intense and irrational fear
_____	4. clinical interview	d.	feeling that you are under the gun
_____	5. *DSM*	e.	he needed more elbow room
_____	6. anxiety	f.	inability to tell right from wrong
_____	7. phobia	g.	cultural influences in mental health
_____	8. somatoform disorder	h.	mental disorders likened to diseases
_____	9. *taijin kyofusho* (*TKS*)	i.	most common form of diagnosis
_____	10. why Dahmer moved	j.	symptoms without physical causes

Mastering the material... Which answer makes the statement true?

_____ 1. The main issue in the Jeffrey Dahmer trial was whether Dahmer
   a. actually killed 15 young men, or only the one he was arrested for
   b. was under the influence of drugs when he killed
   c. knew the difference between right and wrong when he killed
   d. really intended to kill the five men who said they got away

_____ 2. The difference between the terms insanity and mental disorder is that
   a. insanity is more severe than a mental disorder
   b. insanity is a legal term while mental disorder is a medical term
   c. mental disorders are specific forms of insanity
   d. mental disorders do not qualify for insurance reimbursement

_____ 3. All of the following are approaches to understanding and treating mental disorders *except*
   a. statistical frequency
   b. medical model
   c. psychoanalytic
   d. cognitive-behavioral

_____ 4. All of the following are yardsticks for defining abnormal behavior *except*
   a. statistical frequency
   b. deviation from social norms
   c. maladaptive behavior
   d. slips of the tongue

_____ 5. The most commonly used tool for diagnosing mental disorders is the
   a. Rorschach inkblot test
   b. neurological examination
   c. psychological test
   d. clinical interview

_____ 6. The reason why psychiatrists in the John Hinckley trial disagreed with each other is that
   a. Hinckley was clever enough to tell each doctor a different story
   b. the government was able to pressure some psychiatrists to agree with the prosecution
   c. psychiatry is more an art than a science
   d. Hinckley showed symptoms of several disorders, making precise diagnosis difficult

_____ 7. The most widely used system of psychological classification is the
- a. *Freudian Psychoanalytic System (FPS)*
- b. *Diagnostic and Statistical Manual of Mental Disorders (DSM)*
- c. *Disordered Mind Standards (DMS)*
- d. *Federal Uniform Code of Psychopathology (UCP)*

_____ 8. A recent large-scale study showed that _________ of all Americans had at least one mental disorder during their lifetimes
- a. only one-tenth
- b. about one-third
- c. fully two-thirds
- d. almost 100 percent

_____ 9. The anxiety disorder that causes the greatest terror and suffering is
- a. panic disorder
- b. simple phobia
- c. generalized anxiety disorder
- d. obsessive-compulsive disorder

_____ 10. Shonda is so afraid of being out in public that she stays at home all the time now; Shonda suffers from
- a. a simple phobia
- b. a social phobia
- c. agoraphobia
- d. claustrophobia

_____ 11. Remember the case of Shirley, who had to do everything exactly 17 times? The theory is that she was trying to
- a. reduce or avoid anxiety, in this case about being dirty
- b. obey inner voices which told her God loves cleanliness
- c. cleanse her mind of confusing hallucinations
- d. please her mother, who used to punish her severely whenever she got her clothes dirty while playing

_____ 12. When 250 children performing at a concert suddenly became ill, the cause was determined to be mass
- a. hallucination
- b. delusion
- c. conversion disorder
- d. somatization disorder

_____ 13. The key feature of somatoform disorders is
a. pretending to be sick to avoid school or work
b. real physical symptoms but no physical causes
c. imagining physical symptoms that aren't really there
d. psychological problems but no physical symptoms

_____ 14. Of all the mental disorders we know, it's a good bet you don't have to worry about getting *TKS*—mainly because you
a. are in college, and therefore too old to get it
b. are in college, and therefore too intelligent to get it
c. got shots for it as a child
d. don't live in Japan

_____ 15. All of the following are techniques for treating phobias *except*
a. gradually exposing clients to the feared situation
b. administering antidepressant drugs to clients
c. hospitalizing clients until their fears begin to diminish
d. teaching clients to become aware of their thoughts about the feared situations

Module 28: Disorders II

Use this

Outline

to organize your studying. Write notes on it. Turn it into a personalized aid for effective learning.

I. Mood disorders

A. Three ways mood can be abnormal

1. **Major depression**

2. **Dysthemic** disorder

3. **Bipolar** disorder (depression alternating with mania)

B. Causes of depression

1. Biological theory

2. Cognitive theory (Aaron Beck)

C. Treatment of mood disorders

1. **Psychotherapy**

a. Cognitive-behavior therapy

b. Interpersonal therapy

2. **Antidepressant drug** therapy (monoamine theory)

3. **Electroconvulsive** (shock) therapy (ECT)

a. Seizures

b. Side effects

4. Lithium treatment of bipolar depression and mania

II. **Personality** disorders

A. **Antisocial personality** disorder]

B. Other personality disorders

III. **Schizophrenia**

A. Two varieties in the course of schizophrenia

1. Acute

2. Chronic

B. Symptoms of schizophrenia

1. Disorders of thought

2. Disorders of attention

3. Disorders of perception

4. Motor disorders

5. Emotional (affective) disorders

C. Subtypes of schizophrenia

1. **Paranoid**

2. **Disorganized**

3. **Catatonic**

D. Causes of schizophrenia

1. Genetic factors

2. Brain factors — **dopamine** theory

3. Environmental factors — **diathesis-stress** theory

E. Treatment of schizophrenia

1. Antipsychotic drugs

2. Side effects (**tardive dyskinesia**)

F. Long-term outcomes of schizophrenia

For psych majors only...

Now, boys and girls, can *you* say "diathesis-stress theory?"

This chapter is tough, but getting a handle on the material now will help you in all your subsequent psychology courses, especially abnormal psychology.

One reason the chapter is tough is that the subject involves the technical terminology of medical science and the concept of the medical model of illness. You must learn to think and talk like a doctor. Another complicating factor is that it touches on the most difficult challenge faced by psychology: how to understand why things go wrong for troubled people and how to help them.

Have you noticed how frequently new discoveries about the causes and treatment of mental illnesses are in the news? The field of abnormal psychology is developing right before your eyes. Memorize what you must in this chapter, but keep your eyes on the big picture, too.

Yes, this chapter is tough, but it presents psychology at its most real.

IV. **Dissociative** disorders

- A. Psychogenic **amnesia**
- B. Psychogenic **fugue**
- C. **Multiple personality**

V. *Applying/Exploring:* Mild depression

- A. The vicious circle of depression
- B. How to break out of the circle
  1. Focus on positive events
  2. Give yourself credit
  3. Take some action

Now take the

Self-Tests

to check your understanding and mastery of this module.

Getting the general idea... Is the statement true or false?

_____ 1. William Styron knew exactly what caused his depression, so he was able to cure it himself

_____ 2. The most serious mood disorder is major depression.

_____ 3. At the opposite pole from depression is mania.

_____ 4. The discovery of antidepressant drugs made treatment of schizophrenia by psychotherapy obsolete.

_____ 5. The treatment of choice for mania is lithium.

_____ 6. People suffering from antisocial personality disorder are extremely shy and attempt to avoid other people.

_____ 7. People suffering from acute schizophrenia have a better chance for recovery than those suffering from chronic schizophrenia.

_____ 8. Dissociative disorders and how they work: psychogenic amnesia, forget; psychogenic fugue, flee; multiple personality, split off.

_____ 9. Antipsychotic drugs are effective, but they have serious side effects.

_____ 10. Although many people experience occasional mild depression, there is little they can do except tough it out.

Knowing the essential vocabulary... Which phrase matches the term?

	Term		Phrase
_____	1. mood disorder	a.	psychopath, possibly a serial killer
_____	2. depression	b.	loss of contact with reality
_____	3. bipolar disorder	c.	sad, depressed, energyless, suicidal
_____	4. monoamine theory	d.	shock treatment
_____	5. antipsychotic drugs	e.	out of this world
_____	6. schizophrenia	f.	neurotransmitter levels affect mood
_____	7. diathesis-stress theory	g.	tardive dyskinesia
_____	8. antisocial personality	h.	prolonged emotional state
_____	9. ECT	i.	genetics – environment interaction
_____	10. ET	j.	alternately manic and depressive

Mastering the material... Which answer makes the statement true?

_____ 1. Rod Plotnik uses the example of William Styron's illness to show that
a. alcoholism is a huge psychiatric problem in America
b. depression is a terrifying, crippling disorder
c. anyone can become depressed at almost any time
d. creative people are more likely to become mentally ill

_____ 2. All of the following are mood disorders *except*
a. major depression
b. bipolar disorder
c. antisocial personality disorder
d. dysthymic disorder

_____ 3. Science now says the cause of depression is
a. mainly biological
b. mainly cognitive
c. mainly personal (optimistic versus pessimistic)
d. both biological and cognitive

_____ 4. Is psychotherapy as effective as drug therapy in treating major depression? The study reported in the textbook found that
a. drug therapy was much more effective
b. psychotherapy was much more effective
c. neither drugs nor psychotherapy had lasting effects
d. both drugs and psychotherapy can be effective

_____ 5. ECT is a controversial treatment for depression because it
a. has serious side effects, such as memory loss
b. terrifies patients
c. works on the brain, yet no one knows how
d. is prescribed by psychiatrists but not by clinical psychologists

_____ 6. The most common treatment for bipolar disorder and mania is
a. ECT
b. monoamine
c. lithium
d. dopamine

____ 7. ____________ is a famous example of an extreme case of antisocial personality disorder
a. John Hinckley
b. William Styron
c. Ted Bundy
d. the Genain quadruplets

____ 8. A key feature of schizophrenia not present in the other disorders is
a. odd or eccentric behavior
b. loss of contact with reality
c. inability to remember important personal information
d. giddy excitement or excess energy

____ 9. All of the following are symptoms of schizophrenia *except*
a. disorders of thought
b. disorders of attention
c. disorders of perception
d. disorders of moral character

____ 10. Rod Plotnik tells us about the famous Genain quadruplets to illustrate the fact that
a. science is filled with amazing coincidences
b. there must be a genetic factor in schizophrenia
c. children can "learn" to be schizophrenic from close contact with family members who are ill
d. schizophrenia strikes in a random, unpredictable fashion

____ 11. According to the ____________ theory, schizophrenia is caused by abnormalities in neurotransmitters in the brain
a. dopamine
b. diathesis-stress
c. monoamine
d. frontal lobe

____ 12. Most patients taking antipsychotic drugs report feelings of
a. euphoria and often a sudden rush of energy
b. calmness and peace
c. some pain, but renewed hope for recovery
d. physical discomfort and mental dullness

_____ 13. The difference between suffering from psychogenic amnesia and psychogenic fugue is that

a. in the former you stay in contact with reality while in the latter you become schizophrenic

b. in the former you have memory gaps while in the latter you may wander away and assume a new identity

c. in the former you forget more than in the latter

d. these are really two different terms for the same experience

_____ 14. A common factor in multiple personality disorder appears to be

a. physical trauma, such as a head injury

b. unstable parents who give their children mixed messages about what they expect

c. a flighty personality along with a tendency to overdramatize every situation

d. severe psychological or physical abuse and/or sexual trauma during early childhood

_____ 15. If you are trying to break out of the vicious circle of common depression, Rod Plotnik suggests all of the following *except*

a. focus on positive events

b. don't think about your problems

c. give yourself credit

d. take some action

Answers for Chapter 14

Module 27

True-False	Matching	Multiple-Choice
1. F	1. f	1. c
2. T	2. h	2. b
3. F	3. a	3. a
4. T	4. i	4. d
5. F	5. b	5. d
6. F	6. d	6. d
7. F	7. c	7. b
8. T	8. j	8. b
9. T	9. g	9. a
10. F	10. e	10. c
		11. a
		12. c
		13. b
		14. d
		15. c

Module 28

True-False	Matching	Multiple-Choice
1. F	1. h	1. b
2. T	2. c	2. c
3. T	3. j	3. d
4. F	4. f	4. d
5. T	5. g	5. a
6. F	6. b	6. c
7. T	7. i	7. c
8. T	8. a	8. b
9. T	9. d	9. d
10. F	10. e	10. b
		11. a
		12. d
		13. b
		14. d
		15. b

Chapter 15: Therapies

The contribution of psychodynamic psychology to therapy

Psychotherapy is one of the great inventions of this century. Whether you consider it an art or a science, it is a young and constantly evolving process. Rod Plotnik discusses four current approaches to psychotherapy, each with numerous varieties and special techniques.

At the heart of most forms of psychotherapy lies a basic assumption and a fundamental process that come from psychodynamic psychology and the work of a great pioneer, good old You Know Who. Both the assumption and the technique are inherent in Freud's theory of dreams, about which you read way back in Chapter 5.

Manifest content and latent content

The key idea is the distinction between manifest content and latent content. The manifest content of a dream is the story (however bizarre) we remember in the morning. The latent content is the disguised, unconscious wish hidden in the apparently meaningless story of the dream. The challenge to the dreamer, perhaps a patient in psychotherapy, is to gain insight into that latent content because it is a direct line [Freud called it the *via regia*, or royal road] to the unconscious. With the help of the therapist, the patient examines thoughts and feelings connected to the dream in the expectation that these associations will suggest an underlying meaning, a meaning that provides insight into the patient's 'dynamics,' or psychological life.

This key idea has broad implications. Freud saw dreams and other unconscious acts (slips of the tongue, losing things, forgetting, accidents) as miniature neuroses, reflecting the larger neuroses of which we all have more than a few. Therefore, we can interpret *any* behavior like a dream. Here's the formula. First, examine the behavior (a comment, an act, even a thought) very carefully. Exactly what happened? That's the manifest content. Next, search the manifest content for clues about what the *latent* content might be. Why did you forget the assignment? Lose your keys? Call your honey the wrong name? Bingo! Insight into how your unconscious mind works.

A model for understanding psychotherapy... and life

This fundamental idea of psychodynamic psychology underlies most forms of therapy, and can be used as a model for understanding almost anything in life from the meaning of Shakespeare's plays to why your roommate is driving you crazy. Whenever you want to understand some behavior, whether your own or someone else's, just ask and answer two questions: What is the manifest content? What is the latent content?

Effective Student Tip 15

High Grades Count Most

Here is a hard truth. Unfair, maybe, but true. Anyone who looks at your transcript, whether for admission to another school or for employment, is going to be looking for the *high* grades. It's difficult for them to tell exactly what C means. In some schools, C may only mean you attended class. The grade B begins to say more about your abilities and character, but it is an A that is really convincing. No matter what course or what school, an A says you did everything asked of you and did it well. That's a quality admissions people and personnel officers look for.

Tailor your work toward earning high grades. Take fewer courses, stay up later studying, write papers over, ruthlessly cut fun out of your life [just kidding].

Earning high grades in a few courses beats getting average grades in many courses. The fastest route toward your goal is a conservative selection of courses in which you do well, resulting in a good record and confidence in your effectiveness as a student.

Module 29: Therapy I

I. Psychotherapy

A. History

1. Story of "**Anna O.**"

2. Lunatics and asylums

3. Reform movement (Dorothea Dix)

4. **Deinstitutionalization** (antipsychotic drugs)

5. Uneven care today

a. Private treatment and hospitals

b. Community mental health centers

c. Homeless mentally ill

B. Psychotherapists

1. **Psychiatrist**

2. **Clinical psychologist**

3. Counseling psychologist

C. Approaches to psychotherapy

1. Major schools of psychology: psychodynamic, cognitive, behavioral, humanistic, etc.

2. Current trend: **eclectic** blend of several schools

D. Effectiveness of psychotherapy

Use this

Outline

to organize your studying. Write notes on it. Turn it into a personalized aid for effective learning.

II. **Psychoanalysis** (Sigmund Freud)

A. Freud's major discoveries

1. **Unconscious conflict** (example: Freudian slips)
2. Necessity of **interpretation**
3. Technique of psychoanalysis

B. How psychoanalysis works

1. Overcoming defenses
2. Achieving insight

C. Four main techniques used in psychoanalysis

1. **Free association**
2. **Dream** interpretation
3. Analysis of **resistance**
4. Analysis of **transference** (and countertransference)

C. Psychoanalysis today

1. Decline in influence and use since 1950s
2. Continues to be model for insight therapies
   a. Psychodynamic approach
   b. **Brief dynamic psychotherapy**

D. Cultural diversity: the balian, a local healer in Bali

1. Assumes problem comes from outside, not inside
2. Healing power of ritual

III. *Applying/Exploring:* What factors make psychotherapy effective?

A. **Nonspecific factors**

1. Therapist (personal and professional qualities)
2. Client (internally motivated)
3. Partnership (helping and supportive client-therapist relationship)
4. Commitment (time and openness to change)

B. Skills of the psychotherapist: ability to...

1. Create accepting and compassionate atmosphere
2. Deal with client's emotional feelings

C. Choosing a psychotherapist

1. Referral
2. Being a careful consumer

Now take the

Self-Tests

to check your understanding and mastery of this module.

Getting the general idea... Is the statement true or false?

_____ 1. The main ingredient of most forms of psychotherapy is talk.

_____ 2. The history of treatment is a story of continual improvement in the treatment of the mentally ill.

_____ 3. There are three types of psychotherapists: psychiatrists, clinical psychologists, and sympathetic laymen who are good listeners.

_____ 4. Today, more psychotherapists see themselves as eclectic than as adhering to one of the traditional schools of psychotherapy.

_____ 5. The basic assumption of psychoanalysis is that since we learn maladaptive behaviors we can unlearn them through training.

_____ 6. A "Freudian slip" can be important because it may reveal an unconscious thought or wish.

_____ 7. Transference is the process by which a patient gives his or her problems to the therapist for analysis and solution.

_____ 8. Although widely criticized, psychoanalysis continues to be a force in psychotherapy today.

_____ 9. The secret of the success of the balian, the local healer of Bali, is that the balian is a very sympathetic listener.

_____ 10. To be effective, the therapist must be able to (1) create an accepting and compassionate atmosphere and (2) keep the client talking about the problem instead of about irrational feelings.

Knowing the essential vocabulary... Which phrase matches the term?

	Term		Phrase
_____	1. deinstitutionalization	a.	typical psychotherapist today
_____	2. eclectic	b.	strong feelings
_____	3. psychiatrist	c.	uncensored expression
_____	4. clinical psychologist	d.	medical training
_____	5. insight therapy	e.	head
_____	6. free association	f.	general aspects of psychotherapy
_____	7. transference	g.	psychoanalysis
_____	8. resistance	h.	doctorate in psychology
_____	9. nonspecific factors	i.	defenses
_____	10. shrink	j.	homeless mentally ill

Mastering the material... Which answer makes the statement true?

_____ 1. Rod Plotnik begins the chapter with the true story of "Anna O." to make the point that
a. Freud had some notable failures as well as famous successes
b. talking about your problems seems to help
c. the real credit for inventing psychoanalysis should go to Dr. Breuer
d. talking won't help unless the client also does something positive

_____ 2. In the history of the treatment of mental illness, Dorothea Dix is famous for
a. charging admission to watch the crazy antics of the "lunatics"
b. inventing early treatment techniques like the strait jacket and bleeding
c. publicizing the terrible living conditions and cruel treatment of the mentally ill
d. emptying the mental hospitals of almost half of their patients

_____ 3. The discovery of antipsychotic drugs led directly to
a. deinstitutionalization
b. the reform movement
c. reinstitutionalization
d. the community mental health center

_____ 4. In order to become a ______________, you need a medical degree and a residency with further training in psychopathology and treatment
a. clinical psychologist
b. counseling psychologist
c. social worker
d. psychiatrist

_____ 5. When asked which approach they use in therapy, the majority of psychologists indicated a preference for the ______________ approach
a. psychodynamic
b. behavioral
c. eclectic
d. cognitive

____ 6. How effective is psychotherapy? Studies suggest that psychotherapy is
a. an effective treatment for many mental disorders
b. no more effective than just waiting
c. no more effective than doing nothing
d. successful in about 85% of all cases

____ 7. The reason why free association is crucial in psychoanalysis is that
a. in a long-term therapy, the patient is bound to stumble over the solution eventually
b. since the cost of psychoanalysis is so high, the patient should have the right to speak his or her mind
c. the unconscious resists associating with the ego
d. the unconscious, by definition, cannot be known directly

____ 8. The only one of the following who was a patient of Freud's was
a. Anna O.
b. the Rat Man
c. Dorothea Dix
d. Joseph Breuer

____ 9. All of the following are techniques of psychoanalysis *except*
a. free association
b. dream analysis
c. analysis of performance
d. analysis of transference

____ 10. Those embarrassing little slips of the tongue (or Freudian slips) can actually be valuable in therapy because they
a. reveal material you had decided not to tell your therapist
b. reflect thoughts and wishes that were unconscious
c. provide occasional lighter moments — a sort of comic relief
d. remind you that no one is perfect

____ 11. Analysis of transference is so important in psychoanalysis because
a. strong feelings are aroused, and they could get out of hand
b. loving or hating the therapist could torpedo the therapy
c. the transference relationship shows whether the client has the capacity for love
d. the transference relationship is a model of the client's actual past and present relationships

_____ 12. All of the following are true about psychoanalysis today *except*
   a. fewer clients seek psychoanalysis today
   b. psychoanalysis has been proven ineffective in treating mental disorders
   c. psychoanalysts are isolated in their "ivory towers"
   d. many clients receive drug treatment instead of psychoanalysis today

_____ 13. Rod Plotnik's fascinating example of the *balian*, a local healer in Bali, suggests that Western psychotherapy
   a. is another example of the superiority of modern medicine
   b. is superior because it assumes the problem is inside the sufferer
   c. may have evolved from the knowledge of folk healers like the balian
   d. may be a ritual of our own culture

_____ 14. All of the following are nonspecific factors in psychotherapy *except*
   a. a therapist who is sensitive to the client's thoughts and behaviors
   b. a client who is internally motivated to make changes
   c. a therapist who is intelligent enough to figure out what is wrong with the client
   d. a helping and supportive partnership between client and therapist

_____ 15. In order to be effective, the therapist needs two skills: (1) the ability to provide a good relationship, and (2) the ability to
   a. help the client deal with emotional feelings that come with transference
   b. spell out what the client is doing wrong, even if it is embarrassing or painful to the client
   c. analyze and explain the meaning of the client's dreams
   d. tolerate the abuse that clients often heap on their therapists

Module 30: Therapy II

I. **Behavior therapy**

A. Behavioral approach (classical and operant conditioning) applied to psychotherapy

1. Story of "**Little Albert**" (John B. Watson)

2. Emphasis on modifying observable behaviors

B. Treatment of phobias

1. **Desensitization**

a. Relaxation

b. Stimulus hierarchy

c. Desensitization training

2. **Flooding**

C. Behavior therapy today

1. Advantages

a. Strong experimental foundation

b. Emphasis on evaluation of results

c. Widespread applications

2. Criticisms

a. Failure to examine underlying factors

b. Neglect of therapist-client relationship

c. Neglect of cognitive factors [rise of cognitive-behavior therapy]

Use this

Outline

to organize your studying. Write notes on it. Turn it into a personalized aid for effective learning.

II. **Cognitive therapy**

A. Basic assumptions

1. Our thoughts shape our emotions and our actions

2. Our beliefs and assumptions shape how we perceive and interpret events

3. Our distorted thoughts can lead to a number of different kinds of disorders

B. **Rational-emotive therapy (Albert Ellis)**

1. Problem is irrational interpretation of experience

2. **ABC theory of emotions**

a. **A**ctivating event

b. **B**elief triggered by the event

c. **C**onsequent emotional feelings

C. **Cognitive therapy (Aaron Beck)**

1. Negative automatic thoughts

2. Treatment of depression

III. Humanistic therapy

A. Basic assumptions: emphasis on...

1. Positive, creative side of human nature

2. Personal growth and **self-actualization**

3. Freedom of choice and importance of the future

B. **Person-centered therapy (Carl Rogers)**

1. Nondirective, supportive

2. Therapist's characteristics

   a. Empathy

   b. Positive regard

   c. Genuineness

3. Influence on psychotherapy and counseling

IV. Review of psychotherapy

A. Major schools of psychotherapy

1. **Psychoanalysis**

2. **Person-centered** therapy

3. **Behavior** therapy

4. **Cognitive** therapy

B. Effectiveness of psychotherapy

1. Specific applications

2. **Nonspecific factors** (common to all therapies)

V. *Applying/Exploring:* Cognitive-behavior techniques

A. **Thought stopping**

1. Self-monitoring (to establish baseline) of depressive thoughts

2. Yelling "stop" and counting to ten

3. Substituting positive thoughts

B. **Thought substitution**

1. Self-monitoring of irrational thoughts

2. Composing matching list of rational thoughts

3. Practice (and reward) substituting rational thoughts whenever irrational thoughts occur

Now take the
Self-Tests
to check your understanding and mastery of this module.

Getting the general idea... Is the statement true or false?

_____ 1. In the case history transcripts Rod Plotnik quotes, the therapists all sound very much alike.

_____ 2. The desensitization technique is essentially an unlearning experience.

_____ 3. Flooding is like desensitization, just all at once.

_____ 4. Critics charge that behavior therapy devotes too much time and energy into discovering the hidden causes of problem behaviors.

_____ 5. Critics also charge that behavior therapy neglects the way clients think about their problems.

_____ 6. Behavior therapy attempts to modify behavior: cognitive therapy attempts to modify thoughts and ideas.

_____ 7. Humanistic therapy starts with the idea that people have an innate tendency to grow through developing their natural potential.

_____ 8. Person-centered therapy avoids giving directions, advice, or disapproval.

_____ 9. Throughout the history of modern psychology, psychoanalysis has been the dominant form of psychotherapy.

_____ 10. Every specific form of treatment must solve the problem of how to overcome the "nonspecific factors" in psychotherapy.

Knowing the essential vocabulary... Which phrase matches the term?

	Term		Phrase
_____	1. behavior therapy	a.	Albert Ellis
_____	2. desensitization	b.	your worst nightmare, all at once
_____	3. flooding	c.	Carl Rogers
_____	4. behavior therapy	d.	problems are learned and unlearned
_____	5. rational-emotive therapy	e.	cramming for the exam
_____	6. cognitive therapy	f.	relaxation and stimulus hierarchy
_____	7. person-centered therapy	g.	desensitization
_____	8. thought stopping	h.	be more realistic
_____	9. thought substitution	i.	Aaron Beck
_____	10. thought numbing	j.	just say no

Mastering the material... Which answer makes the statement true?

____ 1. Rod Plotnik begins the module with the famous case of Little Albert to show that
a. the ethical standards of psychological research are much more stringent today
b. psychological problems affect babies as well as children and adults
c. the fear of rats is almost natural and may be inborn
d. psychological problems can be viewed as learned behavior

____ 2. Behavior therapy differs from psychoanalysis in all of the following ways *except*
a. it creates a warm and supportive therapeutic atmosphere
b. it is based on the principles of classical and operant conditioning
c. it emphasizes treatment of specific behaviors
d. it does not focus on mental events or underlying unconscious factors

____ 3. Which one of the following is *not* a step in the desensitization procedure?
a. relaxation
b. stimulus hierarchy
c. stimulus sensitizing
d. desensitization training

____ 4. The flooding technique works because
a. when it's sink or swim, you are likely to swim
b. if you can cut down the number of sessions, you can save a lot of money, so you are more highly motivated to change
c. you feel silly doing something like holding a container of blood for several hours, so you agree to give up the phobia
d. you can't stay terrified indefinitely, so you learn that you aren't really hopelessly afraid of the phobic object

____ 5. Desensitization and flooding are similar procedures in that they both
a. proceed gradually
b. are techniques of exposure
c. force clients to face up to their fears
d. get at underlying unconscious causes of fear

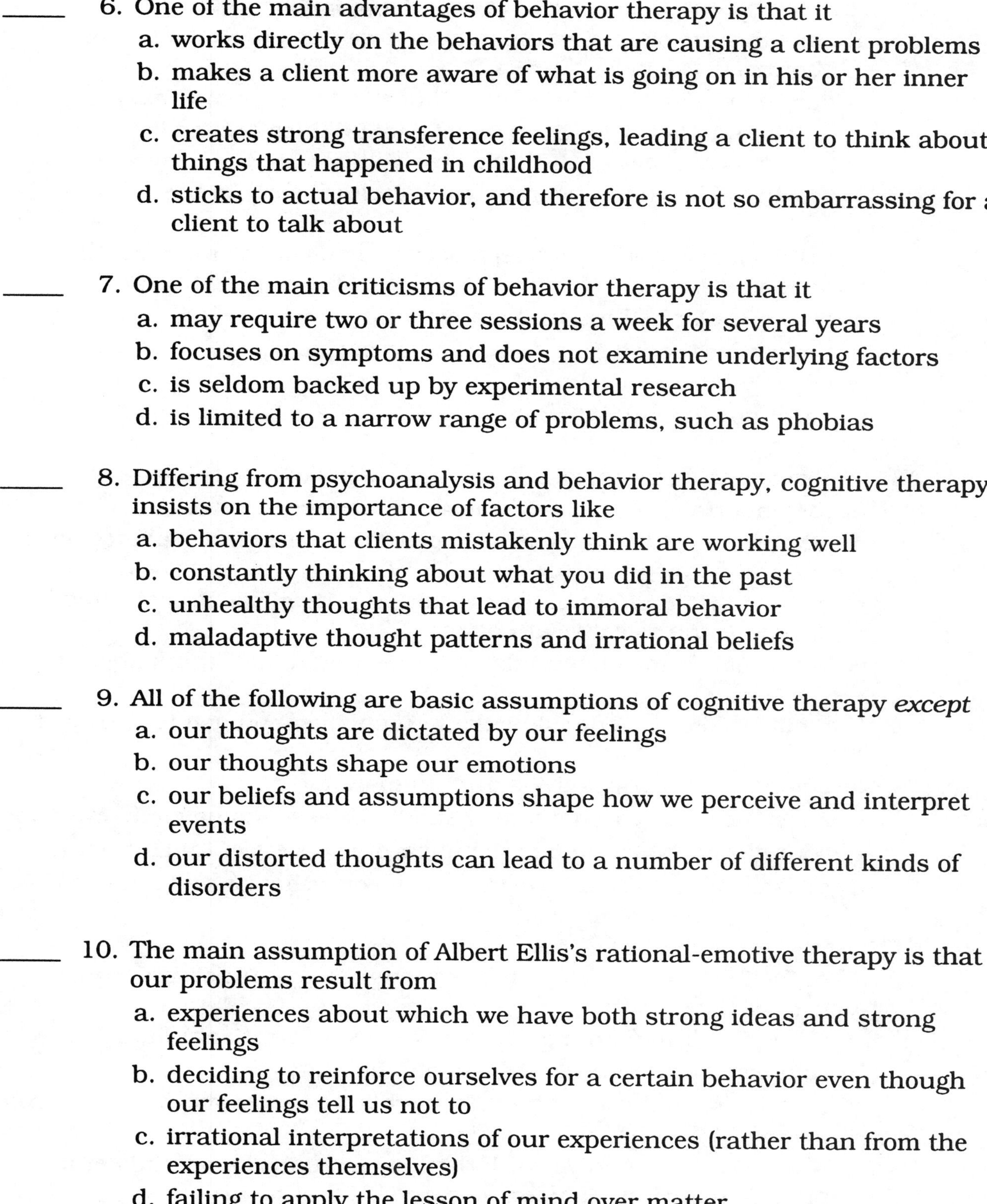

_____ 6. One of the main advantages of behavior therapy is that it
a. works directly on the behaviors that are causing a client problems
b. makes a client more aware of what is going on in his or her inner life
c. creates strong transference feelings, leading a client to think about things that happened in childhood
d. sticks to actual behavior, and therefore is not so embarrassing for a client to talk about

_____ 7. One of the main criticisms of behavior therapy is that it
a. may require two or three sessions a week for several years
b. focuses on symptoms and does not examine underlying factors
c. is seldom backed up by experimental research
d. is limited to a narrow range of problems, such as phobias

_____ 8. Differing from psychoanalysis and behavior therapy, cognitive therapy insists on the importance of factors like
a. behaviors that clients mistakenly think are working well
b. constantly thinking about what you did in the past
c. unhealthy thoughts that lead to immoral behavior
d. maladaptive thought patterns and irrational beliefs

_____ 9. All of the following are basic assumptions of cognitive therapy *except*
a. our thoughts are dictated by our feelings
b. our thoughts shape our emotions
c. our beliefs and assumptions shape how we perceive and interpret events
d. our distorted thoughts can lead to a number of different kinds of disorders

_____ 10. The main assumption of Albert Ellis's rational-emotive therapy is that our problems result from
a. experiences about which we have both strong ideas and strong feelings
b. deciding to reinforce ourselves for a certain behavior even though our feelings tell us not to
c. irrational interpretations of our experiences (rather than from the experiences themselves)
d. failing to apply the lesson of mind over matter

_____ 11. The idea behind Ellis's "ABC" theory of emotions is that
  a. emotions are simple to understand if we don't try to be too logical about it
  b. our feelings are mainly the result of our beliefs about things
  c. we should Always Be Calm (most people get so excited by every problem that they can't think clearly about it)
  d. we should learn to understand our feelings early in life

_____ 12. Aaron Beck discovered that depressed people tend to interpret the world through
  a. carefully planned negative statements
  b. thoughtless repetitions of what other people believe
  c. secretly hostile beliefs
  d. negative automatic thoughts

_____ 13. In his cognitive therapy, Beck attempts to make clients aware of
  a. the importance of education in the contemporary world
  b. adaptive thought patterns like open-mindedness, acceptance, love, and will power
  c. maladaptive thought patterns like overgeneralization, polarized thinking, and selective attention
  d. how much better they could be if they would just "think about it"

_____ 14. The main difference offered by the humanistic approach to therapy is its
  a. emphasis on the positive side of human nature
  b. insistence that psychotherapy should be essentially free to everyone
  c. courageous exploration of the unsavory aspects of human nature
  d. insistence that therapy keep its focus on behavior and not become lost in the mental maze of thoughts

_____ 15. All of the following are steps in the thought substitution procedure *except*
  a. through self-monitoring, write a list of your irrational thoughts
  b. compose a matching list of rational thoughts
  c. practice substituting rational thoughts whenever you have irrational ones
  d. whenever you catch yourself thinking irrationally, administer a predetermined punishment (e.g., no TV that night)

For psych majors only... Reviewing the story

In this chapter you meet many famous and intriguing characters from the history of psychology. People like Anna O., the Rat Man, and Little Albert (almost sounds like a circus, doesn't it?).

If you were to arrange these names in historical order, as I have done below, you could construct a capsule history of the development of modern psychotherapy.

Try it. Match each name to the most appropriate phrase. As you do so, see if you can tell yourself the story of how the four strands of modern psychotherapy emerged, and how they differ from each other.

_____	1. Dorothea Dix	a. free association and transference
_____	2. Anna O.	b. conditioned to fear a rat
_____	3. Sigmund Freud	c. overcoming depressive thoughts
_____	4. the Rat Man	d. hysterical symptoms
_____	5. John B. Watson	e. "I'll get you, you dirty rat!"
_____	6. Little Albert	f. counteracting irrational thinking
_____	7. Carl Rogers	g. cruel treatment of lunatics
_____	8. Albert Ellis	h. all behavior is learned
_____	9. Aaron Beck	i. bizarre nature of the unconscious
_____	10. James Cagney	j. development of full human potential

Answers for Chapter 15

Module 29

True-False	Matching	Multiple-Choice
1. T	1. j	1. b
2. F	2. a	2. c
3. F	3. d	3. a
4. T	4. h	4. d
5. F	5. g	5. c
6. T	6. c	6. a
7. F	7. b	7. d
8. T	8. i	8. b
9. F	9. f	9. c
10. F	10. e	10. b
		11. d
		12. b
		13. d
		14. c
		15. a

Module 30

True-False	Matching	Multiple-Choice
1. F	1. d	1. d
2. T	2. f	2. a
3. T	3. b	3. c
4. F	4. g	4. d
5. T	5. a	5. b
6. T	6. i	6. a
7. T	7. c	7. b
8. T	8. j	8. d
9. F	9. h	9. a
10. F	10. e	10. c
		11. b
		12. d
		13. c
		14. a
		15. d

For psych majors only...Reviewing the story

1. g 2. d 3. a 4. i 5. h 6. b 7. j 8. f 9. c 10. e

Chapter 16: Social Psychology

The chapter that was difficult because it was so easy

Well, not really easy — you'll have to study this chapter as carefully as the others — but obvious, in a sense. One of the difficulties in studying social psychology is that so many of the facts and ideas it presents seem like things you already know. That makes it hard to get a handle on what to "learn." Here's an idea that may make it easier.

Because you are a human being, you have been a social psychologist all your life. If there is one essential human skill, it is how to live with each other. I don't mean this in a preachy way, but in the sense that our instincts, what few we have, tell us very little about interacting with others. Therefore, we must learn to observe, understand, and predict what other people will do (and what we will do) in any given situation. We soon become experts in human interaction. See? You've been studying this stuff all your life.

The beauty of social psychology is that it can take us outside ourselves and help us see our behavior more objectively, and hence more clearly. Such awareness, which social psychology owes to anthropology and sociology, helps correct the tendency of psychology to focus too much on individual, internal factors. There's a price you pay for this insight, however. Theories in social psychology typically involve fancy names and complicated explanations. Don't be afraid. The social psychologists you'll study are talking about what you do every day. Try to understand it that way. Give yourself credit for understanding what seems obvious. Translate what does not seem clear into the language of your own experience.

Effective Student Tip 16

Take Teachers, Not Courses

Take some courses far from your major area of study. Some advisors will urge you to take only courses that fit into your major, but that can be a mistake. One of the purposes of higher education is to broaden your horizons and show you worlds you scarcely know exist. When else will you have the opportunity to investigate ancient history, nutrition, figure drawing, astronomy, women's literature, and other fascinating but unrequired subjects?

Graduate students, who have been through it all and know all there is to know (just ask them), often say you should "take teachers, not courses." What they mean is that you should sign up for professors with reputations as especially stimulating teachers, without too much regard for how well the interesting courses fit into your official program.

You will come to know quite a bit about the faculty at your school. Some professors will begin to stand out as people you would like to study with and get to know. Try to give yourself at least a few of these experiences. You might learn more from an inspired teacher in an unrequired course than from an average teacher in the course that fits so neatly into your major.

P.S.

Whew! We have almost reached our destination. I hope it has been as interesting and productive a journey for you as it has been for me. The thought of you working through this Study Guide kept me going as I struggled to finish it. I also hope you will use some of the ideas in the "Effective Student Tips" in your new courses next term.

Meanwhile, good luck on your finals! You've gotten this far, so I am sure you will do well.

Module 31: Social Cognition

Use this

Outline

to organize your studying. Write notes on it. Turn it into a personalized aid for effective learning.

I. Person perception

  A. Ingredients of perceiving people

    1. Hidden characteristics

    2. Two-way process

    3. Seeking causes

    4. Social consequences

  B. **Stereotypes**

    1. Prejudice

    2. Discrimination

  C. **Schemas**

    1. Kinds of schemas

      a. Person schemas

      b. Role schemas

      c. Event schemas (or **scripts**)

    2. Functions of schemas

      a. Influence social interactions

      b. Influence memory

      c. Persist and resist change

    3. Schemas and sexism

II. **Attribution** — explaining to ourselves why people behave as they do

A. Implicit personality theories (people as naive scientists)

B. Attribution theory (process of finding causes for people's behavior)

1. Disposition

2. Situation

C. Factors that influence attributions

1. Basic question: is the explanation **dispositional** or **situational**?

2. How we should answer the question: according to the **covariation principle** (Harold Kelley), we should look for...

a. Consensus

b. Consistency

c. Distinctiveness

D. Biases and errors in attribution

1. **Cognitive miser model**

2. Typical cognitive shortcuts

a. **Fundamental attribution error**

b. **Actor-observer effect**

c. **Self-serving bias**

E. Attributions and grades — how attributions influence behavior

III. **Attitudes**

A. Components of attitudes

1. Cognitive

2. Affective

3. Behavioral

B. Attitudes and behavior

1. Predicting behavior
2. Functions of attitudes
    a. Utilitarian
    b. Defensive
    c. Social-adjustive
    d. Value-expressive

C. **Persuasion**

1. Two routes to persuasion
    a. Central
    b. Peripheral
2. Elements affecting persuasion
    a. Source
    b. Message
    c. Audience

D. Attitude change

1. **Cognitive dissonance** (Leon Festinger) — *attitudes determine behavior*
    a. Adding new beliefs or changing old beliefs
    b. **Counterattitudinal behavior** (lying about a boring task)
2. **Self-perception theory** (Daryl Bem) — *behavior determines attitudes*

IV. *Applying/Exploring:* Making an impression

A. **Impression management** (or **self-presentation**)

1. Motivation

a. Self-esteem

b. Self-consistency

2. Success and failure

B. Attractiveness — *what is beautiful is good*

For psych majors only...

The classic experiments in social psychology are among the most elegant in psychology, if not in all of science, but they may seem complicated on first reading. Go through the explanations in the text more than once, and make sure you understand the logic of each experiment. The research Rod Plotnik writes about is well worth understanding and remembering. These experiments are important building blocks of modern psychology, and you will come across them repeatedly in your further studies.

Now take the **Self-Tests** to check your understanding and mastery of this module.

Getting the general idea... Is the statement true or false?

_____ 1. When we perceive another person, we feel a strong need to be able to explain *why* the person behaves as he or she does.

_____ 2. The words "prejudice" and "discrimination" mean the same thing.

_____ 3. A schema is an unfair stereotype we apply to a person who is different.

_____ 4. Attributions are our attempts to understand and explain people's behavior.

_____ 5. The "fundamental attribution error" is the tendency to explain behavior by choosing dispositional causes over situational causes.

_____ 6. An attitude is a tendency to respond to others in a quirky, overly-sensitive manner.

_____ 7. Advice for all you budding politicians: if the facts are on your side, take the central route to persuasion, if not, take the peripheral route.

_____ 8. Cognitive dissonance occurs when an audience hears so many contradictory arguments that they lose sight of the main issue.

_____ 9. Social psychologists agree that attitudes and behavior are closely related, but they disagree about whether attitudes determine behavior or behavior determines attitudes.

_____ 10. Humankind, in its eternal folly, adheres to the rule that what is beautiful is good.

Knowing the essential vocabulary... Which phrase matches the term?

	Term		Phrase
_____	1. stereotypes	a.	central route and peripheral route
_____	2. schema	b.	behavior determines attitudes
_____	3. attribution	c.	good
_____	4. attitude	d.	they lied for only a dollar
_____	5. persuasion	e.	that last psych test
_____	6. cognitive dissonance	f.	information filter
_____	7. self-perception theory	g.	to maintain our self-esteem
_____	8. impression management	h.	honors student = nerd; jock = dumb
_____	9. beautiful	i.	cognitive, affective, and behavioral
_____	10. ugly	j.	explains causes of behavior

Mastering the material... Which answer makes the statement true?

_____ 1. Rod Plotnik writes about the female neurosurgeon who was subjected to sexual harassment in order to make the point that
   a. pioneers in any previously closed field are always subjected to ill treatment
   b. men just can't imagine a woman being a neurosurgeon
   c. how people behave is more significant than what they believe
   d. how we perceive and evaluate others has powerful consequences

_____ 2. All of the following are negative aspects of person perception *except*
   a. stereotypes
   b. schemas
   c. discrimination
   d. prejudice

_____ 3. We often ask someone we have just met, "What do you do?" so that we can get more information about the person by drawing on
   a. person schemas
   b. role schemas
   c. event schemas
   d. scripts

_____ 4. A social psychologist might speculate that the female neurosurgeon's male colleagues called her "honey" because
   a. their schemas about women were sexist
   b. their perception of her was strongly influenced by her obvious attractiveness
   c. in high pressure situations like surgery people diffuse tension by using blunt language
   d. their schemas about the profession of medicine called for informality and closeness among doctors on the job

_____ 5. When you read about the female umpire who can't get into the major leagues, the social-psychological process called ______________ made it impossible for you to think, "I don't understand why she is stuck in the minors and I don't care."
   a. person perception
   b. scripting
   c. attribution
   d. stereotyping

_____ 6. Social psychologists say that whenever we try to understand a person's behavior we ask
a. what schema best explains the person's motivation
b. what reinforcements and punishments the person has experienced in the past
c. whether our answer should emphasize distinctiveness or consistency
d. whether the explanation should be dispositional or situational

_____ 7. The fundamental attribution error is explaining behavior by
a. choosing dispositional causes over situational ones
b. choosing situational causes over dispositional ones
c. citing the actor-observer effect
d. falling back on the self-serving bias

_____ 8. "I creamed the chem exam because I studied my a— off! The psych exam I flunked? Well, you know he always asks real tricky questions." [Sounds like the _____________ in action, doesn't it?]
a. fundamental attribution error
b. actor-observer effect
c. self-serving bias
d. whiner effect

_____ 9. An attitude has each of the following *except*
a. a cognitive component
b. a genetic component
c. an affective component
d. a behavioral component

_____ 10. Terri's strong attitudes about animal rights made her shun the use makeup; this is an example of the _____________ function of attitudes
a. utilitarian
b. defensive
c. social-adjustive
d. value-expressive

____ 11. Roberta Reformer, who has an excellent plan for better government, will take the ______________ route to persuasion; her opponent, Boss Bluster, who plans to label her a bra-burning radical, will take the ______________ route

a. direct ... indirect
b. honest ... dishonest
c. central ... peripheral
d. logical ... emotional

____ 12. In Leon Festinger's famous experiment about a boring task, the subjects who were paid only $1 to tell other students it was interesting (a lie) dealt with their cognitive dissonance by

a. convincing themselves that it was somewhat interesting after all
b. finding the students they lied to and explaining that it was just part of the experiment
c. insisting that they should also be paid $20 for telling the lie
d. begging Festinger and his assistants not to reveal their names

____ 13. Daryl Bem (self-perception theory) would interpret the above experiment somewhat differently, based on his belief that

a. we first consult our attitudes, then adjust our behavior accordingly
b. we first observe our behavior, then infer what our attitudes must be, given that behavior
c. we constantly observe our emotional state and adjust our attitudes to take account of our feelings
d. experiments based on deception may not reveal the truth about human behavior

____ 14. Most professors work at it, fraternities and sororities deliberately teach it... heck, we all do it — we're talking about

a. counterattitudinal behavior
b. self-consistency
c. impression management
d. self-concealment

____ 15. Call it depressing if you wish, but again and again research has shown that people are susceptible to the stereotype that

a. once a person makes up his or her mind, nothing will change it
b. insecure people will do anything to make a good impression
c. nothing succeeds like success
d. what is beautiful is good

Module 32: Social Behavior

I. Public and private self

A. Self-monitoring

1. **High self-monitors**

2. **Low self-monitors**

B. **Self-handicapping**

II. Social influences

A. **Conformity** (Solomon Asch)

1. **Compliance**

2. **Foot-in-the-door technique**

B. **Obedience** (Stanley Milgram)

1. The famous experiment on giving electric shocks

2. Interpreting Milgram's results

3. A new ethics of laboratory research

III. Group dynamics

A. Powerful influence of **group** membership

1. Group cohesion

2. Group norms

B. Why people form groups

1. Need for love and belonging (Maslow)

2. **Social comparison theory** (Festinger)

Use this **Outline** to organize your studying. Write notes on it. Turn it into a personalized aid for effective learning.

C. Types of groups [guess which one you should pick to study in!]

1. **Task oriented**

2. **Socially oriented**

D. Group behaviors — effects of the presence of others

1. **Social facilitation**

2. Crowds (**deindividuation**)

3. **Bystander effect**

a. Informational influence theory

b. Diffusion of responsibility theory

E. Group decisions

1. **Group polarization**

2. **Groupthink**

F. Helping (**prosocial behavior** and **altruism**)

1. Motivations for helping

a. Empathy

b. Feelings of personal distress

c. Norms and values

2. Explanations of the decision to help

a. **Decision stage model** (go through 5 stages)

b. **Arousal-cost-reward model** (calculate costs and rewards of helping)

IV. Aggression

A. Explanations of **aggressive behavior**

1. Biological theory
2. **Frustration-aggression hypothesis**
3. Social learning theory (observation, imitation, reinforcement)
4. Cognitive theory (**scripts**)

B. Sexual aggression — **rape**

1. Kinds of rapists
   a. Power rapist
   b. Sadistic rapist
   c. Anger rapist
   d. Date rapist
2. **Rape myths**

V. *Applying/Exploring:* Controlling aggression

A. **Catharsis** (draining off or releasing emotional tension)

B. Anger control in children

1. Social-cognitive deficits
2. Program to teach children how to control their anger and aggressive behavior

C. Anger control in adults

D. Avoiding date rape and sexual aggression

1. Knowing the risk factors

2. Strategy of increasingly forceful rejection of unwanted advances

3. Assertiveness training

Now take the **Self-Tests** to check your understanding and mastery of this module.

Getting the general idea... Is the statement true or false?

_____ 1. If you have gotten this far in the *Study Guide*, it is unlikely that you engage in self-handicapping behavior.

_____ 2. Group pressure can make a person conform to a statement or "fact" that is clearly and obviously incorrect.

_____ 3. The famous "electric shock" experiment showed that if you pay people enough they will follow just about any orders.

_____ 4. You might benefit from preparing for the psych final by joining a study group — just be sure to pick a friendly, socially oriented group.

_____ 5. It is the social-psychological phenomenon of deindividuation that can make a crowd dangerous.

_____ 6. Because of the pooling of many talents and ideas, group decisions are usually superior to individual decisions.

_____ 7. The arousal-cost-reward model of prosocial behavior provides a good example of altruism in action.

_____ 8. Healthy women cannot be raped against their will.

_____ 9. Since aggression is an inborn biological fact, it is almost impossible to get aggressive children to change their behavior.

_____ 10. Good advice on how to avoid date rape: know the risk factors and meet unwanted advances with increasing forcefulness.

Knowing the essential vocabulary... Which phrase matches the term?

_____	1. high self-monitors	a. "Well, I guess line #3 is the same"
_____	2. self-handicapping	b. behavior in a riot
_____	3. conformity	c. getting stoned before the final exam
_____	4. obedience	d. the teens didn't tell about the murder
_____	5. group cohesion	e. final exams are coming up
_____	6. task oriented	f. "Who was that masked man?"
_____	7. deindividuation	g. laugh at jokes they don't find funny
_____	8. groupthink	h. "I've been ordered to give you a shock"
_____	9. altruism	i. more heads don't always work better
_____	10. all-too-truism	j. kind of study group you should join

Mastering the material... Which answer makes the statement true?

____ 1. A social psychologist might cite the ____________ as an example of _____ self-monitors
   a. Cleaver family ... low
   b. Beverly Hillbillies ... high
   c. Jeffersons ... low
   d. Adams family ... low

____ 2. We all know people who engage in obvious self-handicapping behavior, but why do they do it? Most likely to
   a. punish themselves for imagined sins and transgressions
   b. protect their sense of self-esteem from public failure
   c. call attention to their insecurities and fears
   d. gain sympathy and understanding from others

____ 3. The reason why over 900 people died at Jonestown was that they
   a. were machine-gunned to death
   b. believed a magic spell would protect them from harm
   c. thought the poison they were drinking was a harmless punch
   d. did what they were told

____ 4. When Solomon Asch had his confederates deliberately choose an obviously incorrect matching line, the lone naive subject in the experiment _________ went along with the group
   a. always
   b. never
   c. often
   d. rarely

____ 5. Tell you what... before you quit just do one more of these questions, O.K.? [I'm using the ____________ technique on you in my efforts to get you to do all the questions.]
   a. foot-in-the-door
   b. compliance
   c. conformity
   d. soft-soaping

_____ 6. In Stanley Milgram's electric shock experiment, most subjects continued to give shocks
a. only up to the point they considered dangerous
b. even beyond the point they believed was dangerous
c. only if they had been paid a considerable amount to participate in the experiment
d. only as long as the shocks seemed to be helping the "learner" do better

_____ 7. Milgram's experiment, one of the most famous in social psychology, could not be conducted today because
a. a new code of ethics screens experiments for potential harm to the subjects
b. the experiment has been so widely written about (as in your textbook) that everyone is in on the secret
c. psychologists have gained such a reputation for deception that few would be fooled by the fake lab
d. after the rebellious sixties and the "me" generation, people just aren't inclined to obey orders anymore

_____ 8. American troops were stunningly effective in the Gulf War. A social psychologist might attribute their success to all of the following *except*
a. group cohesion
b. group norms
c. social orientation
d. task orientation

_____ 9. The phenomenon of _______________ helps explain why people will do things in a mob that they would never do on their own
a. social facilitation
b. deindividuation
c. social inhibition
d. the bystander effect

_____ 10. Why do most people walk around a person lying on a crowded street and not stop to help? Social psychologists have cited all of the following *except*
a. the bystander effect
b. the informational influence theory
c. the diffusion of responsibility theory
d. the cynical citizen effect

_____ 11. Which one of the following decisions is a prime example of groupthink?
a. the atomic bombing of Japan in World War II
b. the assassination of President Kennedy
c. the Bay of Pigs invasion of Cuba
d. the withdrawal of Ross Perot from the presidential race

_____ 12. Altruism is one kind of prosocial behavior, different in that it is
a. done without expectation of material or social reward
b. an outcome of the decision stage process
c. an outcome of the arousal-cost-reward process
d. a sudden, spontaneous deed that the actor often cannot explain later

_____ 13. Which one of the following statements about aggression would social psychologists be *least* likely to accept today?
a. aggression occurs when our goals are blocked and we become frustrated and angry
b. aggression is learned through observation and imitation
c. aggression can be controlled by draining off or releasing emotional tension
d. aggression is directed by mental scripts stored in memory and used as guides for behavior and social problem solving

_____ 14. The reason why rape is so prevalent in our society is that
a. there are several motivations for rape — the least of which is sexual drive
b. women are much bolder today, yet still like to be actively pursued, a situation that leaves men confused about what women really want
c. advertising, cable TV, provocative clothing, etc., keep our sexual urges in a state of almost constant arousal
d. unfortunately, rape is as natural as male hormones and female flirtatiousness — but it probably gets reported more often today

_____ 15. Good advice for avoiding date rape would include all of the following *except*
a. learn, and avoid, the risk factors associated with date rape
b. only date men you have met once or twice before
c. learn to recognize the cues and clearly put a stop to unwanted sexual advances
d. use a strategy of increasing forcefulness, finally including physical force, if necessary

Answers for Chapter 16

Module 31

True-False	Matching	Multiple-Choice
1. T	1. h	1. d
2. F	2. f	2. b
3. F	3. j	3. b
4. T	4. i	4. a
5. T	5. a	5. c
6. F	6. d	6. d
7. T	7. b	7. a
8. F	8. g	8. c
9. T	9. c	9. b
10. T	10. e	10. d
		11. c
		12. a
		13. b
		14. c
		15. d

Module 32

True-False	Matching	Multiple-Choice
1. T	1. g	1. d
2. T	2. c	2. b
3. F	3. a	3. d
4. F	4. h	4. c
5. T	5. d	5. a
6. F	6. j	6. b
7. F	7. b	7. a
8. F	8. i	8. c
9. F	9. f	9. b
10. T	10. e	10. d
		11. c
		12. a
		13. c
		14. a
		15. b

Guide for Nonnative Speakers

by Laurie Blass

INTRODUCTION

This Guide for Nonnative Speakers is intended for students whose first language is not English. It is also appropriate for native speakers who feel they could benefit from additional language help. The guide includes the following features:

- **Idiomatic Expressions**, definitions of phrasal verbs and other idioms frequently not found in dictionaries
- **Guessing from Context**, an exercise that develops the skill of guessing new word meanings in context
- **Structural Clues**, exercises designed to increase reading speed and comprehension by helping students recognize difficult grammatical points and rhetorical devices such as the passive voice, cause-effect relationships, and transitional words and expressions
- **Terms in Cultural Context**, background information on cultural terms that are not defined in the text
- **Informal Usage**, which points out the use of slang expressions
- **Vocabulary** and **Concept Review** exercises

We recommend the following procedure for using this guide with *Introduction to Psychology*:

Step 1: Do a quick review of the assigned chapter. Familiarize yourself with the contents by reading heads, subheads, picture captions, and marginal text. Don't read the chapter word-for-word, and use the dictionary as little as possible at this point.

Step 2: Read through the corresponding material in this guide. Pay particular attention to the **Idiomatic Expressions** and **Cultural**

Concepts sections; find these items in your text using the page references and study their contexts.

Step 3: Now do a careful, word-for-word reading of the chapter.

Step 4: Complete the remaining exercises in this guide, including the **Vocabulary** and **Concept Reviews.**

Step 5: Read the text carefully a second time. This time, do the Summary Self-Tests and the Concept Glossary quizzes, and do the corresponding material in the regular *Study Guide* (that is, preceding this Guide for Nonnative Speakers).

Note: You may also find it useful to form study groups with native speakers.

Chapter 1: Discovering Psychology

IDIOMATIC EXPRESSIONS

Many idiomatic expressions in English are actually **phrasal verbs**, verb phrases composed of one or more verbs and a preposition. An example is *to touch on,* on page 5 of your text. As the author uses it in your text, it means to talk about something.

It's not always easy to guess the meanings of phrasal verbs in context (that is, as a part of the whole sentence or paragraph in which they occur). There are many of these expressions throughout the text; the most difficult in Chapter 1 are listed here. Some of them have more than one meaning; the definition given here on the right is for the way the author uses the expression in this chapter.

Phrasal verbs:

to get along with someone (p. 4)	To have a good relationship with someone
to focus on (p. 5)	To examine; to study
to fight off (p. 6)	To resist
to break down (p. 12)	To separate into categories
to build something **into** something (p. 18)	To make it a part of
to keep track of (p. 18)	To keep a record of
to make up (p. 26)	To invent
to rule out (p. 32)	To eliminate

Other expressions in Chapter 1:

to run in families (p. 20)	To be hereditary
to bring an amount of money (p. 24)	To be worth

to pinpoint something (p. 28)	To indicate something specific
to keep someone **in the dark** (p. 36)	Not to reveal information

GUESSING FROM CONTEXT

You won't find the following words and expressions from Chapter 1 in the Concept/Glossary section (at the end of each chapter), but they are useful in reading, writing, and talking about psychology and other academic subjects. See if you can guess their meanings by studying their contexts (their relationship to the words around them).

To do this, first find the word or expression in your text and guess its meaning using the clues in the context. You may find clues in an explanation that immediately follows the word, in a synonym that appears nearby, or in the form of examples.

Sometimes, this is easy. **Artificial intelligence** (p. 17) is an example—when you first see the term, you may not know what it means. But if you continue to read, you see that it is defined in the material that follows it—it's something that combines "knowledge of the brain's functions with computer programming to duplicate 'human' thinking and intelligence."

Other terms are a little harder to figure out. For example, you may not understand **megadose** (p. 22) when you first see it, but if you continue to read the entire section on Linus Pauling, you find the word two more times, and the meaning becomes clearer and clearer in each context—it's a large amount of something you take, such as a vitamin or a drug.

Now, write down your own definitions of the following words. Then ask a native speaker what they mean, or look them up in a dictionary to see if your guesses were correct.

to dread (p. 3)

stressors (p. 6)

rigorous (p. 9)

pioneering (p. 11)

compelled (p. 34)

safeguards (p. 36)

STRUCTURAL CLUES

Academic writers, particularly those in the natural and social sciences, tend to use the **passive voice** in constructing sentences. In a passive sentence, the object of the main verb in the sentence is in the subject position (the beginning of the sentence). In addition, the verb is in the form of *to be* + past participle. The **agent** of the verb (the person or thing causing the action of the verb) is often not stated.

Here's an example of the passive voice from Chapter 1 of your textbook:

Object of verb-->	Five-year-old Patrick
Verb-->	is considered a "high-functioning" autistic child . . . (p. 3)

When you read a sentence like this one, you know it's in the passive voice because of the verb form— "is considered." The sentence doesn't say *who* considers Patrick a high-functioning autistic child, but we can easily guess ("doctors," "psychologists," "experts," etc.). Social science writers often don't mention the agent when it isn't important.

Passive constructions can sometimes slow down your reading and comprehension if you get confused about "who's doing what to whom." The best way to avoid this confusion is to note whether the main verb is in the past participle form and is preceded by a form of *to be*. If so, the sentence is probably passive and the agent is probably not as important as the *object* of the main verb. With practice, you can quickly identify the passive sentences you encounter and increase your reading speed and comprehension.

Practice this skill by reading the following sentences. Some of the sentences are passive, and some are active. Underline the main verb (including all forms of *to be*), and write "passive" or "active" on the lines that follow the sentences.

1. The negative side is that our behaviors might be controlled without our knowledge or intention. (p. 4) ________________________

2. These kinds of study habits would be greatly improved by the behavioral approach . . . (p. 7) ________________________

3. Unlike Wundt, who divided the mind into distinct elements, James viewed mental activity as a continuous flow . . . (p. 12)

____

4. The basic ingredient of rhino horn, keratin, has been shown to have no proven medicinal powers. (p. 24) ________________________

5. A success story of this use of correlations involves cigarette smoking. (p. 28) ________________________

TERMS IN CULTURAL CONTEXT

Do you know the following cultural terms and concepts? Guess their meanings first, and then look at the explanations on the right.

inner-city (p. 10)	The central part of a large city; often unattractive or dangerous.
marathon runners (p. 13)	People who run long-distance races, called marathons.
the Super Bowl (p. 28)	The final and most important football game of the season. The Super Bowl game is played by the teams from each league (the National Football League and the American Football League) that have won the most games that season.

INFORMAL USAGE

Are you familiar with the following informal expressions? Study them in context. Try to guess their meanings, and then look them up in a current dictionary or ask a native speaker.

a quack (p. 22) **to cram** (p. 39)

VOCABULARY REVIEW

Use each of the following terms in an original sentence. Your sentences can be about something in your personal life or about the chapter topic.

to focus on	**to rule out**
to pinpoint something	**to run in someone's family**
rigorous	**interact**

CONCEPT REVIEW

Below, you will see references to particular material in Chapter 1. Review the material, and then answer the questions by giving examples from your culture and/or your personal experience.

(p. 10, pars. 1-8): Have cultural differences ever created problems for you in classroom situations? If so, give an example.

(p. 15, pars. 1-2): Are you planning a career in psychology? If so, in what area?

Chapter 2: Biological Bases of Behavior

IDIOMATIC EXPRESSIONS

The following are some of the more difficult phrasal verbs and idiomatic expressions in Chapter 2. Some of them have more than one meaning; the definition given here on the right is for the way the author uses the expression in this chapter.

Phrasal verbs:

to carry out a job, an activity (p. 42)	To perform
to account for (p. 44)	To be responsible for
to ride on (p. 52)	To depend on
to shrug something **off** (p. 56)	To ignore
to figure out (p. 60)	To determine
to die out (p. 67)	To disappear
to carry on a conversation (pp. 70, 82)	To participate in a conversation
to carry out (a plan) (p.71)	To fulfill; complete
to take off (p. 75)	To leave quickly

Other expressions in Chapter 2:

to be in working order (p. 44)	To be in a state of working well
an ironclad rule (p. 49)	A rule that has no exceptions
a threefold (or any number plus "fold") **increase** (p. 68)	Three times bigger

one's **train of thought** (p. 70)	A chain of related thoughts
to turn (someone) **into a vegetable** (p. 71)	To become unable to think, or in some cases, to move

GUESSING FROM CONTEXT

See if you can guess the meanings of the following terms by studying their contexts. Write down your own definitions, and then ask a native speaker what the words mean or look them up in a dictionary to see if your guesses were correct.

voluntary (p. 41)

to surpass (p. 42)

deterioration (p. 52)

severed (p. 54)

curb (p. 71)

localized (p. 81)

STRUCTURAL CLUES

Many English words are made of a main word part and additional word parts added to the beginnings and endings. The main word part is called the **stem**; the additional word parts are called **prefixes** and **suffixes**. Prefixes come at the beginnings of words, and suffixes come at the ends. Knowing the meanings of prefixes, stems, and suffixes can help you understand new words and increase your reading speed.

Look at this example, the word **involuntary**, on page 46 of your text:

in	**volun**	**(t)ary**
prefix	stem	suffix

In means "not," **volun** means "will" or "choice," and **(t)ary** means "having the qualities of" (and, therefore, means the word is an adjective). So if your body has an involuntary movement, it's one that happens without your control.

Study the following list of common prefixes, and then guess the meanings of the terms that follow the list.

Prefix	Example	Meaning
inter-	interaction	between
pre-	prefix	before
in-, im-	involuntary	not
dis-	disappear	not
un-	uninsulated	not
re-	regrow	again
non-	nonfunctional	not
anti-	antisocial	against

Now find the following words in the text, and use your knowledge of prefixes to guess their meanings.

interconnect (p. 80) **prewired** (p. 46)

immobile (p. 56) **disconnected** (p. 82)

unaware (p. 52) **reanalyzed** (p. 67)

nonharmful (p. 77) **anticonvulsant** (p. 82)

TERMS IN CULTURAL CONTEXT

Do you know the following cultural terms and concepts? Guess their meanings first, and then look at the explanations on the right.

Jell-O (p. 42) — The trade name of a gelatin dessert; the trade name has become the generic (or general) name for any product like it.

Michael Jordan, a play-off game, lay-up shots (p. 62) — Michael Jordan is a basketball player; a play-off game is a game played at the end of the basketball season that decides the best teams from each league; a lay-up shot is when the player throws the ball into the basket when he or she is very close to it. (It therefore has a good chance of getting into the basket.)

INFORMAL USAGE

Are you familiar with the following informal expressions? Study them in context. Try to guess their meanings, and then look them up in a current dictionary or ask a native speaker.

to boast (p. 41)

to tough it out (p. 50)

belly (p. 66)

VOCABULARY REVIEW

Use each of the following terms in an original sentence. Your sentences can be about something in your personal life or about the chapter topic.

to figure out

to carry out

a train of thought

voluntary

unaware

indispensable

CONCEPT REVIEW

Below, you will see references to particular material in Chapter 2. Review the material, and then answer the questions by giving examples from your culture and/or your personal experience.

(p. 46, pars. 1-3): Describe a situation in which having quick reflexes would be an advantage.

(p. 67, pars. 1-7): What are some myths regarding brain size and/or intelligence in your native culture or country?

Chapter 3: The Senses

IDIOMATIC EXPRESSIONS

The following are some of the more difficult phrasal verbs and idiomatic expressions in Chapter 3. Some of them have more than one meaning; the definition given here on the right is for the way the author uses the expression in this chapter.

Phrasal verbs:

to break down (p. 91)	To cause a chemical change
to follow up on something (p. 96)	To act further on
to line up (p. 98)	To place in a row
to pick up (a sound) (p. 107)	To perceive
to set off something (p. 109)	To cause to happen
to make out (p. 111)	To perceive with difficulty
to wear out (p. 113)	To be reduced to a useless state
to give off something (p. 115)	To send out

Other expressions in Chapter 3:

a wave of panic (p. 102)	A strong feeling of panic (uncontrollable fear)
to blurt out something (p. 102)	To say something suddenly, without thinking
to go deaf (p. 111)	To become deaf

GUESSING FROM CONTEXT

See if you can guess the meanings of the following terms by studying their contexts. Write down your own definitions, and then ask a native speaker what the words mean or look them up in a dictionary to see if your guesses were correct. Use your knowledge of prefixes wherever possible.

invisible (p. 88)

unassembled (p. 94)

dischromatic (p. 97)

simultaneously (p. 109)

unintelligible (p. 111)

innate (p. 113)

STRUCTURAL CLUES

As you saw in Chapter 2, many English words are made of a stem and prefixes and suffixes. Suffixes come at the ends of words and tell you what part of speech a the word is. For example, in the word **involuntary** (on page 46 of your text), the suffix **ary** means "having the qualities of"; in other words, it makes the word an adjective. So **involuntary** in this case describes an action that is out of one's control.

Recognizing suffixes can help you understand new words and increase your reading speed.

Study the following list of common suffixes, and then guess the meanings of the terms that follow the list.

Suffix	Example	Meaning	Part of Speech
-tion	adaptation	condition	noun
-ate	demonstrate	to do	verb
-al	visual	having the qualities of	adjective

-ly	excitedly	in this manner	adverb
-ment	treatment	cause, means, result (of an action)	noun
-ness	loudness	condition, quality, or degree	noun
-ity	sensitivity	the quality of or being an example of	noun
-ic	characteristic	having the qualities of	adjective

Find the following words in the text, and use your knowledge of suffixes to guess their meanings.

electrically (p. 87) **cortical** (p. 94)

dramatic (p. 98) **vibrations** (p. 107)

intensity (p. 109) **deafness** (p. 110)

stimulate (p. 115) **treatment** (p. 116)

TERMS IN CULTURAL CONTEXT

Do you know the following cultural terms and concepts? Guess their meanings first, and then look at the explanations on the right.

a switch hitter,
batting average (p. 98)

These are baseball terms. A **switch hitter** is a person who can swing a baseball bat either right-handedly or left-handedly. A **batting average** is the ratio of a batter's hits to his or her times at bat. (A high batting average indicates a good player.)

a scratch-and-sniff advertisement (p. 121) — A magazine ad, usually for perfume, that has a strip of paper soaked in a scent. You release the scent by scratching the paper with a sharp object, such as a fingernail.

INFORMAL USAGE

Are you familiar with the following informal expression? Study it in context. Try to guess its meaning, and then look it up in a current dictionary or ask a native speaker.

a sure bet (p. 113)

VOCABULARY REVIEW

Use each of the following terms in an original sentence. Your sentences can be about something in your personal life or about the chapter topic.

to follow up on	**simultaneously**
to pick up	**innate**
to blurt out	**to stimulate**

CONCEPT REVIEW

Below, you will see references to particular material in Chapter 3. Review the material, and then answer the questions by giving examples from your culture and/or your personal experience.

(p. 114, par. 1): What foreign foods might be disgusting to someone from your native country or culture? What tastes good to you that might be disgusting to someone from another country or culture?

(p. 115, par. 3): What food odor reminds you of a festive family gathering?

Chapter 4: Perception

IDIOMATIC EXPRESSIONS

The following are some of the more difficult phrasal verbs and idiomatic expressions in Chapter 4. Some of them have more than one meaning; the definition given here on the right is for the way the author uses the expression in this chapter.

Phrasal verbs:

to hold back something (p. 123)	To keep from happening
to make sure (p. 123)	To be certain
to stand out (against something) (p. 129)	To be easily seen
to keep track of (p. 142)	To keep oneself informed about something or someone
to show up (p. 151)	To appear
to draw on (p. 152)	To use
to account for (p. 155)	To explain; to give a reason for

Other expressions in Chapter 4:

to bring something **to life** (p. 128)	To make it seem more real
(to have a condition) **from early on** (p. 129)	From a young age
to pay good money (p. 136)	To pay a lot of money
a quirk of nature (p. 141)	An accident of nature
to take something **for granted** (p. 152)	To accept it without asking questions

GUESSING FROM CONTEXT

See if you can guess the meanings of the following terms by studying their contexts. Write down your own definitions, and then ask a native speaker what the words mean or look them up in a dictionary to see if your guesses were correct. Use your knowledge of prefixes and suffixes wherever possible.

awareness (p. 126)

distorted (p. 135)

stationary (p. 138)

convex (p. 139)

concave (p. 139)

rehabilitation program (p. 147)

media (p. 149)

perplexed (p. 152)

STRUCTURAL CLUES

In Chapters 2 and 3 you saw that knowing the meanings of different word parts can help you read faster and increase your vocabulary. In this chapter, you'll learn about word **stems.** Stems are the core parts of words. You can attach prefixes and suffixes to them. Learning the meanings of some common stems will help you understand the general meaning of the words you find them in. For example, in the word **involuntary** (on page 46 of your text), **volun** means "will" or "choice." When you combine this stem with the prefix **in** and the suffix **ary**, you have an adjective describing an action that happens without a person willing (or wanting) it to.

Study the following list of common stems; then guess the meanings of the terms that follow the list. (See Chapter 13 of this Study Guide for more examples.)

Stem	Meaning	Example
-anthro-	(hu)man	anthropology
-auto-	self	automobile
-ced(e)-	go, move, surrender	precede
-ology-	study of	psychology
-sequ-, -secu-	follow	consecutive
-tech-	skill	technique
-vers-	turn	converse
-vis-, -vid-	see	vision

Find the following words in the text, and use your knowledge of stems to guess their meanings.

automatically (p. 129) **nonreversible** (p. 129)

recede (p. 135) **technology** (p. 139)

sequence (p. 139) **visual** (p. 152)

anthropologists (p. 152)

TERMS IN CULTURAL CONTEXT

Do you know the following cultural term? Guess its meaning first, and then look at the explanation on the right.

a pitcher (p. 141) The player on a baseball team who throws (pitches) the ball to the batter on the other team.

INFORMAL USAGE

Are you familiar with the following informal expression? Study it in context. Try to guess its meaning, and then look it up in a current dictionary or ask a native speaker.

squiggly (p. 153)

VOCABULARY REVIEW

Use each of the following terms in an original sentence. Your sentences can be about something in your personal life or about the chapter topic.

to keep track of	**to draw on**
to take for granted	**perplexed**
to recede	**sequence**

CONCEPT REVIEW

Below, you will see references to particular material in Chapter 4. Review the material, and then answer the questions by giving examples from your culture and/or your personal experience.

(p. 149, pars. 2-4): Is there a difference between the ideal weight for people in your culture and that for North Americans?

(p. 153, par. 1): Have you noticed any differences between North American cartoons and cartoons in your native country?

Chapter 5: States of Consciousness

IDIOMATIC EXPRESSIONS

The following are some of the more difficult phrasal verbs and idiomatic expressions in Chapter 5. Some of them have more than one meaning; the definition given here on the right is for the way the author uses the expression in this chapter.

Phrasal verbs:

to give rise to (p. 161)	To cause
to drift off (p. 165)	To fall asleep slowly
to make sense of (p. 172)	To understand
to file out (p. 178)	To exit in an orderly fashion, as in a line
to be caught up in something (p. 181)	To be completely involved or interested in
to cut down on something (p. 184)	To use less of

Other expressions in Chapter 5:

to snap at someone (p. 159)	To respond angrily
to be on "automatic pilot" (p. 160)	To function without making any effort
to out of sync (with) (p. 163), **to be out of step** (with) (p. 163)	Not to be operating in agreement with something or somebody else
to keep one's head (p. 170)	To remain in control
a crackdown (on) (p. 185)	Action against unlawful activity

GUESSING FROM CONTEXT

See if you can guess the meanings of the following terms by studying their contexts. Write down your own definitions, and then ask a native speaker what the words mean or look them up in a dictionary to see if your guesses were correct. Use your knowledge of prefixes, suffixes, and stems wherever possible.

a vegetative state (p. 161)

deprivation (p. 170)

disregard (p. 171)

admissibility (p. 182)

an upsurge (p. 191)

cessation (p. 192)

STRUCTURAL CLUES

Transitions are words (or phrases) that show a relationship between two ideas in a text. Transitions prepare you for information that is about to come; they let you know that the next idea may be a contrast, a conclusion, or an example of the previous idea. They appear between two parts of the same sentence, between two sentences, or between two paragraphs. Being able to recognize and understand transitional words and phrases will increase your reading speed and comprehension. Take a look at this example from your text:

"If you went to work everyday and were exposed only to regular indoor lighting, your biological clock would take ten days to fully adapt. If, ***however***, . . . " (p. 163)

Without reading on, if you understand the function of the word *however*, you know that a contrasting idea is about to be presented. You can almost guess that the contrasting idea will have something to do with *lighting*. Now read the rest of the sentence:

" . . . you spent 6 to 8 hours of the first two days outside in bright sunlight, you would reset your biological clock and cause your circadian rhythm to be on local clock time."

The following table lists some common transitions and their functions:

Transition	Function
however, but, on the hand, rather	present a contrasting idea
for example, for instance	present an example to illustrate the preceding idea
in addition, additionally	present another idea, similar to the preceding one
as a result, therefore	present a result or conclusion

Find the following pairs of sentences in Chapter 5. Read the first sentence. As soon as you come to the transition at the beginning of the second sentence, stop and guess what will come next. Then read on to see of you were correct.

p. 169, caption, beginning with: "From infancy to adolescence, . . ." ("For example . . . ")

p. 172, par. 3, beginning with: "Because dreams may contain wishes . . ." ("For instance . . . ")

p. 181, par. 6, beginning with: "Essentially, this theory says . . ." ("Rather . . .")

p. 187, par. 4, beginning with: "According to researcher Frank Gawin (1991), . . ." ("As a result, . . . ")

p. 191, par. 7, beginning with : "Medium to higher doses . . ." ("In addition, . . . ")

TERMS IN CULTURAL CONTEXT

Do you know the following cultural term? Guess its meaning first, and then look at the explanation on the right.

a No-Doz tablet (p. 188)	A nonprescription drug that contains caffeine.

INFORMAL USAGE

Are you familiar with the following informal expressions? Study them in context. Try to guess their meanings, and then look them up in a current dictionary or ask a native speaker.

grumpy (p. 164)

weed, reefer (p. 190)

VOCABULARY REVIEW

Use each of the following terms in an original sentence. Your sentences can be about something in your personal life or about the chapter topic.

to give rise to

to be caught up in

to be out of sync

a crackdown

disregard

cessation

CONCEPT REVIEW

Below, you will see references to particular material in Chapter 5. Review the material, and then answer the questions by giving examples from your culture and/or your personal experience.

(p. 171, pars. 3-5): Do you have any cultural or personal beliefs about dreams coming true or the meanings of dreams?

(p. 188-189): What are the some popular legal drugs in your native country or culture?

Chapter 6: Learning

IDIOMATIC EXPRESSIONS

The following are some of the more difficult phrasal verbs and idiomatic expressions in Chapter 6. Some of them have more than one meaning; the definition given here on the right is for the way the author uses the expression in this chapter.

Phrasal verbs:

to ward off something or someone (p. 208)	To keep away
to turn to something (p. 208)	To go to next
to jut out (p. 216)	To protrude; to stick out
to pay off (p. 217)	To give a reward
to rear up (p. 217)	To stand on the hind legs (refers to a four-legged animal)
to turn in something (p. 219)	To submit; to hand in
to run through something (p. 228)	To be a part of
to hit on something (p. 228)	To discover

Other expressions in Chapter 6:

to be at the heart of something (p. 202)	To be an important part of or to have an important place in
to be laced with (p. 208)	To be mixed with
to give a boost to (p. 209)	To promote; to encourage
to keep one's mind off (of)	To try not to think about something (p. 210)

to perform on cue (p. 214)	To act when a special signal is given
to weigh in at (an amount) (p. 214)	To weigh
to coin a term (p. 215)	To invent a term
to be on the safe side (p. 223)	To be cautious

GUESSING FROM CONTEXT

See if you can guess the meanings of the following terms by studying their contexts. Write down your own definitions, and then ask a native speaker what the words mean or look them up in a dictionary to see if your guesses were correct. Use your knowledge of prefixes, suffixes, and stems wherever possible.

internally (p. 202)

unknowingly (p. 204)

initially (p. 204)

phobia (p. 204)

decondition (p. 204)

antinausea medication (p. 210)

contingent (p. 217)

restraints (p. 229)

STRUCTURAL CLUES

One way you can make textbook reading a little easier is to get an idea of the content of a chapter before you read it word-for-word. This is called "previewing." One technique of previewing a chapter is to read the first sentence of every paragraph. Usually (but not always) the first sentence of a paragraph is the **topic sentence**, the sentence that presents the main idea of the paragraph. If you read the topic sentence of every paragraph, you can get a pretty good idea of what the whole chapter is about just by reading a fraction of the sentences. Then when you go back and read the chapter word-for-word, your job will be easier because of your prior knowledge.

Practice this skill by reading the following topic sentences from Chapter 6. Then choose the statement (a, b, or c) that best describes what you think the rest of the paragraph is about.

1. Topic sentence: "Skinner believed and demonstrated that our daily lives are filled with examples of operant conditioning, some more obvious than others."

The paragraph probably:

a. explains that instances of operant conditioning are difficult to observe in everyday life.
b. gives examples of some of Skinner's laboratory experiments that demonstrate operant conditioning.
c. gives examples of everyday occurrences of operant conditioning.

Find the paragraph on page 222 and see if your guess was correct. (The correct answer is "c.")

2. Topic sentence: "In discussing an organism's capacity for classical, operant, or cognitive learning we must also consider biological factors, which are innate tendencies that may either facilitate or inhibit certain kinds of learning."

The paragraph probably:

a. shows how biological factors are irrelevant in learning.
b. gives an example of how biological factors affect learning.
c. explains how computers "learn."

Read the paragraph on page 229 and see if your guess was is correct. (The correct answer is "b.")

3. Topic sentence: "Support for information theory over the stimulus substitution theory comes from a number of findings."

The paragraph probably:

a. explains how the information theory and the stimulus substitution theory are equally valid in explaining how classical conditioning works.
b. presents an example of how the information theory is better than the substitution theory to explain how classical conditioning works.
c. discusses the qualifications of the researchers who discovered these two theories on classical conditioning.

Now find this paragraph on page 206 and see if your guess was correct. (The correct answer is "b.")

These exercises should have been fairly easy. Textbooks are usually written with clear topic sentences. Try reading further chapters of *Introduction to Psychology* using this technique.

TERMS IN CULTURAL CONTEXT

Do you know the following cultural term? Guess its meaning first, and then look at the explanation on the right.

Tilt-a-Whirl (p. 208)	An amusement park ride. Riders sit on chairs attached to a circular platform that rotates like a carousel; the chair itself also rotates, so the riders "tilt" from side to side.

INFORMAL USAGE

Are you familiar with the following informal expression? Study it in context. Try to guess its meaning, and then look it up in a current dictionary or ask a native speaker.

to boot (someone) **out** (p. 219)

VOCABULARY REVIEW

Use each of the following terms in an original sentence. Your sentences can be about something in your personal life or about the chapter topic.

to pay off

to hit on

to give a boost to

to be on the safe side

decondition

contingent

CONCEPT REVIEW

Below, you will see references to particular material in Chapter 6. Review the material, and then answer the questions by giving examples from your culture and/or your personal experience.

(p. 201, par. 7): What are your feelings about going to the dentist? What, if any, associations with the dentist's office bring on these feelings?

(p. 225, par. 1): Do you have any fears that you think you learned by observing others?

Chapter 7: Memory

IDIOMATIC EXPRESSIONS

The following are some of the more difficult phrasal verbs and idiomatic expressions in Chapter 7. Some of them have more than one meaning; the definition given here on the right is for the way the author uses the expression in this chapter.

Phrasal verbs:

to turn out (p. 237)	To happen to be in the end
to pick out something or someone (p. 253)	To choose
to be borne out (p. 253)	To be proven
to get around something (p. 257)	To avoid
to level off (p. 257)	To become constant
to veer off (p. 263)	To turn or change direction

Other expressions in Chapter 7:

a packed house (p. 237)	An event in a theater or lecture hall so popular that every seat is occupied
to slip one's mind (p. 238)	To be forgotten
(a) one in a million (p. 241)	Rare
to hold one's attention (p. 246)	To be interesting
a common thread (p. 263)	A common idea or theme
to be dubbed (p. 268)	To be named
an airtight case (p. 268)	A legal case that is easy to prove

GUESSING FROM CONTEXT

See if you can guess the meanings of the following terms by studying their contexts. Write down your own definitions, and then ask a native speaker what the words mean or look them up in a dictionary to see if your guesses were correct. Use your knowledge of prefixes, suffixes, and stems wherever possible.

fixate (p. 239)

deliberate (p. 242)

reconstructing (p. 256)

underlie (p. 265)

culprit (p. 268)

bias (p. 269)

STRUCTURAL CLUES

Making **predictions** about *what* you are reading *as* you are reading helps you read more quickly. Good readers are good guessers; they supply missing information as they read, based on their previous knowledge of the subject, their knowledge of transitional vocabulary (see Chapter 5), and their life experiences. You saw in Chapter 6 how to preview text material by reading topic sentences and predicting what each paragraph might be about; in this chapter, you'll review this skill and apply it to a word-for-word reading of a text.

Practice your predicting skills by choosing the letter of the statement that best describes the information that will follow the beginning of each sentence.

1. "If you do not pay attention to the raw information in sensory memory, it automatically ______________." (p. 238)

   a. becomes a part of your permanent memory

   b. disappears without a trace

The correct answer is "b"; your life experiences in paying attention allowed you to guess what happens when you *don't* pay attention.

2. "One of the intriguing findings on patients with brain damage is that some memory functions are lost while ______________." (p. 244)

a. others are spared

b. others disappear

The correct answer is "a"; since you knew that "while" precedes a contrasting idea, you chose the opposite of "lost." Answer "b" of course, makes no sense.

3. "As you already know, a common strategy to keep information in short-term memory is to use maintenance rehearsal, which is simply ______________." (p. 247)

a. associating new information with previously acquired information

b. repeating or rehearsing the information

The correct answer is "b"; you knew this because you already read about maintenance rehearsal on page 240 of your text. If you haven't read the chapter yet, you may be able to guess based on your understanding of the terms "maintenance" and "rehearsal."

Practice your predicting skills as you read this chapter and those that follow.

TERMS IN CULTURAL CONTEXT

Do you know the following cultural term? Guess its meaning first, and then look at the explanation on the right.

a lineup (p. 252) — A process to help witnesses select a criminal suspect. The suspect, along with a certain number of other people of the same sex, are lined up in a special viewing room at a police station.

INFORMAL USAGE

Are you familiar with the following informal expression? Study it in context. Try to guess its meaning, and then look it up in a current dictionary or ask a native speaker.

hot (p. 263)

VOCABULARY REVIEW

Use each of the following terms in an original sentence. Your sentences can be about something in your personal life or about the chapter topic.

to pick out	**to slip one's mind**
to get around	**deliberate**
a common thread	**underlie**

CONCEPT REVIEW

Below, you will see references to particular material in Chapter 7. Review the material, and then answer the questions by giving examples from your culture and/or your personal experience.

(p. 249, par. 4): What major event in recent history do you have a very clear memory of? What were you doing when it occurred?

(p. 256, pars. 1–2): Are there cultural differences in classroom schema? Do you think your idea of a classroom is the same as a North American's?

Chapter 8: Intelligence, Thought, and Language

IDIOMATIC EXPRESSIONS

The following are some of the more difficult phrasal verbs and idiomatic expressions in Chapter 8. Some of them have more than one meaning; the definition given here on the right is for the way the author uses the expression in this chapter.

Phrasal verbs:

to swear in someone (p. 273)	To have someone promise to act or judge responsibly, as in a court
to drum something **into** someone (p. 273)	To repeat something to someone continually
to end up (**with**) something (p. 274)	To have as a result
to flunk out (p. 279)	To be forced to leave school because of bad grades
to put up with (p. 292)	To tolerate
to build on something (p. 298)	To use as a basis

Other expressions in Chapter 8:

to keep an open mind (p. 273)	To be accepting of new ideas
to give the nod to someone (p. 274)	To indicate approval
to lump together (p. 274)	To put together
a dead end (p. 282)	Something that has no future
to shed light on something (p. 306)	To help the understanding of something

GUESSING FROM CONTEXT

See if you can guess the meanings of the following terms by studying their contexts. Write down your own definitions, and then ask a native speaker what the words mean or look them up in a dictionary to see if your guesses were correct. Use your knowledge of prefixes, suffixes, and stems wherever possible.

correlated (p. 276)

differentiate (p. 277)

antisocial (p. 288)

generate (p. 298)

convert (p. 302)

facilitate (p. 303)

fluent (p. 306)

STRUCTURAL CLUES

In Chapter 6 you learned a technique for recognizing main ideas in a text. This is useful in approaching a text for the first time, as preparation for your reading. Often, however, such as when you are preparing for a test, you need to identify specific information (or supporting ideas) quickly and easily. The technique for doing this is called *skimming.*

To skim a text, read it quickly and locate only the specific information you are looking for. You do this by hunting for the key words associated with the subject you are studying. You don't read anything else. Key words might be names, numbers, or whole phrases.

Practice this by locating and underlining the following items in the paragraph below, taken from your text: *validity, WAIS-R, IQ score, 0.30 to 0.70, IQ tests,Terman, very high IQs, 30%, 2%.* Work as quickly as you can and read as few of the other words in the text as you can.

A good test must also have validity, which means that the test measures what it is supposed to measure. To a large extent, the validity of an intelligence test depends on the definition of intelligence. If we define intelligence as the ability to perform well in academic settings, then the WAIS-R is a valid test because it predicts academic performance reasonably well. The correlation between IQ score and performance in academic settings ranges from 0.30 to 0.70 (Jensen, 1980). Nevertheless, the cognitive abilities measured by IQ tests do not account for all of a person's performance in academic settings. For instance, when Terman followed the lives of individuals with very high IQs (an average of 151), he discovered that about 30% never finished their college degrees and 2% actually flunked out.

Now, skim the paragraph again and answer this question: Do people with very high IQs always do well in college?

The answer is is "no." To find this, you should have skimmed the passage for the key phrase "very high IQs." You had to read only the sentence containing these words to get the answer.

Answer the following questions about information from your text by skimming the paragraphs indicated, and indicate what key words you used to help you find the information:

1. What IQ score is usually associated with someone who has above-average intelligence? (p. 281, par. 3)

2. What percentage of creative individuals in Kay Jameson's study had been treated for mood disorders? (p. 299, par. 4)

3. How did B. F. Skinner believe that children acquired language? (p. 303, par. 5)

Answers: 1. Above 130; key words: "above average intelligence." 2. Thirty-eight percent; key words: "Kay Jameson," "mood disorders," or "%" (percent).

3. Skinner believed that children acquired language according to the principles of operant conditioning (or reinforcement); key words: "B. F. Skinner."

TERMS IN CULTURAL CONTEXT

Do you know the following cultural terms? Guess their meanings first, and then look at the explanation on the right.

a class action suit (p. 282)	A legal action on behalf of a group of people who feel that some injustice has been committed against them. If they win they suit, every member of the group benefits.
Ellis Island (p. 285)	A reception station in the harbor of New York City through which most European immigrants passed at the beginning of the 20th century.

INFORMAL USAGE

Are you familiar with the following informal expressions? Study them in context. Try to guess their meanings, and then look them up in a current dictionary or ask a native speaker.

dirt-poor (p. 273) **street smart** (p. 275)

VOCABULARY REVIEW

Use each of the following terms in an original sentence. Your sentences can be about something in your personal life or about the chapter topic.

to put up with	**to shed light on**
to end up with	**differentiate**
to give the nod to	**facilitate**

CONCEPT REVIEW

Below, you will see references to particular material in Chapter 8. Review the material, and then answer the questions by giving examples from your culture and/or your personal experience.

(p. 303, par. 3): At what age did you learn English? Was your age an important factor in making the learning experience easy or difficult?

(p. 306, par. 5): Is there a word or expression in your native language that cannot be translated precisely into English?

Chapter 9: Motivation and Emotion

IDIOMATIC EXPRESSIONS

The following are some of the more difficult phrasal verbs and idiomatic expressions in Chapter 9. Some of them have more than one meaning; the definition given here on the right is for the way the author uses the expression in this chapter.

Phrasal verbs:

to revolve around (p. 333)	To be concerned with
to work out a problem (p. 337)	To solve a problem
to kick in (p. 344)	To start to work
to track down (p. 350)	To find

Other expressions in Chapter 9:

to be dead and buried (p. 314)	To be forgotten (usually refers to an idea)
to strike a balance between (p. 316)	To give equal importance to two things
to run in the family (p. 339)	To be hereditary
to spark interest (p. 345)	To cause interest
to drop charges (p. 350)	To stop blaming someone for breaking the law

GUESSING FROM CONTEXT

See if you can guess the meanings of the following terms by studying their contexts. Write down your own definitions, and then ask a native speaker what the words mean or look them up in a dictionary to see if your guesses were correct. Use your knowledge of prefixes, suffixes, and stems wherever possible.

energize (p. 314)

hierarchy (p. 316)

celibate (p. 331)

cognitive (p. 342)

physiological (p. 342)

appraising (p. 344)

elicit (p. 351)

STRUCTURAL CLUES

In Chapter 5, you saw some common transition expressions, words and phrases that show you the relationship between two ideas in a text. One of these was *as a result*, which shows a **cause and effect** relationship. When you see *as a result*, you know the next sentence contains the **effect** (or **result**) of the previous one.

Two more expressions that show cause and effect are *X results from*, and *X results in*. Look at these example sentences, and underline the cause in each:

> Researchers believe that homosexuality **results from** a complex interaction between biological and social-learning factors. (p. 329, par. 1)
>
> According to cognitive appraisal theory, interpreting or appraising a situation as having a positive or negative impact on our lives **results in** a subjective feeling that we call an emotion. (p. 344, par. 1)

In the first sentence, the cause is "a complex interaction . . . ." In the second, the cause is ". . . interpreting or appraising a situation . . . ."

Results from and *results in* can be confusing unless you pay close attention to the preposition in each—*from* and *in*. *Results from* lets you know that the next sentence part contains the **cause;** *results in* tells you the next sentence part contains the **result.**

Practice determining the causes and effects in the following sentences with *results from/in*. First find and circle *results in* or *results from.* Then draw a line under the **cause** in each sentence and draw two lines under the **result.**

1. We can conclude that feelings of being hungry or feeling full result from a combination of peripheral and central cues, as well as from the influence of learned and social-cultural cues. (p. 319, par. 10)

2. According to the James-Lange theory, emotions result from specific changes in our bodies, and each emotion has a different physiological basis. (p. 342, par. 2)

3. Today researchers argue that emotions may result not only from situational or environmental cues but also from our own cognitive processes, such as thoughts, interpretations, and appraisal. (p. 345, par. 1)

4. In Chapter 13, we'll discuss how emotions may result in physical and psychological problems . . . (p. 347, par. 3)

TERMS IN CULTURAL CONTEXT

Do you know the following cultural term? Guess its meaning first, and then look at the explanation on the right.

an over-the-counter drug (p. 331)	A drug you can buy without a doctor's prescription.

INFORMAL USAGE

Are you familiar with the following informal expressions? Study them in context. Try to guess their meanings, and then look them up in a current dictionary or ask a native speaker.

and then some (p. 336) **crammed** (p. 350)

VOCABULARY REVIEW

Use each of the following terms in an original sentence. Your sentences can be about something in your personal life or about the chapter topic.

to draw on **to spark interest**

to work out **hierarchy**

to strike a balance **elicit**

CONCEPT REVIEW

Below, you will see references to particular material in Chapter 9. Review the material, and then answer the questions by giving examples from your culture and/or your personal experience.

(p. 349, par. 2): Think of examples of display rules from your native culture that are different from those in North America.

(p. 353, item 9, question): What are common stereotypes foreigners have about people from your native country or culture?

Chapter 10: Child Development

IDIOMATIC EXPRESSIONS

The following are some of the more difficult phrasal verbs and idiomatic expressions in Chapter 10. Some of them have more than one meaning; the definition given here on the right is for the way the author uses the expression in this chapter.

Phrasal verbs:

to drop out (of) (p. 359)	To quit or leave
to slough off (p. 361)	To get rid of
to go through something (p. 363)	To experience
to come about (p. 379)	To develop
to act out (p. 388)	To express (thoughts, fears, etc.) in actions and behavior instead of words
to push somebody **around** (p. 390)	To treat someone roughly or unfairly

Other expressions in Chapter 10:

to make one's way to (p. 361)	To arrive at slowly or with some difficulty
to be at the heart of (p. 373)	To be an important part of
to be bound to (p. 385)	To be likely to
to lay the groundwork for something (p. 385)	To prepare for
to make inroads (p. 388)	To progress

GUESSING FROM CONTEXT

See if you can guess the meanings of the following terms by studying their contexts. Write down your own definitions, and then ask a native speaker what the words mean or look them up in a dictionary to see if your guesses were correct. Use your knowledge of prefixes, suffixes, and stems wherever possible.

gestation (p. 355)

nature (p. 357)

nurture (p. 357)

microscopic (p. 360)

encounter (p. 378)

resilient (p. 386)

STRUCTURAL CLUES

In Chapter 6, you saw a technique for previewing text material by reading the topic sentences of paragraphs. Another way to preview text material is to read the **pre-reading** questions that appear throughout the text *before* you read the text word-for-word. It's tempting to skip them altogether, but they're there for a purpose—to make the reading task easier.

By reading these questions, you get a pretty good idea of the information on that page. But don't just read them. It's a good idea to try to answer these questions as best as you can before you start to read; then as you read, you can find out whether or not your answer was correct. Reading with a purpose makes reading easier.

The pre-reading questions are usually in *italics* and they appear at the beginning of a paragraph. Some pre-reading questions are **called out**; that is, reprinted with a larger typeface in a box elsewhere on the page.

For example, turn to page 362 of your text. Look for and read the following pre-reading questions:

- What happens during the fetal period?
- What effect do drugs have on the fetal period?

Practice using pre-reading questions to preview chapter material by finding the following questions on the pages indicated. Guess the answers *before* you read the material on the page. Then read the material word-for-word and see if your guesses were correct.

1. How much did the world's tiniest surviving infant weigh at birth? (p. 355)
2. What can an infant do in the first weeks of life? (p. 364)
3. Why are some babies so smiley? (p. 369)
4. Does day care result in social problems? (p. 375)
5. How does an infant develop into a social being? (p. 384)
6. When do you know whether you're a boy or a girl? (p. 388)
7. How similar are gender roles in Australia, Japan, Peru, and the United States? (p. 390)
8. Are there gender differences in verbal abilities? (p. 391)

You may have noticed that there was no specific answer to some of the questions; in some cases, they're there just to get you interested in the subject. But whether you found an answer or not, it should have been fairly easy to read the text after reading and answering the pre-reading questions. Use this technique to preview the rest of the chapters in *Introduction to Psychology.*

TERMS IN CULTURAL CONTEXT

Do you know the following cultural term? Guess its meaning first, and then look at the explanation on the right.

kindergarten (p. 372) — The first year of school in the United States; it prepares children around five to six years old for the following twelve years of school by training them in social and pre-academic skills.

INFORMAL USAGE

Are you familiar with the following informal expression? Study it in context. Try to guess its meaning, and then look it up in a current dictionary or ask a native speaker.

spunky (p. 355)

VOCABULARY REVIEW

Use each of the following terms in an original sentence. Your sentences can be about something in your personal life or about the chapter topic.

to act out	**to make inroads**
to push around	**encounter**
to lay the groundwork for	**resilient**

CONCEPT REVIEW

Below, you will see a reference to particular material in Chapter 10. Review the material, and then answer the question by giving examples from your culture and/or your personal experience.

(p. 389, par. 5): To what extent does the media (especially television programs and television commercials) portray men and women in stereotypic careers in your native country?

Chapter 11: Adolescence and Adulthood

IDIOMATIC EXPRESSIONS

The following are some of the more difficult phrasal verbs and idiomatic expressions in Chapter 11. Some of them have more than one meaning; the definition given here on the right is for the way the author uses the expression in this chapter.

Phrasal verbs:

to count something **against** somebody (p. 397)	To blame someone for something
to go through (a developmental phase) (p. 399)	To experience
to take hold (p. 402)	To become permanent
to show off (p. 403)	To act in a such way as to get attention or admiration from others
to give up something (p. 404)	To stop having or doing something
to lay down (a rule) (p. 407)	To state firmly or clearly
to wipe out (p. 410)	To eliminate completely
to hand out (a sentence) (p. 411)	To give
to figure on (p. 412)	To expect
to border on something (p. 416)	To be close to
to break up (p. 424)	To end a relationship (usually romantic)

Other expressions in Chapter 11:

to make great strides (p. 401)	To make a lot of progress

to play into something (p. 407)	To manipulate; to behave in in such a way as to get expected results
(verbal) **give-and-take** (p. 407)	Both sides having equal opportunities
level-headed (p. 412)	Practical; realistic
right off the bat (p. 416)	Immediately
to open the door to something (p. 431)	To make vulnerable

GUESSING FROM CONTEXT

See if you can guess the meanings of the following terms by studying their contexts. Write down your own definitions, and then ask a native speaker what the words mean or look them up in a dictionary to see if your guesses were correct. Use your knowledge of prefixes, suffixes, and stems wherever possible.

a role model (p. 397)

terminal (p. 408)

antisocial behavior (p. 409)

accelerate (p. 414)

encoding (p. 416)

withdrawing (p. 425)

banning (p. 431)

STRUCTURAL CLUES

Being able to recognize the uses of punctuation in a text can help you understand what you read. Some punctuation types you should be familiar with are **quotes, colons, semicolons,** and **commas.**

Quotes have two uses in your text:

1. To indicate direct speech.

Example: The night after Tommy Smith's suicide he [Jerry] told his mother, "I can't understand how anyone would commit suicide—that was the coward's way." (p. 408, par. 8)

2. To emphasize a special name or way of referring to something.

Example: As soon as the passion dies and the intimacy fades, the individuals no longer feel "in love" and go their separate ways. (p. 424, par. 8)

Colons have two uses in your text:

1. To introduce lists.

Example: One such approach is Robert Sternberg's (1986) triangular theory of love, which divides love into three components: passion, intimacy, and commitment. (p. 424, par. 3)

2. To introduce an idea that illustrates, clarifies, or gives further information on the preceding one. In this text, **semi-colons** have a similar use.

Example **(colon)**: Researchers are no longer searching for what should occur (great emotional problems) but rather are studying what actually occurs: how adolescents change, adapt, and grow. (p. 397, par. 6)

Example **(semicolon)**: Adolescence is a developmental period lasting from about ages 12 to 18 that marks the end of childhood and the beginning of adulthood; it is a transitional period of considerable biological, cognitive, and social changes. (p. 397, par. 6)

Commas separate a series of items.

Example: These individuals do well in school, develop rewarding friendships, and participate in social activities. (p. 401, par. 2)

Practice using your knowledge of punctuation. First, read each of the following questions about material in your text. Locate the material using the page and paragraph numbers indicated, and skim to find the punctuation clue. (Note: This is also an opportunity to practice skimming.)

1. What was Jerry's nickname? (quotes) (p. 408, par. 8)

2. What does Katharine Hepburn say about women's brains? (quotes) (p. 416, par. 3)

3. According to the traditional view of gender roles, why does someone rated high on one pole of the continuum have to be low on the other? (colon) (p. 422, par. 1)

4. What are the secrets of the Russians, Pakistanis, and Ecuadoreans who tend to live to 100? (serial comma) (p. 415, par. 3)

5. What is intimacy, and how does it develop? (semicolon) (p. 424, par. 5)

TERMS IN CULTURAL CONTEXT

Do you know the following cultural terms? Guess their meanings first, and then look at the explanations on the right.

oldies (p. 408)	Popular music (usually rock and roll) from the past; for example, Elvis Presley's "Blue Suede Shoes," popular during the 1950s, is an oldie.
a prom queen (p. 412)	A prom is a formal dance that high school students attend; a prom queen is a female student, elected to be "queen" of the prom. She wears a crown and is seated in a place of honor during the evening.

INFORMAL USAGE

Are you familiar with the following informal expressions? Study them in context. Try to guess their meanings, and then look them up in a current dictionary or ask a native speaker.

blah, blah, blah (p. 397) **do drugs** (p. 407)

VOCABULARY REVIEW

Use each of the following terms in an original sentence. Your sentences can be about something in your personal life or about the chapter topic.

to show off	**to figure on**
to make great strides	**level-headed**
terminal	**accelerate**

CONCEPT REVIEW

Below, you will see references to particular material in Chapter 11. Review the material, and then answer the questions by giving examples from your culture and/or your personal experience.

(p. 407, pars. 1-5): Do you think there are cultural differences in parenting styles? Is the predominant style of your culture similar to either Christopher's or Ida's situation?

(p. 427, pars. 1-4, and chart, lower left corner): How do you think love ranks in your culture? How do you explain its ranking?

Chapter 12: Personality

IDIOMATIC EXPRESSIONS

The following are some of the more difficult phrasal verbs and idiomatic expressions in Chapter 12. Some of them have more than one meaning; the definition given here on the right is for the way the author uses the expression in this chapter.

Phrasal verbs:

to pick on someone (p. 435)	To choose someone to punish or blame
to be kicked out of something (p. 435)	To be asked to leave
to come up with something (p. 438)	To think of
to take on something (p. 438)	To begin to have
to add up to something (p. 442)	To indicate
to break away from something (an idea or a school of thought) (p. 449)	To go in another direction
to live up to (p. 451)	To meet expectations
to take in (p. 455)	To include
to touch on something (p. 455)	To consider
to put off (doing) something (pp. 456, 461)	To avoid doing; to procrastinate
to bring out something (p. 467)	To cause to be seen

Other expressions in Chapter 12:

to make an about-face,	To make a dramatic change

to turn over a new leaf (p. 435)	
to bring to mind something (p. 435)	To make one think of something
to pick an argument (p. 441)	To start an argument
butterflies in the stomach (p. 455)	A feeling in the stomach caused by nervousness
to take into account (p. 467)	To consider
to be in sight (p. 467)	To be near

GUESSING FROM CONTEXT

See if you can guess the meanings of the following terms by studying their contexts. Write down your own definitions, and then ask a native speaker what the words mean or look them up in a dictionary to see if your guesses were correct. Use your knowledge of prefixes, suffixes, and stems wherever possible.

revert (p. 435)

underlying (p. 437)

assess (p. 446)

resettle (p. 453)

exemplifies (p. 462)

exhaustive (p. 465)

easygoing (p. 471)

STRUCTURAL CLUES

In Chapter 10, you saw that some pre-reading questions appear in italics in this text, and that others appear in a large-sized typeface. You saw that familiarity with the uses of typeface in a textbook can often help you find information quickly.

This textbook also uses typeface variations to indicate new terms and their definitions. In *Introduction to Psychology*, new terms appear in **bold type**, and their definitions follow in *italics*. Find this example from page 435 of your text:

Personality *refers to a combination of lasting and distinctive behaviors, thoughts, and emotions that typify how we react and adapt to other people and situations.*

Not only does this system tell you that this sentence is important (it's the answer to question #1 in the Concept/Glossary on page 447), but it also makes reviewing easy. For example, when you're studying for an exam or checking your understanding by doing the Concept/Glossary quiz, all you have to do is search in the text for words in bold or italic type.

Practice skimming for definitions using typeface clues by completing the following chart. Skim the text for the terms listed on the left. Indicate the page number on which you find each one, and the paragraph it's in. Read the definition, and for further practice, paraphrase it (say it in your own words). The first one has been done for you.

Term	On Page #	In Paragraph #	Paraphrased Definition
Freudian slips	437	6	Mistakes that supposedly indicate our true feelings
graphology			
sublimation			

trait theory			
heritability			
a projective test			
observational learning			

TERMS IN CULTURAL CONTEXT

Do you know the following cultural terms? Guess their meanings first, and then look at the explanations on the right.

reform school (p. 458) A school for young people under the age of 18 who have committed a crime.

ex-con (p. 458) An "ex-convict," a person who has been convicted of a crime, and has spent time in prison as a result.

INFORMAL USAGE

Are you familiar with the following informal expressions? Study them in context. Try to guess their meanings, and then look them up in a current dictionary or ask a native speaker.

a bully (p. 435) **to "mouth off"** (p. 443)

VOCABULARY REVIEW

Use each of the following terms in an original sentence. Your sentences can be about something in your personal life or about the chapter topic.

to live up to **to put up with**

to turn over a new leaf **to bring to mind**

revert **exhaustive**

CONCEPT REVIEW

Below, you will see references to particular material in Chapter 12. Review the material, and then answer the questions by giving examples from your culture and/or your personal experience.

(p. 453, pars. 4-7): What are some primary values of your culture? Are they relevant to academic success? Explain.

(p. 476, pars. 3-9): What is your personal opinion of astrology? Graphology? Are they considered invalid as means of personality assessment in your native culture or country?

Chapter 13: Stress and Health

IDIOMATIC EXPRESSIONS

The following are some of the more difficult phrasal verbs and idiomatic expressions in Chapter 13. Some of them have more than one meaning; the definition given here on the right is for the way the author uses the expression in this chapter.

Phrasal verbs:

to pass out (p. 481)	To become unconscious, e.g. to faint
to break out in something (p. 481)	To show suddenly (especially on one's skin)
to come to (p. 481)	To regain consciousness (after passing out)
to wind up (p. 485)	To be in a certain state accidentally
to come down with (an illness) (p. 497)	To have an illness
to act up (p. 497)	To cause problems
to dole out (p. 498)	To give

Other expressions in Chapter 13:

to busy oneself with something (p. 481)	To occupy oneself
a full-blown case (of an illness) (p. 487)	Fully developed
to lay a foundation for something (p. 490)	To create a basis for something that will follow
to tackle something **head on** (p. 491)	To deal with something forcefully

to bear in mind (p. 493)	To remember; to consider
to slave over something (p. 498)	To work hard
to make ends meet (p. 498)	To live (just barely) on one's income
gang-buster (children) (p. 498)	Very active children
to make time for someone (p. 499)	To allow time for
the flip side of something (p. 501)	Another way of looking at something

GUESSING FROM CONTEXT

See if you can guess the meanings of the following terms by studying their contexts. Write down your own definitions, and then ask a native speaker what the words mean or look them up in a dictionary to see if your guesses were correct. Use your knowledge of prefixes, suffixes, and stems wherever possible.

deliberation (p. 482)

trigger (p. 484)

suppress (p. 491)

hinder (p. 505)

buffer (p. 507)

obese (p. 510)

STRUCTURAL CLUES

As you saw in Chapters 2, 3, and 4, knowing the meanings of prefixes, suffixes, and stems can help you understand new words and increase your reading speed. This chapter presents some additional stems to add to your repertoire.

Chapter 13 contains several words with scientific stems derived from Greek. You'll encounter these stems often if you continue to study psychology, but you'll also see them in other scientific and social scientific contexts.

Take the term **psychosomatic** (on page 486) for example. As the text states, *psyche* comes from the Greek word for "mind" and *soma*, also a Greek word, means "body." If you knew these stems already, you could guess that that **psychosomatic** might have something to do with a mind-body relationship.

Study the following chart of scientific stems derived from Greek appearing in Chapter 13:

Stem	**Meaning**	**Example**
-para-	resembling, beside	paramedic (p. 483)
-physio-	body	physiological (p. 484)
-sym-	with	sympathetic (p. 485)
-pathy-	feeling	parasympathetic (p. 485)
-soma-	body	psychosomatic (p. 486)
-gen-	become, produce, bear	genetic (p. 488)
-hyper-	high	hypertension (p. 489)
-bio-	life	biofeedback (p. 495)

Now, find each example in the chart in your text. Guess the meanings first, and then check your guesses in a dictionary.

TERMS IN CULTURAL CONTEXT

Do you know the following cultural term? Guess its meaning first, and then look at the explanation on the right.

dinette (p. 498) — A small, informal dining table designed to fit into small spaces, such as a kitchen corner.

INFORMAL USAGE

Are you familiar with the following informal expressions? Study them in context. Try to guess their meanings, and then look them up in a current dictionary or ask a native speaker.

a putdown (p. 486) **hassles** (p. 500)

VOCABULARY REVIEW

Use each of the following terms in an original sentence. Your sentences can be about something in your personal life or about the chapter topic.

to come down with **to act up**

to tackle head on **to bear in mind**

trigger **suppress**

CONCEPT REVIEW

Below, you will see references to particular material in Chapter 13. Review the material, and then answer the questions by giving examples from your culture and/or your personal experience.

(p. 502, col. 3): Have you experienced cultural stress as a student? If so, what factors caused it? Are there any services on your campus for foreign, immigrant, and minority students suffering from cultural stress? Have you used these services? Why or why not?

(p. 510, pars. 1-3): Are close family relationships important in your native culture or country? Are they important to you personally? Why or why not?

Chapter 14: Disorders

IDIOMATIC EXPRESSIONS

The following are some of the more difficult phrasal verbs and idiomatic expressions in Chapter 14. Some of them have more than one meaning; the definition given here on the right is for the way the author uses the expression in this chapter.

Phrasal verbs:

to look on something (p. 519)	To consider; to view
to spell out something (p. 524)	To explain carefully
to break out of something (pp. 539, 550)	To escape from
to pick up someone (p. 541)	To become friendly with someone one meets in a public place, usually with sexual intentions

Other expressions in Chapter 14:

a broken home (p. 517)	A family in which the parents have divorced
to con someone **into** (doing) something (p. 517)	To convince someone to do something that is illegal or not to his or her advantage
clear-cut (p. 520)	Easy to understand
to be under the gun (p. 525)	To be under pressure
to lose touch with reality (p. 542)	Not to be able to tell what is real and what isn't

to scrape up (money) (p. 550) — To find or collect with difficulty

GUESSING FROM CONTEXT

See if you can guess the meanings of the following terms by studying their contexts. Write down your own definitions, and then ask a native speaker what the words mean or look them up in a dictionary to see if your guesses were correct. Use your knowledge of prefixes, suffixes, and stems wherever possible.

obsessed (p. 520)

imbibe (p. 536)

grandeur (p. 543)

plateau (p. 546)

antipsychotic (p. 547)

psychogenic (p. 548)

STRUCTURAL CLUES

You have seen how a knowledge of prefixes, suffixes, and stems can help you guess the meanings of new words in context. An additional and related technique is to know word families, groups of words that come from the same stem, but are different parts of speech. As you saw in Chapter 3, suffixes usually indicate what part of speech a word is (noun, verb, adjective, or adverb). An example of this in Chapter 14 is **obsession** (a noun), and **obsessive** (an adjective), on page 528 of your text.

See if you can fill in the missing forms of the following words from Chapter 14, and then test your understanding of them by using their correct forms in the sentences that follow the chart. Use a dictionary, if necessary.

All forms for the first example in the chart are given as an example. (Note: The page number is given for the form that appears in Chapter 14. "X" means that there is no form for that category. Also, some categories may have two forms.)

Nouns	Verbs	Adjectives	Adverbs
recurrence	recur	recurring (p. 517)	X
			legally (p. 517)
	X	statistical (p. 519)	
	deviate(s) (p. 519)	X	X
		general, generalized (p. 525)	
conversion (p. 529)			X
confrontation (p. 532)			
	distort (p. 538)		X

Fill in the blanks with the correct forms of the words from the chart. The first one is done for you.

1. (recurring) The recurrence of a problem that interferes with an individual's ability to live a satisfying life is one sign of a mental disorder.

2. (deviate) It's necessary to consider changes in social norms over time when determining ______________ from social norms.

3. (statistical) ______________ are sometimes useful in determining abnormal behavior.

4. (generalized) Fred didn't have a specific fear; rather he was ______________ apprehensive about many things in life.

5. (conversion) In a conversion disorder, emotional conflicts are ______________ to physical symptoms.

6. (confrontation) Some phobics are encouraged to ______________ the situations they fear the most in order to change their behavior.

7. (distort) A depressed individual's view of reality may be a ______________.

8. (legally) The ______________ definition of insanity is not knowing the difference between right and wrong.

TERMS IN CULTURAL CONTEXT

Do you know the following cultural term? Guess its meaning first, and then look at the explanation on the right.

a self-help book (p. 532) — A book written to help people solve their psychological or behavioral problems; people sometimes choose self-help books instead of consulting a counselor or psychologist.

INFORMAL USAGE

Are you familiar with the following informal expressions? Study them in context. Try to guess their meanings, and then look them up in a current dictionary or ask a native speaker.

a wimp (p. 537) **the blues** (p. 550)

VOCABULARY REVIEW

Use each of the following terms in an original sentence. Your sentences can be about something in your personal life or about the chapter topic.

to rule out **to spell out**

clear-cut **to be under the gun**

obsessed **plateau**

CONCEPT REVIEW

Below, you will see a reference to particular material in Chapter 14. Review the material, and then answer the questions by giving examples from your culture and/or your personal experience.

(p. 531, pars. 1–7): Are you aware of any disorders that appear in your native culture or country that don't appear anywhere else?

Chapter 15: Therapies

IDIOMATIC EXPRESSIONS

The following are some of the more difficult phrasal verbs and idiomatic expressions in Chapter 15. Some of them have more than one meaning; the definition given here on the right is for the way the author uses the expression in this chapter.

Phrasal verbs:

to work through something (p. 563)	To resolve; to have a good result
to come to something (p. 563)	To happen
to reach out to someone/**into** someplace(p. 564)	To have contact with; to communicate with
to go over something (p. 565)	To review; to study
to break off (a relationship) (p. 567)	To end
to speak up (p. 573)	To say what one is thinking; to be assertive
to carry off something (p. 573)	To be successful (at)
to hang on to someone or something (p. 580)	To keep; to possess
to make up for something (p. 580)	To compensate

Other expressions in Chapter 15:

topnotch (p. 557)	Of the highest quality
to stay on course (p. 563)	To proceed according to a plan
to fall on difficult times (p. 565)	Not to be in favor

a driving force (p. 570)	An important cause
to be walked (or **stepped**) **on** (p. 573)	To be taken advantage of; to be treated disrespectfully

GUESSING FROM CONTEXT

See if you can guess the meanings of the following terms by studying their contexts. Write down your own definitions, and then ask a native speaker what the words mean or look them up in a dictionary to see if your guesses were correct. Use your knowledge of prefixes, suffixes, and stems wherever possible.

halfway houses (p. 557)

maladaptive (p. 561)

"ivory towers" (p. 564)

termination (p. 565)

internally motivated (p. 569)

ascribe to (p. 580)

selective attention (p. 585)

STRUCTURAL CLUES

In Chapter 14, you saw how recognizing word forms can help you guess the meaning of unfamiliar vocabulary. This skill depends largely on your knowledge of suffixes, which often tell you what part of speech a word is. Sometimes, however, there may be two forms for the same part of speech. This is especially true for nouns, many examples of which you can find in Chapter 15. For example, on page 555 of your text, you'll find both *therapy* and *therapist*; both are nouns, but one denotes a person or practitioner(*therapist*); the other a thing or field (*therapy*). The distinction between person and thing noun forms is commonly found in discussions of professions and occupations.

Review suffixes in Chapter 3, and the word formation chart in Chapter 14 of this study guide. Then see if you can fill in the missing forms of the following words from Chapter 15.

(Note: "X" means there is no form for that category.)

Nouns	Verbs	Adjectives	Adverbs
1. ________ (the person) 2. ________ (the thing)		humanistic (p. 555)	
1. ________ (the person) 2. psychoanalysis (p. 555)			
1. schizophrenic (p. 556) 2. ________ (the thing)	X		X
1. psychiatrist (p. 558) 2. ________ (the thing)	X		X
1. counselor (p. 558) 2. ________ (the thing)			X

1. ________
(the person)

2. interpretation
(p. 561)

____

Now test your understanding of these forms by using them in the following sentences. The first one is done for you.

1. (interpretation) Freud interpreted his patients' dreams as a psychoanalytic technique.

2. (humanistic) As a ______________, Carl Rogers disagreed with the pessimistic nature of the psychoanalytic approach.

3. (psychiatrist) Future psychiatrists must earn not only an M.D., but also must complete a residency in the ______________ department of a hospital.

4. (counselor) ______________ psychologists often find positions in "real-world" settings.

5. (schizophrenic) ______________ may have genetic or environmental causes.

6. (psychoanalysis) Traditional ______________ rarely take an active role in the therapeutic process.

TERMS IN CULTURAL CONTEXT

Do you know the following cultural term? Guess its meaning first, and then look at the explanation on the right.

a cabbie (p. 562) — A person who drives a taxi.

INFORMAL USAGE

Are you familiar with the following informal expression? Study it in context. Try to guess its meaning, and then look it up in a current dictionary or ask a native speaker.

"F___ you!" (p. 562)

VOCABULARY REVIEW

Use each of the following terms in an original sentence. Your sentences can be about something in your personal life or about the chapter topic.

to speak up | **to make up for**

to stay on course | **to be walked on**

maladaptive | **ascribe to**

CONCEPT REVIEW

Below, you will see a reference to particular material in Chapter 15. Review the material, and then answer the questions by giving examples from your culture and/or your personal experience.

(p. 583): In your opinion, should therapists take their patients' cultural backgrounds into consideration when choosing therapeutic techniques? Explain your answer.

Chapter 16: Social Psychology

IDIOMATIC EXPRESSIONS

The following are some of the more difficult phrasal verbs and idiomatic expressions in Chapter 16. Some of them have more than one meaning; the definition given here on the right is for the way the author uses the expression in this chapter.

Phrasal verbs:

to strike up (a conversation) (p. 590)	To start
to be passed over for something (p. 595)	Not to be considered
to break down (p. 596)	To eliminate
to fit in (p. 599)	To conform
to stand out (from) (p. 599)	To be different
to stand up for something (p. 599)	To defend one's beliefs
to take out (an emotion) **on** someone (p. 624)	To express an emotion (usually negative) to someone

Other expressions in Chapter 16:

a pigeonhole (p. 592)	A compartment; a category
to be in a time warp (p. 593)	To have old-fashioned ideas
out-and-out (p. 602)	Extreme
to cut (classes) (p. 602)	To miss
an inside track (p. 607)	An advantage

a snap judgment (p. 608)	A judgment made without considering all the facts
white lies (p. 611)	Lies told to avoid embarrassment in social situations

GUESSING FROM CONTEXT

See if you can guess the meanings of the following terms by studying their contexts. Write down your own definitions, and then ask a native speaker what the words mean or look them up in a dictionary to see if your guesses were correct. Use your knowledge of prefixes, suffixes, and stems wherever possible.

naive (p. 594)

shun (p. 599)

affective (p. 600)

renounced (p. 602)

naturalistic (p. 621)

erroneous (p. 622)

STRUCTURAL CLUES

You have learned a variety of techniques for increasing your reading speed and your understanding of unfamiliar vocabulary. In this last chapter, practice all of your skills by reading the following passage and filling in the missing information. To do this, you will use your abilities to predict and to make guesses. Read the passage one time without writing. The second time, fill in the blanks. Then find the passage in your text (referenced at the end of the exercise) to check your answers. Even if your words are not exactly the same as those in the text, you have done a good job if the general meaning is the same.

After 13 seasons and 2,000 games in the minor leagues, this umpire was passed over ____________ promotion to the major leagues and released. An evaluation report by the Office ____________ Umpire Development claimed that this umpire's ____________ had "deteriorated in areas of enthusiasm and execution," ____________ though earlier in the ____________ the rating had been "____________ than average." What is ____________ about this umpire is that she is a ____________.

(p. 594)

TERMS IN CULTURAL CONTEXT

Do you know the following cultural term? Guess its meaning first, and then look at the explanation on the right.

an umpire (p. 594)	An official in a baseball game who determines when a player makes a point, commits a foul, or is out of the game.

INFORMAL USAGE

Are you familiar with the following informal expression? Study it in context. Try to guess its meaning, and then look it up in a current dictionary or ask a native speaker.

nerd (p. 591)

VOCABULARY REVIEW

Use each of the following terms in an original sentence. Your sentences can be about something in your personal life or about the chapter topic.

to be passed over | **to fit in**

an inside track | **a snap judgment**

naturalistic **erroneous**

CONCEPT REVIEW

Below, you will see a reference to particular material in Chapter 16. Review the material, and then answer the questions by giving examples from your culture and/or your personal experience.

(p. 591, pars. 1-6): What are some negative stereotypes that people from your native culture or country have about North Americans (or whites)? What are the positive stereotypes?